A Dame Full of Vim and Vigor

Women in Science

Series Editor

Marilyn Bailey Ogilvie, *History of Science Collections, University of Oklahoma, USA*

Editorial Board

Pamela Gossin, *School of Arts and Humanities, University of Texas at Dallas, USA*
Joy Harvey, *Independent Scholar*
Catherine Hobbs, *Rhetoric/Composition/Literacy, University of Oklahoma, USA*
Sylvia McGrath, *Department of the History of Science, University of Oklahoma, USA*

A Dame Full of Vim and Vigor: A Biography of Alice Middleton Boring; Biologist in China
Marilyn Bailey Ogilvie and Clifford J. Choquette

This book is part of a series. The publisher will accept continuation orders which may be cancelled at any time and which provide for automatic billing and shipping of each title in the series upon publication. Please write for details.

A Dame Full of Vim and Vigor
A Biography of Alice Middleton Boring; Biologist in China

Marilyn Bailey Ogilvie
and
Clifford J. Choquette

harwood academic publishers
Australia • Canada • China • France • Germany • India • Japan
Luxembourg • Malaysia • The Netherlands • Russia • Singapore
Switzerland

Amsteldijk 166
1st Floor
1079 LH Amsterdam
The Netherlands

British Library Cataloguing in Publication Data

Ogilvie, Marilyn Bailey
  A dame full of vim and vigor : a biography of Alice
  Middleton Boring : biologist in China. – (Women in science)
  1. Boring, Alice Middleton 2. Women biologists – United
  States – Biography   3. Biologists – United States – Biography
  4. Women biologists – China – Biography
  I. Title II. Choquette, Clifford J.
  570.9′2

ISBN: 90-5702-575-2
ISSN: 1028-7191

CONTENTS

LIST OF ILLUSTRATIONS
(between pages 120 and 121)

PREFACE TO THE SERIES

For many years it was assumed that women had little or no part in scientific enterprise. However, during the last two decades, the interest in women and/or gender and science has increased. Research indicates that even in remote antiquity there have been women who were scientists. It is tantalizing to attempt to determine the special circumstances that existed in the lives of these women that made them able to overcome an often hostile environment. In order to reach a better understanding of these unique women, it is vital to study their lives and their works. Recognizing the importance of providing a publication outlet for scholarly works that will provide answers to some of these questions, Harwood Academic Publishers has established a series on Women in Science. This series provides a forum for the publication of full-length scholarly biographies of women scientists, collective biographies with a specific emphasis, collected works of women scientists, and critical analyses.

The books in this series will appeal to those interested in the history of science, technology, and medicine; women in history; and gender issues in science. Although these books are scholarly, they are written so that they will appeal to a more general audience.

Marilyn Bailey Ogilvie
Series Editor

ACKNOWLEDGMENTS

We are heavily indebted to many individuals and institutions of learning. Without their time, expertise, and encouragement this project would have been impossible. We received the usual superb service from college and university archivists. Lucy Fisher West, Teresa Taylor and incumbent Caroline Rittenhouse supplied not only Bryn Mawr information on Alice Boring, but provided additional valuable advice and leads. Martha Lund Smalley at the Yale Divinity School archives led us to a treasure chest of Yenching documents and photographs, a collection given to them by the United Board for Christian Higher Education in Asia. Wellesley and Radcliffe colleges made available for study the Grace M. Boynton papers which added much to our knowledge of Boring's personality. Clark Eliott at the Pusey Archive Center at Harvard was an invaluable resource as he led us through the Boring family papers. The Rockefeller Foundation provided Ogilvie with a grant to study their rich resources on our subject. The Director, Dr Darwin Stapleton, and most especially the archivist, Dr Thomas Rosenbaum, made the trip to the Archive Center a success. We would also like to thank the archivists at Smith, Mount Holyoke and Haverford colleges.

In Philadelphia, the American Philosophical Society and Free Public Library contributed as did the American Museum of Natural History in New York and the Field Museum of Natural History in Chicago. Librarians at Harvard, the University of Würzburg, the University of Maine at Orono, Johns Hopkins, and the Stazione Zoologica in Naples were also very helpful. Employees of the National Archives, Library of Congress, Franklin D. Roosevelt Library, Harry S. Truman Library, and Dwight D. Eisenhower library served us well.

We thank the staff of the Red Cross National Headquarters in Washington for supplying us with information concerning Boring's trip home in 1943 aboard the neutral ship Gripsholm after months of confinement in a Japanese internment camp for non-combatants. The US Army Military History Institute at Carlisle Barracks, Pennsylvania, gave us a history of the 79th Pennsylvania Regiment of Infantry in which Dr Boring's father served. Professor of Biology, Kraig Adler of Cornell, included Alice Boring in his work *Contributions to the History of Herpetology* as one of 152 scientists of the past who have advanced the study of amphibians and reptiles. He also kindly supplied photographs of Chinese amphibians. Mr Clayton Farraday, historian of the Friends' Central School of Philadelphia was generous with information on Boring's early schooling.

Some people who contributed are no longer with us. Christian Brother C. Edward Quinn, Professor of Biology at Manhattan College was willing to help anytime. With his death, the American Society of Zoologists lost its historian. Mr Dick Ritter, despite his advanced age and infirmity wrote clearly about his experience as history instructor at Yenching as well as his remembrances of Alice Boring. Janet Rhodes called him "a dear, sweet soul." Dr Frederick Kao was one of Boring's former students who became a well-known research physician in the United States and wrote of his recollections of Alice Boring. Dr Kao Ph.D., MD, formerly of the State University of New York Health Science Center in Brooklyn, died before he could see this biography to which he supplied so much important information.

Dr Frank Boring, a nephew of Alice Boring, referred us to Mrs Janet Smith Rhodes whose father had taught at Yenching. Janet turned out to be a 'fairy godmother', adding immensely to our knowledge of Yenching. Through her contacts we established a Yenching grapevine which seemed to grow exponentially. Dozens of Yenchingites produced an abundance of information and referrals. Miss Margaret Speer, Yenching's Dean of Women, gave an oral history to her beloved Bryn Mawr College that included her remembrances of Alice Boring. Mrs Mildred Wiant, widow of Bliss Wiant, Yenching's music director who played the organ at Dr Sun Yat Sen's funeral ceremony was helpful as was Harold Shadick who taught history, philosophy, and literature at Yenching.

Significant contributions came from William Hung's daughter Ruth Beasley; Rose and K.T. Chang; Dr Kenneth Chen, Department of East Asian Languages, UCLA; Dr Langdon Gilkey, author and Professor of Theology, University of Chicago; Mrs L. Carrington Goodrich; Kuo Chen Hsieh, President, Yenching Alumni Association; Katharine H.K. Hsu, MD, Professor Emeritus, Baylor University College of Medicine; Dorothy Wei (Cheng) King, Professor Emeritus, Department of Zoology, National Taiwan University; Chien Liu, MD, Director, University of Kansas Medical Center; Mrs Dorothy (Galt) MacArthur; the late Stephen Tsai, former Assistant Treasurer and Comptroller at Yenching; Mr Leslie Severinghaus, language instructor and soloist, Yenching, 1922–1927; Nai Hsuan (Chang) Shen, Professor of Biology, Georgian Court College; Florence (Giang) and Gene Szutu, MD; J.C. Tao, MD; Chi Hua Wang, Professor of Chemistry, University of Massachusetts; Yang Wang, MD, Department of Medicine, University of Minnesota; Mamie Kwoh Wang, MA, RN, and husband Professor Emeritus Shih Chien Wang, Ph.D., MD; Yan Tim Wong, MD; Laurence T. Wu, MD;

Mrs Nelson Wu (Mu Lien Hsueh); C.C. Tan, MD and Chih Chen (Lin); Brigadier General John L. Fugh, US Army; Mr Edward Rondthaler, III; Mrs Elizabeth R. Hays.

Our gratitude also goes to Tin Yuke Char, MD; Mrs Mary Musgrove; Professor Kao Laing Chow; Chao Chun Hsu; Susan Chan Egan, author, the National Women's History Project; Mrs Catherine G. Curran; Sung Nien Lu, MD; James Sailer; Mark K.H. Wang, MD; James McNamara, Bronx Historical Society; Dr Patricia Brown of Siena College; C. Martin Wilbur, author; Ti Huang; Peter Pang; and Tien Te Wu. The great staff of the Chelmsford Public Library, Oklahoma Baptist University which supplied money for the China trip, and the University of Oklahoma History of Science Collections have all been very supportive. Mrs Paul B. Bien of Georgia; Professor Kuo Ping Chou, University of Wisconsin; Professor Norman C. Li of Maryland; Utah Tsao, widower of the late Hazel A.C. Lin, MD of New Jersey; Shujiang Li of Vancouver, BC; and Jesuit fathers Francis Edwards of Rome and Paul Mech of Paris.

We want to especially thank those who were so kind and helpful when Ogilvie visited Beijing. First, Judge Robert Henry made it possible for Ogilvie to get a visa for a China trip. There are so many people in Beijing and in Xi An to whom we are indebted, we will undoubtedly accidentally omit someone. The help of Ye Dao Chun, now a librarian at Beijing University and an important member of the Yenching Alumnae Association, was vital to the success of the trip. Taking time off from her own work, Miss Ye shepherded Ogilvie around Beijing, including a visit to Boring's old house in the 'Manchu Prince's Garden'. The house had been torn down as unsuitable for the large number of families that it now had to accommodate, but the original gate that opened into the courtyard remained.

Shortly after Ogilvie arrived in Beijing, she was hosted by approximately twelve of Boring's former students and associates at a tea at what was formerly the home of President Leighton Stuart of Yenching. Yenching itself is now a part of Beijing University, but the distinction between Yenching and the rest of the university is evident. The group included not only former students, but others who had known her. Those present at this party were Wu Jie-Ping, Wang Xiu-Ying, Hou Ren Zhi, Jiang Lijin, Lin Chi Wu, Ye Dao Chun, Sun You Yun, Lu Niangao, and three former Boring laboratory helpers. Sun You Yun had done most of the arrangements for the tea, and later hosted Ogilvie at an excellent lunch at her house and provided the opportunity for her to meet Bin Xin, a famous writer, who was a member of Boring's 'Friday Lunch' group and who took her to an exhibit of Bin Xin's work. Lin Chang Shan escorted Ogilvie around the former campus of Yenching University. It superficially resembled the building as it was when Lin entered in 1931, and with his help it was possible to reconstruct the earlier appearance. The biology building of Boring's time was currently being used for chemistry. The formerly spacious laboratories had been partitioned into smaller laboratories. The general biology laboratory where Lin had learned so much about the scientific method from Boring was half its original size. Chemical apparatus and supplies cluttered the area formerly occupied by preserved specimens and biological models. The former invertebrate zoology laboratory had been divided into four small laboratories. Boring's office remained much as it was when she called in hapless students to discuss their problems.

On another day, Ogilvie visited the Peking Union Medical College where a group of seven of her former students gathered in the still beautiful PUMC to share their recollections with Ogilvie. All seven individuals (Miss Wang Xiu Ying, Dr Zhou Hua Kang, Dr Feng Chuan Yi, Dr Fan Qi, Dr Tang Ji Xue, Dr Jin Yin Chang, and Dr Liu Shilian), now recognized authorities in their fields, unanimously agreed that Boring was a strict, no-nonsense, demanding teacher. After the interviews, Drs Liu Shilian and Feng Chuan Yi gave Ogilvie a tour of PUMC, including the auditorium where Sun Yat Sen's funeral took place.

We especially want to thank historian of science, Li Pei Shan of the Institute for the History of Natural Sciences, for her help.

In Xi An we would like to thank Liu Ming and Qi En Ho (President of the Yenching Alumnae Society) for all of their help. Liu Gian (Liu Ming's daughter) and another young woman, Li Tan, served as guides, taking Ogilvie to various archaeological and historical sites. We are indebted to the physicians whom Ogilvie met at the Fourth Military Medical University College, Dr Li Huan Jang, the head of the hospital who did not go to Yenching until 1950, after Boring had left; Dr Tung Kuong Huan, an endocrinologist at the Second Teaching Hospital; Dr Ma Shu Kun, a cardiologist at the first teaching hospital; Dr Wang Quan, Dr Ma's husband and an associate professor of ENT at the second affiliated hospital; and Dr You Guo Xing, Professor and Chairman of the Department of Neurology at the second teaching hospital; all provided information. They hosted an elegant banquet under the guise of a 'simple Chinese lunch'. Tan Li Zhu of the International Trade, Shanxi Subcouncil, Mr Yuan, and Tan Li Zhu took us to the Music Institute where we met Liu Chang Biao, Professor of the Xi An Conservatory of music and his wife Feng Zhong Hui, Professor of Statistics and Medical Demography. Others who supplied information were Ho Hsi Chen, Shan Yu Hsin, Tan Li Zhu. Drs Feng and Liu provided another excellent lunch. Ogilvie had intended visiting

Ding Han Bo, a herpetologist who works on the herpetofauna of Fujian province, but the logistics were impossible and she had to be content with his informative letters.

NOTE ON CHINESE NAMES

There are two major systems of transliteration for Chinese words, the Pinyin and Wade-Giles. When Alice Boring was in China, the Wade-Giles form was generally used. However, today, the Pinyin form is the dominant one. We have found consistency impossible, and not altogether desirable. Whenever possible, we have used the Pinyin form in this book. However, in many cases, Chinese students of Boring's day transliterated their own names using the Wade-Giles system. They published in English under these names, and we have used their names as they did. An example of a deliberate choice of the Wade-Giles over the Pinyin is in the name of the university where Boring taught. We have, as she did and as graduates of this university still do, used the Wade-Giles, 'Yenching' rather than the Pinyin, 'Yanjing'. On the other hand, we have used the Pinyin 'Beijing' rather than the Wade-Giles 'Peking'.

Introduction:
The Green Grasshopper

During the crisp days of autumn, the lotus flower-filled pool mirrored brilliant orange, red, and yellow trees. The new Yenching University, situated on this former summer garden of the Manchu prince, Jui Wang, included artificial hills, waterways, islands, and flowing streams from the west. The natural beauty of the property was enhanced by Chinese fir, pine trees, and artificial grottoes. From the property's highest hills, a magnificent panorama of the surrounding countryside was visible. When the architectural decision was made regarding the design of the new university's buildings, the committee agreed that Chinese rather than western architecture would be adopted. The biology department was housed in one of the new brightly colored buildings replete with decorative dragons and a hyperbolically shaped tile roof.

In this building, Alice Middleton Boring, a middle-aged teacher with thick glasses and a bright green laboratory coat, provided her small class of Chinese premedical students at Yenching University with detailed laboratory instructions.[1] Quiet, attentive students focused their eyes and minds on the teacher, understanding that "Miss Boring" had the power to determine their acceptance or rejection by the prestigious Peking Union Medical College (PUMC).[2] Even though members of this advanced class were in awe of Boring's knowledge and power, they also realized that beneath a brusque facade dwelled a soft and giving person. This knowledge made them courageous enough to gently spoof their teacher's appearance. Surreptitiously they passed around the room a drawing made by one of the students. This piece of art showed the similarities of their teacher, with her thick glasses and bright green lab coat, to a grasshopper. The students fervently hoped that she would never hear of the nickname, but assumed that if she did they would be forgiven.[3]

Not all of her students had a reason to be so brave. In 1934, a premedical student who fell below the acceptable level was faced with a letter from premedical advisor Boring with a warning that he would probably "not be able to enter PUMC and therefore" should "begin to plan either to drop medicine and take up some other subject or else to enter some other medical school." Although a student would be petrified to be faced with such a letter or, even more daunting, with a meeting with Boring herself, she actually was doing the frightened one a favor by recommending him or her to other less demanding medical schools.

When new students first arrived at Yenching, they were warned that Boring was "strict" and were prepared to find her an uncompromising, demanding, and humorless presence. It was not long, however, before hard-working students realized that Boring cared deeply about them and passionately wanted to see them succeed. A former student, the late Frederick Kao, remarked that she behaved toward her favored students as if they were the children she never had. He was convinced that this attitude was a major strength and enabled her "to devote her life to educating many instead of loving only a few."[4] Those students who relied on first impressions never got to see her softer side. When Lin Chi Wu, a sociology undergraduate who preferred athletics to school work, cast about for a course to satisfy a science requirement he briefly considered taking biology until he heard of Boring's reputation. Those who worked hard and stayed with Boring, such as biologist Lin Chang Shan, recalled that although "we were afraid of her," the training she provided in the scientific method made it possible for her students and her students' students to occupy many of the most prestigious positions in science and the medical professions in China today.

When beginning students received a summons to "see Miss Boring," they were universally unnerved. Her apparent sharp abruptness was a direct result of her sense of efficiency and responsibility as premedical advisor and teacher. By insisting on rigorous standards, she hoped to arm a young generation of Chinese students with resources to attack China's social, medical, and scientific needs. Western science—in which she had unlimited faith—was to be the weapon. The lazy, the incompetent, and, occasionally, the students who "rubbed her the wrong way," were weeded out. On the other hand, diligent, intelligent, and personable students were groomed, courted, and coddled for their mission.

Boring's appearance in a Chinese classroom could not have been predicted from her early life. Exquisitely educated to take a leading role in the development of early twentieth-century biology, her mentors included Thomas Hunt Morgan and Edwin B. Conklin, who played key roles in the development of cytogenetics, as well as Raymond Pearl, known for his development of statistical techniques. Through her relationship as a student and friend of the remarkable Nettie Maria Stevens who provided convincing evidence for the chromosomal theory of heredity, Boring learned that a woman could be a successful scientist. After receiving her Ph.D. degree from Bryn Mawr College, she rose to the rank of Associate Professor at a state university where she proceeded to publish numerous papers. From these beginnings it seemed likely that Boring would continue teaching, publishing, and working on research and make a secure place for herself as a scientist in the United States. However, at the age of thirty-four, she gave up this security to teach in an unstable China. She changed her research focus from "modern" prestigious cellular biology to more traditional taxonomy.

Why did Boring choose to leave the certainty of a steady position and create a career for herself that was even more atypical for a woman than the one she left? What motivated this radical change? Clearly the answers are not simple, but by exploring Boring's fascinating life we may glimpse some of the reasons Boring made the choices that she did, and in so doing generalize from her experiences and unique solutions to challenges that other women scientists have faced.

Some clues to these questions may be found not in Boring's professional training and experience, but in her personality and family background. Boring had never been a conventional person. Knowing her well, her family could not have been surprised when she decided to leave her secure position and accept a temporary post in an unstable China. Inconsistency was a consistent theme. Tension between decorum and impropriety, tradition and innovation surfaced throughout her life. Alice could be upset with a friend who violated protocol by being late to a party, yet could gleefully revel in a Mongolian camping trip where there were no boundaries of convention "as to what one may do or not do—we take shower baths in the morning by rolling naked in the long wet grass."[5] She could demand that her Chinese students learn proper western table manners but annoy her own family at home by refusing to use them herself. During conflicts with the "Great Powers," Boring aligned herself with radical student political protests and helped students make and distribute posters protesting perceived injustices, explaining that their cause superseded academics. Yet when students decided to boycott classes to protest Japanese outrages, she indignantly declared that attention to studies was the best way to show patriotism.[6]

This dissonance between proper social protocol and unconventionality had its origin in Boring's childhood. Alice was the third of four children in an opinionated, strong-willed family. Bound together by ties of blood and behavioral convention, they sometimes overwhelmed each other. The two younger children, Alice, and the only boy, Edwin, were the family scholars. Although at times Alice and Edwin got along well, at other times she found him condescending and derisive. As professor of experimental psychology at Harvard, he was notorious for his exclusionary treatment of his women graduate students. It was much easier for Alice to deal with overbearing Edwin when she was thousands of miles away than when she lived down the street. For his part, Edwin was relieved to be spared the competition of an inflexible, competent sister. He complained that he had grown up in a matriarchy; "in my lifetime women dominated it and the men had inferior status."[7] Apparently from an early age, Alice and her female relatives did not fit into the conventional role of woman. Not a feminine woman according to early twentieth-century standards, she was outspoken, opinionated, adventurous, and idealistic.

The religious background of the family also contributed to the contradictions in Boring's life. One side of the family was Moravian and the other, Quaker. In the Boring household, there was conflict, although neither of these denominations was especially dogmatic. The Borings were conventional in their own way and valued the forms and manners of their culture and, until 1918, when the Chinese opportunity arose, conventionality had the upper hand in Alice's life. Her dissatisfaction with the status quo did not result from onerous rules. Instead, she had been chafing under the tyranny of the commonplace. Her social conscience and her philosophical and political idealism were no doubt inspired by her early education in a Quaker school. When she arrived in China she was definitely antimissionary, for she assumed that missionaries stressed the inconsequential to the exclusion of true Quaker verities. She declared that by concentrating on superficialities such as smoking and drinking and ignoring the social and political effects of poverty and colonialism they missed the important ethical values, namely a respect for the culture they professed to help.

Although idealism no doubt contributed to Boring's desire to go to China, both an appetite for influence and a taste for adventure motivated her to leave a comfortable post at the University of Maine to go to a China dominated by the internecine strife of warlords. Her decision involved risks not encountered by her male colleagues. Although the number of jobs available for women biologists in the United States had increased by 1918, they remained rare and were usually confined to women's colleges. Boring, who was an Associate Professor of Biology at the Maine Agricultural station of the University of Maine, was an exception and would have been well advised by her colleagues to keep this position. Boring had managed to manipulate the state university system successfully, but such success was scarce, and many women biologists would have clutched at the security she was throwing away.

Perhaps Boring herself was surprised by her own audacity. Until 1918, her biological career had been traditional: she received A.B., M.A., and Ph.D. degrees in biology; studied in Europe; published the results of her research; belonged to scientific societies; and advanced up the academic ladder to the rank of associate professor. She clearly liked "teaching the farm boys why they kill potato bugs and their sisters why they put yeast in bread, and other similar useful information, and, incidentally, all unknown to them, trying to instill into their minds some ideas of evolution and heredity...."[8] She considered it "a great game trying to sugar-coat real science so that agricultural students will like it."[9] After eight years, however, the "great game" began to pale. Faced with the prospect of doing essentially the same thing for the rest of her life, she became restless and looked for other options. China provided an alternative which allowed Boring to teach and to feel that she was doing something useful for humanity. She also saw an opportunity to influence policy that she would never have had at home.

The Chinese setting did not harness Boring to the pursuit of power to the exclusion of the relational aspects of science. Science was not an activity to be practiced in isolation, but one to be enjoyed with colleagues, friends, and students. The community setting reflected a large infusion of human and social elements less evident in the American scientific community. Administrators, faculty, staff members, and students developed friendships through informal and formal meetings and parties. Boring truly believed that "objective" science was important *because* of its potential to help people. If she could browbeat, cajole, and threaten students, thereby forcing them to accumulate scientific knowledge, then they would be potentially competent to save their world from the "evils of superstition." The power she wielded through teaching allowed her to influence the course of science and—as she would have seen it—history.

Thus the "Green Grasshopper," a master teacher, travelled many miles, both literally and figuratively, from her academic origins in the eastern United States to teach in China. On September 12, 1918, the thirty-five-year-old zoologist departed from San Francisco Harbor on the China Mail Steamship Company's newly purchased and refurbished *Nanking*.[10] Spectacled, strong-chinned Boring was on her way to teach biology at the pre-medical college of Rockefeller Foundation-funded Peking Union Medical

College, an institution that had opened only the year previous to her sailing.[11] Her position was temporary, so she had no reason to assume that she was making an irrevocable career change. In spite of the experience of many women biologists, Boring with irrepressible confidence never doubted that when she returned to the United States she would be offered a teaching position.

Twelve time zones from Maine in a land where tomorrow is today, Boring might have expected to be lonely. Instead, she encountered other American biologists who were participants in the geographical expansion of western biology. When she met her new colleagues, she found that five had joined the PUMC premedical faculty in 1917 and were friendly, congenial, and shared some of her background experiences. PUMC biology department chairman Charles R. Packard had even studied with her former teacher, the well-known geneticist Thomas Hunt Morgan.[12]

Boring's rich life was filled with academic science; she published papers in both experimental biology and taxonomy, and prepared generations of Chinese students for successful careers in medicine and biology. However, it is clear that these matters, however important, were generously mixed with concerns about her relationships with family, friends, students, and colleagues—especially Yenching University president, Leighton Stuart.

Throughout her early life in both the United States and China, romantic attachments eluded Boring, largely because she was preoccupied with teaching, politics, and research. Men found her desire to control situations and relationships distinctly unfeminine, although they accepted her as a respected colleague. One man, however, seemed to be unbothered by her demeanor, although the nature of their relationship is unclear. From their first meeting, Boring worshiped Leighton Stuart, the handsome president of Yenching University and later United States Ambassador to China. She supported him unquestioningly, and defended him against all detractors. Brother Edwin teased her about her infatuation with Stuart, and students reported seeing Stuart and Boring strolling across a bridge on the Yenching campus holding hands. Her friendship with English teacher Grace Boynton was seriously endangered after a quarrel over Stuart.

In some sense, these personal factors might be considered extraneous to science; clearly Boring thought they were. However, Boring's life and work can be used to support both sides of the current feminist debates about the existence of a special feminine science characterized by family concerns and relationships. While Boring herself would have insisted that she was teaching pure, "objective" biology, the reasons that she gives for teaching science in China are colored by an idealistic vision.

Alice Middleton Boring's contributions belie the myth that women had little importance in the development of science. She is one of many women scientists whose previously unexplored lives show the involvement of women in the discipline. She extrapolated Nettie Stevens' ideas about chromosomal determination of sex to additional organisms and published numerous papers in developmental biology. In China, she worked on the taxonomy of reptiles and amphibians of that country, added information on little-known organisms, and discovered new ones.

What distinguishes Boring from the other women scientists who were students of Morgan, was the venue in which she chose to practice her trade. Candid, blunt Boring would have had little opportunity to exercise power if she had remained in the United States. Although she had absolute control in the classroom, outside its boundaries she was subject to constraints dictated by male colleagues. Even her competently completed research problems in experimental zoology were suggested by others. Third World China allowed her to exercise authority in a new way. Transplanted into a small community of westerners, she was able to appropriate the power largely reserved for men in the American scientific environment. In China she became the biologist-premedical advisor who controlled students' fates. As a part of her university's "inner circle" she participated in the determination of both biology department and university policies, for colleagues and superiors knew that her support would aid their favorite projects.

Historians of science have realized that through reading about the lives of their subjects, they may gain insight into not only the kind of science pursued by the subject, but the relationship between the individual and the science. In the case of Alice Boring this relationship is apparent in the emphasis that she gives to research science and to teaching. It is also clear that Boring lived in an especially interesting time and place in history, and was involved in globe-shattering events. As their biographies indicated, other women scientists in some ways have common experiences with Boring, but her specific orientation in time and place makes her life different from others. Whereas Marie Curie worked with radioactivity, Sofia Kovalevskaia studied mathematics, and Barbara McClintock made important discoveries in genetics, Alice Boring's life and science were distinguished by her commitment to improving the lives of her Chinese students through her teaching and research.

Notes

1. Yenching University was located outside of Beijing, People's Republic of China. Yenching has now been incorporated into Beijing University.
2. The English transliteration "Peking" will be used instead of Beijing when referring to the medical school because it is known as Peking Union Medical College (PUMC) today.
3. Dr. Wu Jie Ping described the incident in an interview with Marilyn Bailey Ogilvie on 13 July 1988. In a letter to Clifford Choquette on 6 November 1988, Nai Hsuan Chang Shen noted that she "always wore different shades of green outfits in classes. Green must be her favorite color."
4. Frederick F. Kao, "Remembering Miss Alice M. Boring." An essay printed on 3 February 1989.
5. Boring to Family, 22 Aug. 1924. Special Collection Archives, Yale Divinity School.
6. A.M. Boring to Family, 14 June 1924, Special Collection Archives, Yale Divinity School; Interview, Wu Jie Ping with Marilyn Bailey Ogilvie, 13 July 1988.
7. Edwin Garrigues Boring, "Edwin Garrigues Boring" (Clark University Press, 1952), Reprinted from *A History of Psychology in Autobiography*, 4, pp. 27–28.
8. Alice. M. Boring, Letter, *Bryn Mawr Alumnae Quarterly*, July 1914.
9. Ibid.
10. Gordon Newell, ed. *The H.W. McCurdy Marine History of the Pacific Northwest* (Seattle, Washington: Superior Publishing Co., 1966, p. 269).
11. PUMC opened on September 11, 1917.
12. Packard had studied with Morgan at Columbia, and Boring with Morgan at Bryn Mawr.

Chapter I
Origins and Early Years

I

Alice Boring's first New World ancestor, John Boreing, presaged Alice's adventurous nature when, as a widower with a young daughter, he abandoned England and emigrated to the fertile colony of Maryland in 1670.[1] He married two more times and, with his third wife, Anne, produced four children, the youngest of whom, Thomas, was Alice's ancestor.

One of Thomas's great grandsons, Ezekiel (1788–1861), began a new religious tradition for the family that would be important in the lives of Alice and her immediate family. Ezekiel became a minister of the United Brethren (Moravian) Church.[2] The church's official toleration of doctrinal differences as long as its adherents held "fast to essentials" carried on through the Boring tradition to Alice. She abhorred religious groups that condemned behaviors such as smoking and drinking and ignored social issues such as the plight of hungry children and oppressed adults. Ezekiel married Catherine Moore, and their eight children included John Dobbins Boring (1811–1884), Alice's grandfather.[3] This Boring, a carpenter and building contractor, moved to Pennsylvania where the Moravian church had achieved more prestige than in Maryland, married Eve Catherine McCurdy, and with her produced six children, one of whom, Edwin McCurdy, became Alice's father.[4]

Five feet eight inches tall, Edwin McCurdy Boring (1839–1920) had gray eyes, a light complexion, and dark hair. He joined the Union army on April 18, 1861 as a private, was discharged on July 26, 1861, reenlisted on September 17, 1861, and was finally discharged again on July 12, 1865. After the war, he moved to Philadelphia, became a well-known pharmacist, and married Elizabeth, the granddaughter of his Quaker pharmacist partner, Edward Briggs Garrigues.[5] The Garrigues family was proud, snobbish, and not altogether happy with the marriage of Elizabeth and Edwin Boring, for they were convinced that she had married beneath herself.[6]

Edwin and Elizabeth never were free from the strong Garrigues influence. Harmony was subordinate to economy as four generations literally lived together. Alice's orthodox Quaker great-grandfather, Edward B. Garrigues, owned the drug store at 10th Street and Fairmount Avenue. He lived next door to the store with his domineering sister, Alice's favorite great-aunt who "was always kind to children." Alice literally lived over the store with her grandmother, blind Hicksite (Liberal) Quaker grandfather, mother and father, two older sisters, and younger brother. The houses were connected, and the two groups had their meals together.[7] The living arrangements of Edwin and Elizabeth and their four children, Lydia Truman, Katharine Genther, Alice Middleton, and Edwin Garrigues influenced the development of each child.

Alice's brother, Edwin G. Boring who became an eminent experimental psychologist at Harvard University, elaborated on the position of the Garrigues and Boring men in the household. Their Hicksite Quaker grandfather's opinions were ignored, for not only had he "gone blind . . ." but "was a business failure" as well. Alice and Edwin's father, "had an additional handicap to being male;" he was also a member of the Moravian Church and thus "counted as an outsider in this Quaker family, which thought he lacked the cultural background of the Garrigueses."[8] Psychologist Edwin asserted that his father compensated for his sense of inferiority by insisting on a college education for his children. Lydia (Ly) graduated from Bryn Mawr College and became a Latin and classics teacher, Katharine (Kat) did not graduate from college but married an educator and minister, Alice (the "Kid" or Alicia) earned a doctorate from Bryn Mawr and became a university professor, and Edwin (Garry or Garri), earned his doctorate from Cornell University and, like his sister Alice, became a university professor. Garry insisted that the three Boring girls were more acceptable than he to their grandparents, and that his appearance as a boy was an "unwelcome surprise."[9]

The social life of the Boring-Garrigues tribe revolved around the family. There were few guests and they seldom went out. The children were not allowed to play with the "rough" children of the "deteriorating" neighborhood, and were left to their own devices to entertain themselves. The sense of adventure that led John Boreing and Jean Garrigues to the New World seemed notably lacking in this generation.

Alice's attitudes toward religion were shaped in this early environment and carried over to her experiences in China. Although doctrinally

Moravians abhorred sectarianism and Quakers stressed the overweening importance of love, she found these ideals strangely missing from the religions practiced in her home. Her experience with religious intolerance led her to deplore it. The family configuration was influenced by religion, involving more than the two denominations, Quaker and Moravian. Different family members belonged to two different Quaker branches, the conservative Orthodox and the liberal Hicksite. Alice's grandmother had been disowned by the Orthodox Quakers for marrying a Hicksite, Alice's blind grandfather. Edwin McCurdy Boring apparently had some influence over the religious direction of his immediate family, for he and Elizabeth were married in a Moravian church and, after their grandfather died, the parents and four children attended Moravian services. The children's educations reflected an additional bit of ecumenism; the girls attended a Hicksite Quaker school and Garry, an Orthodox Quaker school. Although they did not attend a Quaker Church the four children used the "plain language" (thee and thy) to family members throughout their lives. Religion influenced their ethical outlooks. Garry noted that in his childhood there was "much going to church," stressing "a pervasive sense of duty and right whenever decisions were being made."[10]

Perhaps Alice was more influenced by the Quaker ethic than she would have admitted. When the "Great Powers" bullied China after the Boxer Rebellion, her Quaker pacifism was offended. Critical of the forms and minor hypocrisies of established religion, she accepted a broader, more humanitarian approach to life. However, the quarreling Quaker factions of her childhood and their less than idealistic behavior may explain some of her later prejudice toward missionaries.

II

When Alice entered Friends' Central School, a square building at Fifteenth and Race Streets in Philadelphia, she encountered both boys and girls preparing for college but in separate classes, on different floors, and with different teachers. Although Friends' Central was coeducational in name only, it still fulfilled Edwin M. Boring's dream of a progressive educational atmosphere for his girls that would prepare them for college. Alice, president of the class of 1900, could look back on several innovative pedagogical practices within the school. Chemistry, for example, was not a subject to be memorized from a thick, unillustrated, small-print volume but included hands-on laboratory activities. Mixing, measuring, weighing, and heating actual substances inspired Alice and her fellows to want to understand chemical reactions. Smelling the pungent odor of sulfur dioxide was much more impressive than reading in the textbook that sulfur dioxide smelled like rotten eggs! The essential ingredients of laboratory experiences were available to girls as well as boys, even though they were taught chemistry separately.[11]

Laboratory chemistry was not the only area in which Friends' Central was progressive. Although Alice never attended it, the school had opened a kindergarten in 1877 when such early training was a radical idea. During Boring's time at the school, physical education for girls was introduced. The innovations, such as laboratory training in addition to standard curricular offerings, provided Alice with an excellent college preparatory education.[12]

Alice, decision to attend Bryn Mawr College was not only based on its reputation as one of the "Seven Sister" colleges and its Quaker connections, but on the fact that her older sister, Lydia, had graduated from the college in 1896. Its Quaker origins and values, its prestige as one of the Eastern women's colleges where women of "good" families could obtain a high-quality education, and its proximity to Philadelphia all contributed to her decision.

From its origin in 1885, Bryn Mawr reflected the belief of its Quaker physician founder Dr. Joseph W. Taylor that women should have the opportunity for a superior university education in a variety of fields. Graduate courses led to advanced degrees in each department, and Bryn Mawr was the first college in the United States to award a Ph.D. degree to a woman. Its dean and in 1884 first woman president, Margaret Carey Thomas, devoted her life to securing opportunities for higher education for women.[13]

Once Alice decided to apply to Bryn Mawr, she submitted herself to a barrage of entrance examinations. Although she passed all sixteen examinations, her highest scores were in science, mathematics, and French and lowest in Latin, Greek, American History, and English Composition and Punctuation. An observer on the Bryn Mawr campus on the day that Alice arrived would have seen a tall, thin new scholar (she had not yet gained the weight that made her appear rather stout in later photographs) studying the college's geometrically shaped stone buildings with a steady gaze through rimless glasses. Her rather determined chin and firmly set jaw gave the impression of a young woman with decided ideas. Her demeanor was that of a sensible, no-nonsense, no-frills person.[14]

The eight courses that Boring took as a first semester freshman seemed a formidable introduction to college. However, when the first-semester grades were recorded in February 1901, she had performed above average in all of her courses except "physical culture," in which she chalked up simply a "pass." She had decided to major in biology, but her first semester biology grades were not outstanding. By the end of the second semester, she had improved them.[15]

Alice spent increasingly more time in the many-windowed biology laboratory in Dalton Hall. Long tables ran underneath the windows, and students sat for long periods of time in wooden, curved-backed swivel chairs, continually adjusting their microscope mirrors in order to collect the maximum amount of light. The long center table decorated with glass-bottled preserved specimens was useful if one was not using a microscope and did not need the light. Two curved-legged demonstration tables backed by a portable blackboard and a glass-fronted storage cabinet filled with the usual delights of a biology laboratory presided over the front of the room. The demonstration tables were strategically located between metal support columns that marched across the front of the room and were topped with pseudo-Greek capitols.

Bryn Mawr's biology faculty included Nettie Maria Stevens (1861–1912), a Research Fellow who had not yet made a name for herself; and Thomas Hunt Morgan (1866–1945), who was just beginning to acquire an international reputation in cytology and experimental embryology. Boring first encountered Morgan in her freshman biology class. She admired him greatly, writing that "as a freshman I was enthralled by his telling us humble students of his Minor Biology class about the exciting things he had been doing with frogs' eggs the night before."[16] High biology marks during her sophomore year reflected Boring's increased interest and proficiency in the subject.[17]

Bryn Mawr did not require a broad scientific and mathematical background for its biology majors. Biology was the only science Boring studied during her freshman and sophomore years. During her entire college career she took only one mathematics course, a one-hour course, "Fundamental Theorems of Mathematics," audited as a senior. By the time she was a junior with most of her required general education courses behind her, she was required to take three laboratory science courses: physics, chemistry, and biology.[18] The heavy load appeared to challenge rather than daunt, for she received "credits" in physics, and "high credits" in both chemistry and biology. During her junior year, Morgan allowed her to participate in his experiments. Flattered by his trust, she claimed that she became "sold to biology for life." Many years after the fact, she confessed that the "frogs' eggs unfortunately reached the critical stage in the evening after Dalton was closed. . . ." Therefore, the only way to make the critical observations "was to throw pebbles at Dr. Morgan's window until he came down to let me into the building."[19]

The frog adventure was a part of Boring's first major research project. After her nocturnal visit to Dalton Hall, she meticulously used both preserved and living materials to observe and record spatial relationships within the parts of developing non-traumatized frog embryos. She was ecstatic when the collaboration with Morgan resulted in a joint paper in a prestigious German embryological journal.[20]

Morgan and Boring had studied one of the most important problems confronting investigators at the beginning of the twentieth century—the mechanism for cell differentiation. They hoped to clarify the controversy between scientists who thought environment controlled differentiation and those who were convinced that heredity was dominant. Morgan and Boring's research seemed to indicate that, although environmental trauma could alter the course of development, the most important determinants lay within the embryo itself. By studying regeneration, the renewal of lost or damaged parts, Morgan later sought to support his supposition, presuming that the same mechanism operated in normal differentiation and regeneration.[21]

By the time she was a senior, Boring had become sufficiently familiar with research techniques and procedures to work on her own. Proud of her success with the first publication, she resolved to incorporate the results of her new research into another paper. This time, following a suggestion of Morgan and Nettie Stevens, she sectioned, stained, and studied the course of embryonic development in a species of the hydroid genus, *Tubularia, T. crocea*. With the confidence of more experience, she criticized the work of a biologist who had done similar work with a Neapolitan species. Moving from the safety of pure observation, she ventured into interpretation. Carefully observing the formation of a membrane closing the two sections of the stems of *T. crocea* slit with fine scissors, she concluded that the membrane formation was not caused by mitosis (normal somatic [body] cell division).[22] Boring began to gain assurance in her ability to understand and explain what she saw. Work by Morgan again supplied the theoretical framework for the explanation. In his work on regeneration, he had proposed that a small piece of tissue could be remolded into new tissue that eventually would take on the form of the entire organism without mitotic or amitotic cell division. Young Boring was able to demonstrate that this phenomenon, called *morphallaxis* by Morgan, appeared in the fusion of the halves of the tubularian stem. She published this second paper independently in the *Biological Bulletin*, a newly created journal of the Marine Biological

Laboratory at Woods Hole, Massachusetts.[23] Few undergraduates publish papers with their mentors and even fewer publish papers on their own.

Boring divided her academic time between research and class work. During her final year as an undergraduate, she again took three science courses each semester. She studied embryology and chemistry for the entire year, adding meteorology the first semester and oceanography the second. In June 1904, when she received her A.B. degree, she had accumulated an excellent record.[24]

Although Boring remained at Bryn Mawr to work on her Master's degree, this year may have been anticlimactic, for Morgan had left for Columbia University. She found, however, a worthy colleague in the scholarly forty-two-year-old Nettie Stevens. Boring was outgoing and intense, Stevens quiet and shy. Boring enjoyed socializing with her colleagues while Stevens's associations were usually restricted to a professional relationship. The two women's complementary characteristics made for a good professional match.

Stevens had already earned her Ph.D. degree from Bryn Mawr (1903) under Morgan, but remained in college as a Research Fellow while awaiting the results of a grant application to the Carnegie Institution. As her fellowship was assured for only one semester and the fate of her grant application was unknown, she received an appointment from Bryn Mawr for 1904–1905 as Reader in Experimental Morphology.[25] While Stevens was at the Hopkins Seaside Laboratory at Pacific Grove, California, she had performed some experiments on regeneration in a flatworm, *Polychoerus caudatus*, an inhabitant of the underside of stones and shells in shallow tide pools. Boring and Stevens compared the regeneration of this undifferentiated flatworm with the more highly organized freshwater planarian. Stevens collected the material at the Hopkins Seaside Laboratory, classified the specimens, described the external anatomy, and experimented on the regeneration of the parts. She preserved large numbers of these worms, brought them back to Bryn Mawr, and assigned Boring to work on the histology of the group. They concluded that the more differentiated fresh water planarians exhibited both mitosis and morphallaxis along the cut surface, whereas the less differentiated *P. caudatus* showed only morphallaxis.[26]

As Boring and Stevens worked with flatworms, they recognized a variant form that they described as a new species. The result was a second collaborative paper between the two women, a description of the new form *Planaria morgani*, which they named for their mentor, Morgan.[27]

In June 1905, Boring received her Master's degree, having divided her time between physiology (one-third) and morphology (two-thirds).[28] Since Bryn Mawr was not nearly as exciting for Boring without Morgan, when the time came to continue her graduate work she decided to attend another institution close to home, the University of Pennsylvania. At Pennsylvania, she studied with another outstanding scholar, Professor of Zoology Edwin Grant Conklin (1863–1942). He never attained Morgan's renown, but his work in cytology, embryology, and genetics was well respected. Conklin not only was Boring's teacher but became a close, life-long friend.[29] Although she received support from a University of Pennsylvania Fellowship, Boring left after the academic year 1905–1906. Perhaps if Conklin had stayed, she would have remained at Pennsylvania for her doctoral work. He was well qualified to supervise her work, which was divided between morphology (four-fifths) and physiology (one-fifth).[30] However, Conklin moved to Princeton, and Boring applied for admission to the Ph.D. program at Bryn Mawr on November 14, 1906, where Stevens supervised her dissertation.

By the time she applied to the Ph.D. program, Boring had established her own goals. Not only did she recognize that she wanted to continue with her originally declared specialties, "principal subject," morphology, and "subordinate subject," physiology, but she had already begun work on her thesis.[31]

From purely descriptive works on regeneration and embryology, Boring had moved with a host of investigators into an exciting and potentially fruitful area of research, the role of the chromosomes in heredity. During the early part of the twentieth century, scientists were exploring this relationship aggressively. The behavior of the chromosomes during cell division suggested a possible mechanism for the transfer of hereditary traits. The postulate had been proposed as early as 1884 and 1885, but the evidence supporting it, although intriguing, was not convincing. Two men working independently, Theodor Boveri (1862–1915) in 1902 and Walter S. Sutton (1876–1916) in 1903 collected more compelling evidence. They were unable to include actual examples, since no trait had been traced from the chromosomes of the parent to those of the offspring, nor had a specific chromosome been linked with a specific characteristic.[32] Edmund B. Wilson and Nettie M. Stevens independently supplied the missing example. They each traced the behavior of an aberrant chromosome to the inheritance of a specific trait, sex. Stevens first published her interpretation in 1905 on the basis of work on the common meal worm, *Tenebrio molitor*. Since the course of spermatogenesis (sperm formation) differs from insect group to insect group, Stevens needed supplementary evidence from a diversity of forms to confirm her generalizations.

Hoping to find additional information, in the summer of 1905 at Woods Hole Stevens suggested Boring's dissertation problem—to follow the course of spermatogenesis in additional groups of insects.[33] Boring, whom Stevens had known for several years by this time and whose work she respected, seemed ideal to support Stevens's pioneering ideas. Although Boring was spared the frantic search for a topic that often plagues graduate students, she may have lost an opportunity for originality. When she filled out her application for the Ph.D. program, she had already completed much of the research on her dissertation, both with Stevens during the Master's year and the following year with Conklin at Pennsylvania. When the dissertation was completed she had changed the title from the application-form topic, "A Study of the Germ Cells of Several Hemiptera Homoptera" to the more specific title, "A Study of the Spermatogenesis of Twenty-Two Species of the Membracidae, Jassidae, Cercopidae and Fulgoridae," but the general subject remained the same.[34]

After a radically new scientific theory has been propounded, one of the major tasks confronting subsequent investigators is the gathering of additional supporting data. Without this collecting of information, a broad-based scientific theory is impossible. Boring's carefully conceived and executed project supported Stevens's pioneer efforts. By demonstrating a basic consistency undergirding the superficial variations within families, she extended Stevens's work.[35]

Reviewing Stevens's accomplishments, Boring may have felt envious of her mentor's willingness and determination to pursue pure research in a singleminded fashion. As a graduate student, she followed Stevens's example. By choosing Nettie Stevens's favorite research subject, spermatogenesis, as her own topic, Boring showed her admiration both for Stevens and her choice of subject matter. The two women spent many hours together in the laboratory. They also travelled to Europe together in 1908. Interestingly, neither mentions the other in extant documents. Boring credits Morgan with stimulating her interest in biology, but is strangely silent about Stevens. Stevens seldom expressed opinions about people, so her silence was in character, but outspoken Boring's taciturnity seems curious. Boring may have been concerned that she could never match Stevens's major theoretical breakthrough. Even though her capability was apparent as she extended Stevens's work, she may have been dissatisfied. After showing that she could subject herself to the rigid discipline necessary to accomplish a significant piece of research, she may have wondered if it was worth the effort—especially if she could not match Stevens's theoretical facility. Perhaps she began to view herself as Stevens's assistant and resented the position.

Boring distilled several important principles regarding the relationship between chromosome number and taxa. She concluded that chromosome number was not significant for determining either families or genera, but that "the number of chromosomes is constant for each species." She implied, but did not state explicitly in the conclusion, that species represent natural taxonomic entities but families and genera do not. She also indicated the importance of chromosomes in determining taxonomic relationships.[36] Although she sometimes seemed tantalizingly close to an important theoretical conclusion, she stopped short of actually making her point. Unlike Stevens, she found life's variety more exhilarating than pursuing a single project to its conclusion. Teaching, with its concern for people and their relationship to the subject matter, may have offered Boring the diversity she sought.

Outgoing Boring showed an aptitude for teaching during her graduate studies. During 1907–1908 after completing her dissertation (but before receiving her degree), she accepted a position as Instructor in the Biology Department at Vassar College.[37] She remained at Vassar for only one year, however, for graduate students in biology were encouraged to spend part of their graduate tenure at a marine biological station. Boring spent the next academic year, 1908–1909, satisfying that requirement in Europe.[38]

Boring's college German became more useful than she ever had imagined. She was able to use it when she took advantage of the Mary E. Garrett European Fellowship to study at the University of Würzburg and the Naples Zoological Station. Although she had excelled in her one-year class in college German and had passed her senior oral examination, seven years had elapsed since the course. By arriving in the summer before she was to begin the first semester on November 1, she was able to spend six weeks in Eisenach studying German, with time left over to travel.[39]

The two institutions where Boring studied had already attracted many American cytologists and geneticists. Theodor Boveri alternated between Würzburg and Naples and was one of the major attractions for the American workers. His famous sea urchin experiments were important in providing a firm foundation for the chromosomal theory of heredity. Boring was extravagant in her praise of Boveri, advising future Garrett Fellowship holders that Würzburg was an excellent place for American biologists to work because Professor Boveri "departs from the German custom and always gives his students much individual attention and interest."[40]

At the beginning of his career, Boveri had rejected the idea of women working in his laboratory. However, after he met and married Marcella O'Grady, a talented biologist in her own right, he appeared to change his mind. Stevens studied with Boveri during 1901–1902, and he influenced her subsequent work in the chromosomal basis of sex determination. Stevens returned to Würzburg in 1908. After this second visit, Boveri referred to "Miss Stevens and the woman who accompanied her" as "the purest blood suckers."[41] Boveri had become increasingly disillusioned with Americans who came to his laboratories for short periods, absorbed inordinate amounts of his precious research time, and emerged triumphantly with superficial publications. He apparently lumped Stevens and her "companion" into the parasite group that absorbed the benefits of his laboratory without contributing to its success. After Stevens "and the woman who accompanied her" left, each "with one or two completed works, just like Morgan," Boveri vowed "never to take on another person who doesn't remain at least a year."[42]

For the second semester of her Fellowship, Boring moved to the Zoological Station at Naples. Director Anton Dohrn's original concept of an international institute for marine biology had emerged from a nineteenth-century fascination with marine biology. Zoologists were intrigued by the possibility of extending Charles Darwin's theory of natural selection to marine forms. By comparing the development "of the simpler and lower forms, such as most of the species living in the sea," to the "higher, more complex" species, they hoped to chart evolutionary relationships.[43] Systematists, morphologists, embryologists, and physiologists all flocked to the new institution.

Dohrn financed his institute from three sources: the public exhibition aquarium, the sale of preserved marine animals, and the renting of working places to scientific institutions or governments. The last financial source, known as the "Table System," provided Boring with her working space. Such an opportunity had only recently become available to women scientists. During the 1890s, American male zoologists were able to absorb the latest in scientific ideas from Europe, particularly Germany, by participating in research at the Naples Zoological Station. Many institutions such as Harvard, Johns Hopkins, and the Smithsonian Institution supported tables for American research scientists. However, no such tables were available for women until physiologist Ida Hyde (1857–1945) formed a committee in 1897 to work toward subsidizing an American woman. In 1898, Bryn Mawr's Margaret Carey Thomas, enthusiastic about the project, headed a committee called the Naples Table Association for Promoting Laboratory Research by Women. Thomas persuaded women's colleges and individuals to contribute fifty dollars each to under-write this research.[44]

Boring benefitted from this arrangement. Her appointment to the American Woman's Table assured her of not only the right to a working space but also a daily supply of fresh animal material, instruments, reagents, and the use of the library.[45] From March 12 to June 9, 1909, Boring collected and preserved material to analyze later. She also studied Mediterranean plankton daily in order to familiarize herself with as many "forms as possible."[46]

III

Since Boring had completed her dissertation before she had left for Europe, she collected her Ph.D. degree from Bryn Mawr College on her return in 1910.[47] She accepted a position as Instructor in Zoology at the University of Maine's Agricultural College. Armed with a brand-new doctorate, a teaching job at a major state university, and with colleagues who appreciated her accomplishments, Boring seemed well on the way to establishing herself as a university professor with excellent research credentials.

Her dissertation represented the longest piece of work that Boring produced in the areas of genetics and embryology, but the twelve papers that she published while at Maine reflected her continued interest in the subject. The first of these papers resulted from her work at the Zoological Institute in Würzburg during the winter semester, 1907–1908. The topic was suggested by Boveri, who proposed that she repeat an experiment done by three other investigators who had identified an inverse relationship between temperature and size of the nucleus in sea urchin eggs. Convinced that such an inverse relationship did not exist, Boveri encouraged Boring to repeat the earlier experiment, using *Ascaris megalocephala*, a parasitic roundworm subject to great changes of temperature within its life cycle. As predicted by Boveri, but contrary to the work of the previous investigators, the size and number of the nuclei of *Ascaris* embryos remained the same regardless of the temperature. In this paper, as in her previous publications, the idea was suggested by Boring's mentor, but by careful, dependable work she supplied the observational and experimental evidence required to support the hypothesis.[48]

Boring's experience in Naples and Würzburg also resulted in a second small paper. While studying *Ascaris megalocephala*, she used her skill at identifying chromosomes acquired during her work with

Stevens to describe a small chromosome that she assumed was a sex chromosome.[49]

In the remainder of the papers that Boring published while at Maine, she was guided by the interests of Raymond Pearl, then chairman of the department of biology at the Maine Agricultural Experiment Station (1907–1916). Although Boring collaborated with Pearl on several publications, she never became involved in his earlier fascination with the power of eugenics to solve social problems. By the time she worked with him, Pearl had begun to doubt the effectiveness of selection for the "improvement" of organisms, including human ones. He had mounted an attack on both natural and artificial selection as viable mechanisms for producing new types.[50] Boring's contributions remained basically cytological and histological. At the agricultural station, she used Pearl's favored research animals, poultry and cattle, as research subjects.[51]

In her first collaborative paper with Pearl, Boring considered the relationship of the domestic chicken's testicular and ovarian fat deposits to the functional activity of these organs.[52] In a second paper, they collaborated to consider genetic factors involved in the patterning of individual chicken feathers. Observations had indicated that although patterning on individual chicken feathers was inherited in a "clean-cut Mendelian manner," unusual modifications were found. If the feather was removed from the follicle immediately after it was fully grown, a new feather would be regenerated but would not show the same pattern as the original. With continued regenerative activity, the "patterns tend to be broken up, and probably will ultimately be entirely lost as a definite pattern." They concluded that the "pattern factor or gene" may be represented by a limited amount of material in each follicle; when this material is used up, the pattern is lost.[53]

Notes published by Boring and Pearl concerning the problem of determining whether the male or female chicken is homozygous for sex help clarify the professional interaction among Boring, Stevens, and Pearl. Pearl began the work, Boring added to it, and then they sent materials to Stevens at Bryn Mawr for comment. Stevens's death at age fifty-one from breast cancer may have inspired Boring to publish their incomplete data on the subject. After Stevens died, Boring found Stevens's "rough notes and drawings" and decided that they should be published. Although the useful drawings did not provide an unequivocal answer to the question, they illustrate a continued relationship among the three scientists.[54]

As she became known for her research and teaching skills, Boring progressed rapidly up the academic ladder. She was an instructor for part of one year (1911), assistant professor for two (1911–1913), and associate professor for five years (1913–1918). Most early-twentieth-century women's academic careers never proceeded beyond assistant professor, yet Boring made extraordinary progress. If she followed the typical male career trajectory she would have been due for a promotion to professor at any time. Boring was not the only woman to find the Maine Agricultural Experimental Station a congenial place to work. Edith Marion Patch (1876–1954) became head of the department of entomology and published numerous papers. Maynie R. Curtis, Maud DeWitt Pearl (Raymond Pearl's wife), Lottie E. McPheters, Hally Jolivetter Sax, and Anna R. Whiting were all connected with the Station at about the same time and authored or co-authored papers.[55]

Of the eight-hundred students at the agricultural institute one hundred were girls. Boring voiced her preference for male over female students. "I like the job, and I like to teach boys (this statement is based unscientifically upon unequal data–one year at Vassar to five years at Maine)."[56] Her preference for male students did not interfere with her belief in "Votes for Women" and she promised to "claim citizenship in either Pennsylvania or Maine, according to which state grants equal suffrage first."[57]

Neither Pennsylvania nor Maine claimed her citizenship, however. Events in distant China, far from Orono, Maine, eventually laid claim to her future. Boring probably learned of an opportunity to teach in China through her association with the Marine Biological Laboratory, Woods Hole, Massachusetts.

This center for biology was a place where practitioners of both descriptive and experimental disciplines could gather in pleasant surroundings during the summer; work on their individual projects; and, most importantly, be included in the network of personal interactions that made them a part of a biological community.[58] Women were an important part of that community as attested by the number of papers written by women published in the MBL's journal, the *Biological Bulletin*.[59] Unaccompanied women could "walk, collect, and participate in biology without danger to their reputations."[60]

Although conflict between experimental and descriptive biologists disrupted the tranquility of early twentieth-century academic biology, an "era of good feeling" at the MBL muted this antagonism between morphologists and physiologists. The distinction between biological and medical research also was blurred. With distinguished medical experimentalists such as Simon Flexner, Franklin P. Mall, and Jacques Loeb in the MBL's past and with support from the Rockefeller Foundation in its future, the Rockefeller Foundation's new venture in China, the Peking Union Medical

College, probably was discussed by members of the MBL community.[61] Morgan, Pearl, Conklin, and Gilman Drew, men with whom Boring was involved professionally, were a part of the MBL network. Her friend and colleague, Drew, had resigned his position at the University of Maine in 1911 to become full-time Director at the MBL.

Notes

1. On July 14, 1670, Boreing presented his claim for 250 acres of land to the provincial government. Land records of Baltimore County indicate that he made numerous land trades in the vicinity of the Patapsco, Back, and Middle Rivers, including parcels named Boaring's Pasture, Boaring's Passage, and Boaring's Range. Roger S. Hecklinger and Edwin G. Boring, *The Descendants of John Boreing, Maryland Planter* (Mimeographed, 1950), pp. 8–9.

2. Ibid., p. 21. The inclusive nature of this church was evident in its insistence that "inner fellowship with the Brethren should neither involve nor demand separation from any existing Evangelical body." (E.T. Corwin, J.H. Dubbs, and J.T. Hamilton. *A History of the Reformed Church, Dutch, the Reformed Church, German and the Moravian Church in the United States* [New York: The Christian Literature Co., 1895], pp. 439–462; "Unity of the Brethren" [*Unitas fratrum*]. See also *The New Schaff-Herzog Encyclopedia of Religious Knowledge,*" Samuel Macauley Jackson, ed. [New York: Funk and Wagnalls, 1912], 12, pp. 91–93).

3. Hecklinger and Boring, *The Descendants of John Boring*, p. 21.

4. "Diary of the Journey of Rev. L. Schnell and V. Handrup up to Maryland and Virginia, May 29th to August 4, 1747," *The Virginia Magazine of History and Biography*, 12 (July 1904), pp. 55–82.

5. Ibid. Elizabeth Potts Brown to Clifford Choquette, 23 February 1983, Quaker Collection, Haverford College; Edwin McCurdy Boring, "Declaration for Pension," Bureau of Pensions, Dept. of the Interior. See also Frederick H. Dyer, *A Compendium of the War of the Rebellion*. [Dayton, Ohio: The National Historical Society in Cooperation with the Press of Morningside Bookshop, 1979], p. 1600).

6. Edmund Garrigues, compiler 1st ed. (1938) and R.C. and M.L. Garrigues, compilers 2d ed. (1982). *A Genealogy of Matthew and Suzanna Garrigues Who Settled in Philadelphia about the Year 1712, and their Descendants*. With Introductory Notes of Families of the Same Name with an Account of the Family in France, England, Holland, Germany, and Denmark. Additional information on the Garrigues family is available at the Historical Society of Pennsylvania, 1300 Locust St., Philadelphia, PA., 19107.

7. Edwin Boring, *Edwin Garrigues Boring*, Worcester, Mass. (Clark University Press, 1952) pp. 27–28.

8. Ibid.

9. Ibid.

10. Ibid.

11. Clayton L. Farraday to Clifford Choquette, 30 July 1982. Although the school was located at Fifteenth and Race Streets when Boring attended, it moved to suburban Philadelphia in 1925.

12. Ibid.

13. Bryn Mawr College, Office of Public Information. See also James Mellow, in *The Charmed Circle. Gertrude Stein & Company* (New York: Avon Books, 1975), pp. 86–87.

14. Alice M. Boring, Entrance Examination Results. Prepared by Friends' Central School, Philadelphia and in the possession of Bryn Mawr College. Alice scored a 90 in physiology ("high credit" score) and in the 80s in plane geometry, algebra, and French ("credit scores)." Her lowest scores were in the 60s ("passes"), in Latin I & II; Greek I, II, and III; American History; and English Composition and Punctuation. She earned "merit" ratings, scores in the 70s in Latin III, English grammar, and solid geometry.

15. Boring, Undergraduate Transcript. In the possession of Bryn Mawr College. The marks proceeded from "failed" through "conditioned," "passed," "merit," "credit," and "high credit." The only two "high credit" marks that she received were in German grammar and translation. Her first semester biology laboratory grade was a "credit" and the lecture a "merit." By the end of the second semester, she had maintained her "credit" in laboratory but earned a "high credit" in the lecture.

16. Boring, "Thomas Hunt Morgan," *Bryn Mawr Alumnae Bulletin* (February 1946).

17. Boring, Undergraduate Transcript.

18. Ibid.

19. Boring, "Thomas Hunt Morgan." *Bryn Mawr Alumnae Bulletin* (February 1946).

20. Thomas Hunt Morgan and Alice M. Boring, "The Relation of the First Plane of Cleavage and the Grey Crescent to the Median Plane of the Embryo of the Frog." *Archiv für Entwickelungsmechanik der Organismen* 16 (1903), pp. 680–90.

21. Garland Allen, "Morgan, Thomas Hunt," *Dictionary of Scientific Biography*, ed. Charles Coulston Gillispie, 16 vols. (New York: Charles Scribner's Sons, 1974) 9, pp. 515–526 (517–18).

22. She found that mitotic figures were not more common in the slit than in the unslit tubularians.

23. Boring, "Closure of Longitudinally Split Tubularia Stems." *Biological Bulletin* 7 (Aug. 1904), pp. 154–159.

Origins and Early Years   25

24. Boring, Undergraduate Transcript.

25. Ogilvie and Clifford J. Choquette, "Nettie Maria Stevens (1861–1912): Her Life and Contributions to Cytogenetics," *Proceedings of the American Philosophical Society* 125 (Aug. 1981), pp. 293–311 (299–300).

26. Nettie M. Stevens and Boring, "Regeneration in Polychoerus caudatus," *Journal of Experimental Zoology* 2 (August 1905), pp. 336–345.

27. Stevens and Boring, "Planaria morgani n. sp." *Proceedings of the Academy of Natural Sciences of Philadelphia* 58 (May 1906), pp. 7–9.

28. Boring, Graduate Transcript.

29. In 1951, when Conklin was president of the American Philosophical Society, he invited Alice Boring to attend the meeting as his personal guest. Since members were allowed only one guest, "usually their wives, but Conklin was then a widower," it was an honor. Edwin Guerigues Boring, Comment on Clara Woodruff Hull, "Alice Middleton Boring–1904."

30. Boring, Application for Graduate School, Bryn Mawr College.

31. Ibid.

32. Ogilvie and Choquette, "Nettie Maria Stevens (1861–1912): Her Life and Contributions to Cytogenetics," *Proceedings of the American Philosophical Society* 125 (August 21, 1981), pp. 292-311 (199–300).

33. Boring, *A Study of the Spermatogenesis of Twenty-Two Species of the Membracidae, Jassidae, Cercopidae and Fulgoridae*. A Dissertation Presented to the Faculty of Bryn Mawr College for the Degree of Doctor of Philosophy (Baltimore: 1907). Reprinted from *The Journal of Experimental Zoology* 4 (October 1907), pp. 502, 508.

34. Boring, Application for Graduate School; Boring, *A Study of the Spermatogenesis of Twenty-Two Species of the Membracidae, Jassidae, Cercopidae and Fulgoridae.*

35. Ibid.

36. Ibid.

37. Boring, "Curriculum Vitae," Alumnae Association of Bryn Mawr College.

38. Boring, "Report Presented by Holder of European Fellowship to the President and Faculty of Bryn Mawr College."

39. Ibid.

40. Ibid.

41. Ogilvie and Choquette, "Nettie Maria Stevens," p. 298. Archivist Maria Gunther found Boring mentioned in two letters from Boveri to Richard Goldschmidt of 17 May 1909. Boveri wrote, "I will send you along with this letter a short article by Miss Boring (including an appendix of mine) with drawing and figures you might want to use for your archives." In a second letter, 29 October 1909, Boveri noted that "I received the correction of Miss Boring's article with my appendix two days ago." Boveri to Goldschmidt, 29 October 1909. Archives, University of Würzburg.

42. Boveri to Goldschmidt, 29 Oct. 1909.

43. Christine Groeben, *The Naples Zoological Station at the Time of Anton Dohrn. Exhibition and Catalogue*, trans. Richard and Christl Ivell (Edition for the Centenary of the Naples Zoological Station, 1975), p. 12.

44. Margaret W. Rossiter, *Women Scientists in America. Struggles and Strategies to 1940* (Baltimore: The Johns Hopkins University Press, 1982), pp. 47–48.

45. Groeben, *The Naples Zoological Station*, p. 42.

46. Boring, Report Presented by Holder of European Fellowship.

47. Boring, "Curriculum Vitae," Alumnae Association of Bryn Mawr College.

48. Boring, "On the Effect of Different Temperatures on the Size of the Nuclei in the Embryo of *Ascaris megalocephala*, with Remarks on the Size Relations of the Nuclei of univalens and bivalens," *Bryn Mawr College Monographs* 9 (1910).

49. Boring, "A Small Chromosome in *Ascaris megalocephala*." *Archiv zur Zellforschung* 4 (No. 1, 1909), pp. 120–131.

50. Garland E. Allen, "Old Wine in New Bottles: From Eugenics to Population Control in the Work of Raymond Pearl, 231–261" in *The Expansion of American Biology*, eds. Keith Benson, Jane Maienschein, and Ron Rainger, 1991.

51. Franklin Parker, "Pearl, Raymond," *Dictionary of Scientific Biography* 10, pp. 444–45.

52. Raymond Pearl and Boring, "Fat Deposition in the Testis of the Domestic Fowl," *Science* 39 (January 23, 1914), pp. 143–44.

53. Boring and Pearl, "Some Physiological Observations Regarding Plumage Patterns." *Science* 39 (January 23, 1914), pp. 143–44.

54. Boring and Pearl, "The Odd Chromosome in the Spermatogenesis of the Domestic Chicken." *Journal of Experimental Zoology* 16 (January 1914), pp. 53–54.

55. David C. Smith, *An Annotated Bibliography of the Maine Agricultural Experiment Station* (Orono, Maine: Maine Agricultural Experiment Station, Bulletin 808, April 1985). The bibliography lists the publications of the Station from before the Hatch Act to 1985, describes the content, and includes an index.

56. Boring, *Bryn Mawr Alumnae Quarterly* (July 1914).

57. Ibid.

58. Philip J. Pauly, "Summer Resort and Scientific Discipline: Woods Hole and the Structure of American Biology, 1882–1925," in *The American Development of Biology*, eds. Ronald Rainger, Keith R. Benson, and Jane Maienschein (Philadelphia, University of Pennsylvania Press, 1988), p. 131.

59. See early editions of the *Biological Bulletin* for the women who published in this journal.

60. Pauly, "Summer Resort and Scientific Discipline: Woods Hole and the Structure of American Biology, 1882–1925," p. 134.
61. Ibid., p. 141; Frank R. Lillie, *The Woods Hole Marine Biological Laboratory* (Chicago: University of Chicago Press, 1944), pp. 146–47.

Chapter 2
The China Experiment

I

At Wood's Hole on July 25, 1918, Alice Boring received official notification that she had been appointed Assistant in Biology at Peking Union Medical College. When the Rockefeller Foundation first announced the need for premedical teachers for its new medical college in Beijing, she had applied and had been unofficially assured that she would be accepted. Her expectations from the position were firm, simplistic, clear, and unequivocal. She intended to export the best of western biology to Chinese premedical students, thereby providing them with the tools they would need to become successful physicians. They, in turn, would apply what they had learned to help their people. The two-year appointment would begin on August 1, 1918, carry an annual salary of $1,200, and provide "a residence in Peking, probably together with some of the other single ladies of the school."[1]

The expectations of American scientists who crossed the Atlantic Ocean to work in European laboratories were quite different from those who crossed the Pacific. Like many of her colleagues, when Boring returned to the United States from Naples and Würzburg she brought new data from European investigators as grist for scientific papers. Although China might yield data for publications (particularly in the areas of taxonomy and medicine), Boring and other westerners did not envision gleaning ideas from Chinese scientists. They expected the information flow to proceed from the United States to China.[2]

Although Boring had no clear understanding of the past relationship between China and the West, she did not join those westerners who classified modern Chinese as ignorant, superstitious, impoverished, and heathen. She recognized, even though vaguely, that China possessed a rich cultural and intellectual past and was confident that if its people could only be exposed to the "truths" of modern western science, China would have a brilliant future. Other western visitors had varying motives for their interest, including genuine religious conviction, hope for individual aggrandizement, and a vision of Manifest Destiny extended across the Pacific. Most westerners, however, had at least one common belief; they were convinced of the superiority of western civilization.[3]

For its part, proud China was woefully ignorant of the West. Unaware that western technology and social advances were producing traders and missionaries interested in dominating all parts of the globe, the Chinese were unprepared for these incursions. Resting assured that their culture was superior, they were complacent when peculiar, tall barbarians with strange eyes, varying hair colors, and flowing beards landed on their shores. The Portuguese were the first Europeans to develop a sustained relationship with China. Their actions set the stage for the antagonism between China and the West that Boring was to enounter in 1918. One group of arrogant, boorish traders reputedly enslaved their captives, and, according to one Chinese report, "stole or bought little children in order to cook and eat them."[4] Exaggerated though this account might be, the antagonism between the two peoples increased and culminated in Portuguese expulsion in 1522.

The expulsion was not absolute, for the Portuguese were allowed to found a mutually beneficial trading post (Macao) on an uninhabited peninsula at the entrance of the Port of Guangzhou. The Chinese continued to consider Macao a part of Chinese territory, but allowed foreigners to live according to their own laws and customs within their "depot." The Portuguese colony maintained relations with China through a leader who was given a nominal Chinese official rank. The custom was soon extended to include Spaniards, Dutch, and British, for the Portuguese were unable to maintain their monopoly in Chinese trade through Macao after 1600.

The customary Chinese way of interacting with foreign trade emissaries spawned the predatory ideas of extraterritoriality and unequal treaties that became politically important in Alice Boring's lifetime. However, the long-term effect of this policy was not apparent during the seventeenth century. The Chinese were contemptuous of the Europeans who intrigued against each other, confirming their biases that all barbarians were crude, cruel, rude, and ignorant.

The personality of one man, Italian Jesuit missionary Matteo Ricci (1552–1610), provided a new model for Chinese-western relations. With the blessings of Gregory XIII (Pope 1572–1585), Ricci's goal was to "win souls for Christ." However, the method of this gentle, persuasive, intelligent man (who taught himself to read and write Chinese and who understood and respected Chinese customs) was so different from that of his arrogant, dogmatic predecessors that the Chinese were forced to reconsider their generalizations about Christians and westerners. Ricci expanded his diplomatic approach to consider not only religion but mathematics, astronomy, cartography, and mechanics as well. By delving into science and technology, he established a pattern that became pivotal in the relationship between China and the West. He assumed that shown the superiority of western predictive astronomy over their own methods, the Chinese would eventually conclude that Christianity was superior to Confucianism, Taoism, and Buddhism, a postulate that defined the westerners' hopes for China through the mid-twentieth century. Ricci's successors had some tantalizing early successes, but when they began to concentrate their efforts on converting the economically deprived and less educated groups, the total number of Chinese Christians remained stagnant.[5]

The very essence of Chinese tradition became threatened as western ideas and aggressive economic and territorial policies invaded the country. The desperate Manchus (Qings) willingly prostituted themselves for the necessary funds. Western merchants hovered nearby, ready to take advantage of weakness. Illegal trade in opium provided a lucrative income for western merchants who brought the substance to China from India and delivered it to Chinese smugglers. As the demand for opium increased in China the number of addicts became alarming, stimulating the government to take drastic actions to quell the traffic. Incensed at what they perceived to be an encroachment on their right of free trade, the British resoundingly defeated the Chinese in a series of skirmishes known as the Opium Wars (1840–1842). As a result, in 1842 China was forced to negotiate an unfavorable treaty with Great Britain (and during the next two years equally unpalatable ones with France and the United States). These crippling indemnities ("unequal treaties") and special privileges to western nations and their citizens ("extraterritoriality") stimulated protests from the Chinese that later became a factor in Alice Boring's career. If the Chinese emperors appeared arrogant to westerners in the eighteenth century, their views could not match the western insolence regarding Chinese autonomy in the nineteenth century.[6]

The Manchu Dynasty was plagued by internal revolts during the same time period as the western encroachments. One of these revolts, the catastrophic Taiping Rebellion, further eroded confidence in the regime, and presaged the period of the warlords. The rebel army grew into a force of about thirty thousand men and women in 1850 and became powerful enough by 1853 to seize Nanjing and to set up their "heavenly capital."[7] Since local forces of the Qing military organization were ineffective, a new type of armed power, regional armies, developed to control the threat. Eventually the rebellion was squelched, but in its aftermath the new regional armies outside the control of the Qings became increasingly powerful.[8]

Although the Manchu government attempted to regain control over the armed forces, it was unsuccessful. Its failure resulted in humiliation when the Chinese were defeated in the Sino-Japanese War (1894–1895). The Chinese lost not only "face" but territory and money as well in the peace treaty that ended the war. In the settlement, China ceded Manchuria and Taiwan to Japan and paid a large indemnity to the Japanese. Sun Yat Sen (1866–1925), incensed with China's "shame" and the inability of the Manchus to deal with it, advocated the overthrow of the regime and began to work for this end.

Frustration with the western nations as well as with Japan festered in the period before Boring became involved in China. Obviously the territorial and commercial demands made by the West were galling. However, western religion as practiced and taught by the increasing numbers of Christian missionaries also was considered intolerable by many Chinese who abhorred the adulteration of Chinese ways by western ideas of all kinds. This anti-Christian, anti-western spirit erupted into violence as the Boxer Rebellion, originally inspired by a Chinese secret society. Although the rebellion was originally anti-Manchu, Manchu officials moved from opposition to surreptitious support to open endorsement. In 1900, the Boxers exploded into an orgy of church sacking and missionary killing. Finally, they besieged the foreign diplomatic legation quarter in Beijing for two months. Indignant westerners, after the legation was liberated, forced additional humiliation on the Chinese. On September 7, 1901, the Chinese government was forced to sign the Boxer Protocol. This settlement resulted in large indemnities to the western nations, destruction of Chinese forts, the occupation of Chinese territory by western troops, and a restriction against re-arming.[9]

From the time Boring received her doctorate in 1910 to her first voyage to China in 1918, the revolutionary movement had strengthened, and revolts against the Qing Dynasty had occurred in several cities. Power fell into the hands of military men, with Yuan Shih Kai emerging from the 1911 Revolution as the single most powerful individual. However, Sun Yat Sen rather than Yuan became the first president of the Chinese Republic (January 1, 1912).[10] The frail government, fraught with provincial particularism and fettered by a weak power base, achieved one of its major goals, the formal abdication of the Manchu Dynasty (February 12, 1912). In an attempt to ease friction, Sun supported Yuan's claim for the presidency and formally resigned during the beginning of April, 1912.[11]

The republican form of government thwarted Yuan's ambitions and he soon was at odds with both his cabinet and parliament. Sun's nationalistic Guomintang collected the majority of parliamentary seats in the elections of December 1912 and January 1913. The new Prime Minister Song Jiao Ren was assaulted on March 20, 1913 and died on March 22. Although it was certain that Yuan was responsible, the Guomintang did not pursue the case.[12]

Song's death marked the end of the parliamentary experiment and opened the era of Yuan Shi Kai's dictatorship (March 1913–June 1916). With a depleted treasury and surrounded by hostile forces, Yuan became dependent on foreign financiers. Forced to make humiliating concessions in order to get money and never in control of the entire country, Yuan's government was in constant danger. In 1914, he nearly was successful in restoring the monarchy but failed when he signed Japan's notorious Twenty-One Demands. Public outrage produced a determined anti-monarchical movement. Demands for Yuan's resignation were resolved by his death from natural causes on June 6, 1916.[13]

After Yuan's death, the central government became increasingly unstable and virtually powerless. Contests between rival military factions for power and money resulted in attempts by individual warlords to take over the machinery of the central government. At the same time, they attempted to maintain and strengthen regional autonomy.

Familiar with the latter part of China's history, Boring was indignant with the role the United States and the other western powers had played in producing China's predicament. From reading the newspapers and talking with Americans who had returned from China, she instinctively sided with what she perceived to be the interests of the Chinese people. She planned to do her share to right the wrongs perpetrated by extraterritoriality, unequal treaties, and economic injustice by using her teaching skills in whatever area they might be most useful.

Historically, the West has attempted to impose its culture on China in two ways: through force and through providing needed services. Neither of these approaches worked to the West's advantage. The first method, born of western ignorance of Chinese civilization, involved attempts to bully the Chinese into conforming to western ideas. The second, far more sophisticated approach, seemed to harbor seeds of success. By melding into Chinese society, westerners learned which services were valued and provided them through technology. There was always the tacit assumption that the Chinese would automatically recognize that countries with superior technologies would also have preferable religious and trade practices. The second approach was more pernicious than the straightforward first, for the Europeans when convinced that they understood the Chinese tended to deceive themselves. When the seventeenth-century Jesuits proffered their superior astronomical technology, the Chinese accepted this gift, but most refrained from accepting the Christianity that was programmed to follow.

Missionaries from both conservative-evangelical and liberal, social-conscience persuasions agreed that western norms were the only ones to be taken seriously. Even those missionaries who railed against the imposition of western culture on the Chinese were convinced that, under certain circumstances, the good of the people justified some coercion. A book of Mother Goose Missionary Rhymes published by the Presbyterian Board of Foreign Missions for use in Presbyterian Sunday Schools appealed for money with the following rhyme:

> The money went to China
> Where there's ignorance and sin
> Now Mary has another box
> To put more pennies in.[14]

Early-twentieth-century China was especially vulnerable to western onslaught. Proud China cringed under the ineffectual leadership of the Qing Dynasty. A corrupt military, depleted treasury, and domestic revolts had heaped woes upon the regime. Humiliated by the Japanese in the Sino-Japanese War and by the West after the Boxer Rebellion, the Qings no longer were able to flaunt China's historic claim of superiority over the West. The special mandate from Heaven that established the legitimacy of a Chinese Dynasty's rule seemed to be seeping out of the ruling family's hands. The Manchurian Qings constantly had to defend their Heaven-given mandate against claims that they were foreigners descended from Tartars. By the nineteenth century, the emperor could no longer afford to be isolationist and arrogant.

Although the contacts between the West and China had crested and ebbed at different times in history, the Chinese had been, for the most part, content with an isolationist position. Although both China and the West were convinced that their people possessed the "truth," they manifested their convictions in different ways. The Chinese, encouraged by the Confucian attitude of reverence for the Emperor, assumed that the farther one retreated from his presence at Beijing, the more degenerate the society. Although formerly it had been unthinkable for the Chinese to pollute themselves by associating with western barbarians who lived so far from culture's center, the situation in early twentieth-century China forced them into a humiliating position with the West. Westerners, for their part, were convinced that it was they who were blessed with religious, scientific, and economic "truths." Unlike the Chinese, they were obsessed with the possibility of sharing their revelation by persuasion, or if that failed, coercion.

II

Boring was unimpressed by reports of temporarily collaborating scheming local armies, internecine power struggles between warring factions, and victimized workers and peasants. Since she seldom acknowledged fear, her decision to become involved in an unstable China did not include concern for personal safety. Violently opposed to economic and religious exploitation, Boring agreed with those who saw medicine as a perfect wedge for penetrating the Chinese consciousness. As Harvard President Emeritus Charles Eliot explained, "we find the gift of Western medicine and surgery to the Oriental populations to be one of the most precious things that Western civilization can do for the East. . . ."[15]

To her distaste, Boring learned that she was going to have to confront a missionary element at PUMC. She was annoyed by pious, platitude-spouting "goodie goodies" who neglected to confront basic ethical questions. Surprisingly, she found some of the missionaries committed to her own Quaker ideals of social justice, and that the mission movement in China was far more complex than she had first imagined.

Boring knew that missionaries had been involved in Peking Union Medical College's origin. It had been customary in the mission community for the physician and missionary to be the same person. However, the founder of PUMC's ancestral hospital (1861), British physician William Lockhart, claimed that when "a man attempts to follow two professions, . . ." he "always fails signally in one," and "sometimes in both." He adamantly opposed fusing evangelism and medicine.[16]

Nevertheless, it was support from the London Missionary Society that made Lockhart's original hospital in Beijing possible. During the Boxer Rebellion, the entire mission compound was decimated, and nothing remained of the highly ornate, spacious, former Buddhist temple hospital. After the rebellion was squelched, the rebuilding task overwhelmed the single mission. To make the task feasible, the London Missionary Society, the American Presbyterian Mission, and the American Board of Commissioners for Foreign Missions combined to form the North China Educational Union. This institution gave rise to the immediate predecessor of the Peking Union Medical College, the Union Medical College.[17]

The Union Medical College did not retain its autonomy for long. An America that was "feeling its oats" moved from an attempt to alter Chinese consumption and worship habits, to changing Chinese society itself.[18] The establishment of philanthropic foundations, especially the Rockefeller Foundation, made this goal possible. John Davison Rockefeller's (1839–1937) strict American Baptist background made him susceptible to former Baptist minister Frederick T. Gates's idea of "wholesale" philanthropy—giving filtered through a centralized organization. Gates's brain child eventually resulted in the formation of the Rockefeller Foundation in 1913, the organization that made possible the large-scale exportation of American science and medicine to various parts of the world, especially China. When the Rockefeller Commissions explored ways in which the Foundation could best become involved in China's affairs, they concluded that adapting western scientific medicine to China might contribute to America's civilizing mission in China.[19] After the Foundation received its charter from the state of New York in 1913, individuals with diverse interests (business, religion, teaching, and government) met "to consider whether this new agency might be able to carry out a useful work in China, and to advise as to the kind of activity, if any, it might most advantageously undertake." They concluded that "aid in the development of modern medicine" would be an effective service. The Rockefeller trustees sent a study commission to China that resulted in the October 21, 1914, report acknowledging the need for better medical education.[20] The Foundation accepted the report, and organized a special department, the China Medical Board, to take charge of the work.[21]

Medical educational reform in the United States had received impetus after Abraham Flexner issued a scathing report exposing blatant abuses.[22] In an effort to correct their perception of the situation, American physicians went to Germany to study "scientific medicine," and upon returning to the United States attempted to put their German-gained knowledge into practice. One of these physicians, William Henry Welch of the Johns Hopkins University, later became intimately involved in the Rockefeller Foundation's enterprises in China. Welch travelled to Germany in 1876 to study in the laboratory of Carl Ludwig. When he returned to the United States, he converted Johns Hopkins into a model of the "ideal" medical training institution. Like new converts, Welch and the other Johns Hopkins physicians were evangelically certain that their approach was the only acceptable possibility. Since their reform program succeeded in the United States, they assumed that a transplanted program would flourish in China. Because of the political chaos, public health in China was in a dismal state. The Rockefeller Foundation stepped in during this time and blended noble intentions such as a humanitarian interest in the well-being of the inhabitants of poor countries with more ignoble concerns, including the use of philanthropy as an adjunct to the United States' imperial diplomacy.[23]

After surveying medical education programs throughout China, Commission members decided that Beijing was the preferred site for a proposed new medical college, and that the old Union Medical College should be purchased and incorporated into the new structure. Negotiations to purchase the college went smoothly after Wallace Buttrick, the first director of the China Medical Board, convinced the London Missionary Society that its mission work could be continued and would, in fact, be enhanced because of the broadened financial base. The purchase was consummated when the China Medical Board purchased Lockhart Hall and the remainder of the old Union Medical College. In addition to the Union Medical College, the Board purchased an adjoining old Chinese palace and additional property to the west for expansion.[24] On July 1, 1915, the China Medical Board assumed the full support of the College, then called the Peking Union Medical College.[25] Previously this piece of land had belonged to the descendents of the Manchu Prince Dodo, known by the Chinese as Prince Yu. Dodo's descendents squandered his wealth and were eventually forced to sell the property. The beautiful, elaborate old buildings resembling those in the Forbidden City were torn down in order to build the new medical school. The construction began in 1917, one year before Boring arrived in China, and the new buildings were completed for the dedication in 1921 after she had returned to the United States. As beautiful as were the new, eclectic Chinese-western style buildings with their brilliant emerald green tile roofs, they could not compare to those ancient ones torn down in the name of progress.

Given the elitist concept of medicine propounded by the Rockefeller group and the populist approach of the missionaries, conflicts appeared inevitable. Although Rockefeller, Jr., stated that denominational and doctrinal restrictions would not be considered in staff selection, the need to placate was apparent in the make-up of the governing body—an equal number of representatives from the missionary societies and from the China Medical Board.

Although a tenuous truce existed between the missionaries and the Rockefeller employees, hostility festered beneath the surface. Wallace Buttrick, concerned about the effects of this latent antagonism on the quality of medical education, engineered a second China Medical Commission to do investigative work in 1915. Commission member Welch of Johns Hopkins closely monitored the situation at PUMC. A politic man, he was able to defuse many of the anxieties of the missionaries magnified by another commission member, sharp-tongued physician Simon Flexner. Flexner bluntly complained that "the men [mission trained] who have come out as teachers were not teachers and were not trained for their work."[26] Flexner's comments to the missionaries that the responsibility for "creating inferior men" lies firmly "in your hands" caused them to fear for their jobs. A polemical missionary tract published in 1916 began, "A great danger is threatening the Foreign Missions of the Church." The "great danger" was the Rockefeller Foundation which had "captured" the Union Medical College. Vivisection was reputedly among the other evils propounded by the Rockefeller Institute and "Dr. Simon Flexner [one of the Rockefeller Foundation trustees] is one of the most notorious of its vivisectors." Graphic descriptions of cruelty to animals and an affidavit describing the supposed vivisection of babies by Flexner at the Rockefeller Institute followed.[27]

Rampant rumors included the report that the Medical Board would demand the withdrawal of all missionaries from medical facilities. A recommendation that classes be taught in English rather than Chinese also disturbed the missionaries. They feared this innovation would hinder their attempts to create a medical terminology in Chinese and slow their efforts to translate medical techniques into Chinese.[28] The missionaries argued that "Chinese students taught in English" were likely to "be out of touch with the people and will not advance Chinese medicine." The Rockefeller representatives countered that few Chinese translations of medical works were available, and they wanted the students to have the best training possible.[29]

Members of the first China Medical Commission wrangled over the ideal form for Chinese medical education. Abraham Flexner and Charles Eliot disagreed both about its purpose and programmatic implementation. Flexner originally contended that medical schools could best serve China's needs by providing a broad-based practical medical education. He argued that medical education in China need not be based on a core of basic sciences, for "an immense amount of medical treatment can be practiced with a very limited knowledge—or perhaps no knowledge in a wide sense of basic science—of chemistry, physics or biology...."[30] Eliot, on the other hand, insisted that medicine must be firmly grounded in the basic sciences. His arguments were persuasive, and eventually even Flexner conceded that it was both desirable and possible to provide a premedical education similar in nature to the best programs in the United States. The preliminary conflict between Flexner and Eliot over the form medical education should take in China reflected a broader conflict between corporate class interests and those of the common people. Both groups were convinced that their views would benefit society as a whole—the corporate class working through the philanthropic foundations naturally tailored its model of a medical system to fit the needs of a capitalist society, whereas the working class people favored a more populist approach to medicine. The goals of the Rockefeller Foundation for medicine prevailed even in China, where the needs were quite different from those in the United States.[31]

When PUMC was opened, John D. Rockefeller, Jr. described the facility as "the best that is known to Western civilization not only in medical science but in mental development and spiritual culture."[32] Entrance requirements, curricula, and training objectives comparable to those in the finest medical schools in the United States and Europe were introduced into China's traditional agrarian society. The program was designed to train a small number of scientifically oriented medical doctors who, in turn, would train other doctors.[33] The emphasis on higher standards involved larger expenditures for fewer students, making it impossible to address the vast medical needs of the country.[34]

In their quest for "excellence," the Rockefeller representatives scorned traditional Chinese medicine as superstition and scoffed at missionary medical facilities as backward. In justifying the Commission's conclusion, H.P. Judson wrote to Rockefeller, Jr. on May 17, 1914, that in China a "large body of native practitioners" exist who "with practically no knowledge of modern science," depend on "ancient remedies handed down for the most part through family tradition." Although he admitted that "in some cases herbs used had certain beneficial effects," he insisted that many of their treatments were useless and potentially dangerous. He noted a particularly virulent practice, "puncturing the body with a needle."[35]

One of the goals of the new medical education was to eliminate such "nonsensical" folk medicine. Since the Commission hoped to produce a medical school with stringent entrance requirements, students obviously needed better premedical preparation. The Commission report, which was important for Boring's future, described the proposed premedical curriculum of biology, chemistry, physics, mathematics, English, and

Chinese. The standards suggested by the report were unrealistic, for no college in China offered adequate training in the basic sciences. When Commission members examined the available schools, they found few capable of supplying this need. Consequently, they decided to establish a temporary premedical school as a part of the medical school. This school, designed to provide the needed basic training in the pure sciences, was intended to exist only until other premedical centers could upgrade their offerings.

In response to the Commission's recommendation, the new president of Peking Union Medical College, Franklin McLean, supported the establishment of the premedical school as the first program of the new medical college. On December 20, 1916, this program, which provided Boring's initiation to China, was approved, and on September 11, 1917, the premedical college was opened.[36]

The novelty, lack of established routine, and logistical obstacles challenged but did not daunt Boring. Being a part of a new institution just beginning to define itself and operating in a setting where academic constraints were not as well defined as in the United States was liberating, as she had hoped it would be, when she left dull, secure Maine.[37]

In spite of her unsympathetic attitude toward missionaries, Boring may have reaped some benefit from the acceptance of women within their ranks. Women clearly dominated the lay cohort of missionaries. A typical group of one hundred missionaries in 1910 would have included thirty ordained men, twelve laymen involved in nonmedical work, five physicians (including one woman and one of the ordained men), and fifty-five women. Women, although clearly subordinate in the hierarchy, had a considerable amount of practical influence. Although originally mission boards had hesitated to send out single women, by the time Boring arrived in China, the practice had become well accepted.[38]

Officials of the Rockefeller Foundation and of Peking Union Medical College expected that their policies of recruiting single women as teachers and admitting women as students would present potential housing problems. The problem was not immediately critical, however, for, originally, Boring was the only woman on the faculty (Alice Ryder, Assistant in English was appointed after December 31, 1918), although two others, Helen R. Downes in chemistry and Edna M. Wolf in biology, came in 1920, the year Boring left.[39] Roger Greene, the Resident Director, realized the need to build quarters for the single women of the staff.[40] A student nondiscriminatory policy was a part of the original program. Greene explained that in planning for PUMC the "important part that women can and do play in medical work has not been overlooked."[41] President

Franklin C. McLean wrote that "women are to be admitted to the Pre-Medical School on the same terms as men."[42] Greene admitted that having a single school for both men and women might "be regarded as a somewhat radical innovation,..." but noted that experience in which men and women attended the same classes had been successful.[43] In spite of this liberal philosophy, university officials did not plan for many women students. A report discussing the physical education facilities indicated that

> as women would be constituting a small fraction only of the entire student body, it would be expedient for us to make some arrangement for them entirely apart from the provision laid out for the men: as for instance, through the YWCA or a similar organization....

The "fact of having a few women students in attendance" would not justify "buying the costly ground and erecting an entirely independent unit for gymnasium purposes."[44]

The status of women in the new school troubled members of the Board of Foreign Missions of the Presbyterian Church. On the surface, they reported, it seemed as if there would no longer be a need for women's medical colleges, since the China Medical Board announced a resolution that declared that "while the Board of Trustees is not prepared at this time to make detailed plans for the medical education of women, it is the purpose of the Board to admit in due time qualified women students to the Medical College on the same basis as men."[45]

The resolution specified that no special attempts would be made to recruit women nor would special preparation in English be provided so that they would qualify. "The purpose is to leave the matter to its normal development as called for by the desires of those concerned." If qualified young women "shall present themselves for admission, they will be received into the same classes and on the same terms as young men." The Mission Board recognized that such an approach could prove retrogressive for the cause of medical education in China. The mission colleges faced a dilemma; should they "continue to maintain a Medical College for Women with the certainty that the most highly qualified young women who have a knowledge of English will seek their training in the far larger and better equipped College of the China Medical Board?" On the other hand, just as the missions retained medical colleges for young men in the Chinese language, "it may be desirable to make similar provision for women, in view of the probability that a large majority of the young women who wish to study medicine will not have the knowledge of English and perhaps not the scientific training which will enable them to pass the entrance examinations of the Medical College of the China Medical Board."[46]

Male professionals at PUMC differed in their attitudes toward women as colleagues. A contrast between Edmund V. Cowdry's and Roger Greene's perspectives was apparent when Dr. Alice Rohde's applied for a position as Associate Professor of Pharmacy. Cowdry considered her unsuitable on the ground "that she had moved so many times during her scientific career...in addition to her somewhat mature years...." He indicated "that it would be wiser to select one or two young men to carry on the work in a temporary fashion until a more thoroughly suitable candidate for the higher rank could be secured...." Although frequent job changing and age might have indicated a problem having nothing to do with the sex of the employee, Cowdry's statement regarding the young men suggests that he did not think highly of women professionals. In addition, the career trajectories of women academics often involved short-term, non tenure-track appointments. Roger Greene, on the other hand, disagreed with Cowdry's assessment. He argued for Rohde's appointment both from the standpoint of expediency and acceptability. The position needed to be filled immediately, pharmacology was a "somewhat restricted" field, and suitable young men to fill a junior appointment and come to China on short notice might be hard to find. Since the New York officers had reviewed Rohde's qualifications and pronounced her acceptable, Greene was in favor of hiring her. His arguments were accepted by the board, which "RESOLVED...that a cable should be sent approving the appointment of Dr. Alice Rohde as associate professor of pharmacology."[47]

Regrettably for Boring, her tour of duty was over before the formal dedication of the facility occurred. Had she been present at the dedication (1921), she would have heard a speech by Resident Director Greene that returned to haunt Americans. In 1949, several decades later, the Communists used his words to illustrate the racist and paternalistic designs of westerners in China. As did most of the speakers, Greene addressed himself to the pre-eminence of western medicine over Chinese traditional medicine. In an unfortunate choice of words, he explicitly stated what most westerners assumed, that the major reason the West should help China was to help itself. "Those Westerners who are working for the development of China, whether in industry, transportation, education or public health," should recognize that if "they succeeded in promoting the prosperity and happiness of the Chinese people" they would at the same time render an important service to their own countries. More insidious, however, was the "yellow peril" tone that crept into his speech. He indicated that a second reason for improving conditions in China was to keep the Chinese from emigrating, a prospect that might cause "a violent upheaval in the country which they invade."[48] Greene also suggested that PUMC join in the eugenics research movement that intrigued American zoologists at home. The proposed research at PUMC might validate or invalidate the idea of racial biological differences. To give him credit, Greene did not expect to find such differences, but his remarks at the Dedication were subject to misinterpretation in the future.

Most of the Chinese speakers concurred with the Americans about the pre-eminence of western medicine. Although the first two speakers seemed to accept this view unquestioningly, the third and fourth were less willing to discount China's own traditions. The fourth and last Chinese speaker, Minister of Education Ma Lin Yi, suggested a synthesis between western and Chinese medicine.[49] Indicating that "in olden times no difference between the medical theories and practices of the East and West" existed, he concluded that Chinese medicine took a different route from western medicine, "becoming more philosophical, while Western medicine followed the progress of modern science." He implied that he did not want China's traditions to be replaced totally by western scientific thought.[50]

Boring was disappointed to have missed the dedication speeches. She would have preferred Beijing to Boston. Her two years at PUMC had bred into her a new loyalty. It also had given her time to reflect upon her own abilities and interests. As she examined her research output, she fretted that, although she had demonstrated the ability to collect data accurately and to interpret results with understanding, she might lack the spark of originality necessary to transform her research from the mundane into the creative. Participation in the PUMC experiment had, however, confirmed her confidence in her teaching abilities.

When the two years were over, Boring reluctantly left China to begin her new teaching position at Wellesley College. Greene noted in his diary that he had engaged in a conversation with her in which she reported that she had not "attempted to do any research work while in Peking," as she would only be there for a short time and "did not feel that there were any special subjects on which it was worth while to begin work." She indicated a willingness to entertain different alternatives in order to work in China. Explaining that she had "gained some very valuable teaching experience in dealing with Chinese students," and that her stay in China had been "most enjoyable and worth while," she "suggested the possibility that if we required a dean of women some time in the future, she might consider an offer."[51] There may have been another reason why Boring neglected research at PUMC. According to Greene, members of the faculty complained that the teaching load in the premedical school was intolerable. "They feel the preference given to the departments of the medical school proper. Their teaching hours are so heavy that they do not have time for necessary reading, to say nothing of research work, particularly in the department of physics and chemistry." Boring, however, was in the department of biology where "the situation is not so difficult."[52] Boring found the workload acceptable, although it may have hindered her research productivity.

III

When Boring left Beijing with its pastiche of jade green and yellow-tiled palace roofs and violet and pink-hued walls she assumed that China would be relegated to a brief but fascinating interlude in her academic career. Resigned to returning to a "real job" in the United States, she was determined to avoid sinking "into a conscienceless drifting".[53] The square Inner City of Beijing with its fifty-foot-high walls pierced by nine gates enclosing spacious government offices, homes of wealthy citizens, banks, and legations must fade into memory.

With some trepidation she returned to the "real job" that she mentioned, an appointment as Professor of Zoology at Wellesley College. She resolved to succeed at Wellesley even though confronted by an inadequate zoology department budget, apathetic students, and a decided emphasis on the humanities over the sciences (one science, botany, being the exception). By convincing her friend and former Maine colleague Raymond Pearl to give a lecture to the zoology department she hoped to generate some renewed interest in the sciences in general and zoology in particular. The situation was so desperate, she explained to Pearl, that it was embarrassing, but true, that a general college lecture would be impractical as neither faculty nor students would attend. Science, she complained, was completely "downtrodden by the Humanities in this institution...." Boring contended that by aggressively promoting a departmental lecture, Wellesley zoology students and faculty might reverse this attitude. The zoology department might become an academic force to be reckoned with on the campus.[54]

Even if Boring's strategy for elevating the sciences to the level of the humanities worked, the zoology department, which had its building destroyed by fire in 1914, would still have been in trouble. It needed superb publicity, more than could have been generated by a lecture by

Pearl, in order to compete with the botany department. Since funds for the sciences were limited, whenever disputes over resources between the botany and the zoology departments occurred the botany department usually prevailed. The Wellesley zoologists had not yet made names for themselves, but botany could proudly point to the achievements of Margaret Ferguson (1863–1951) in plant physiology and genetics. Officials at Wellesley recognized zoology's problem and sought a solution. In Marian Hubbard's report to Wellesley President Ellen F. Pendleton she indicated her hope that Boring's appointment would be the catalyst needed. Praising Boring's credentials, she anticipated that her achievements would bolster the prestige of the zoology department.[55]

In spite of her good intentions, the anti-zoology milieu at Wellesley affected Boring's research. She began a project on the cytology of termite chromosomes but never completed it. It was difficult, she conceded, to continue to achieve when one's colleagues were content with the status quo. Most discouraging of all was the attitude of the students. In place of the dedicated, enthusiastic Chinese pre-medical students, she found complacent, self-satisfied ones. No specific incident spurred what might appear to be Boring's negative attitude toward American students. In addition to the specific problems in the zoology department at Wellesley, she was confronted by American students who were content with doing the minimum work required to pass; they considered education a right rather than a privilege. Boring suspected that many of the Wellesley young women were only putting in time until they married. On the other hand, most of the Chinese students whom she had so recently left were serious about their work and had ambitious professional goals.

Boring had just returned from an exhilarating two years in China. In China her talents were appreciated, she felt as if she were contributing to creating a better world through teaching interested students and supporting their enterprises, and she did not have to deal directly with her family. At Yenching, she shared an active social life with people of similar interests. It is not surprising that upon returning she found complacent Wellesley failed her standards.

Teaching at Wellesley was only part of Boring's disappointment when she returned to the United States. At home, she was confronted by a tedious plethora of business details that required attention. In China, she had only to consider simple financial problems—budgeting for clothes, food, servants, and vacations. From a distance, brother Edwin (Garry) had taken care of the more complex investment matters while teaching and doing research. Both her father and Garry were obsessively cautious about financial matters, a trait that led to conflict with less financially fastidious Alice. Admitting that even his personal relationships were often defined by money considerations, Garry recognized this preoccupation as a fault.[56] This recognition, however, did not preclude him from scolding Alice when she appeared irresponsible and uninterested in business. Alice's tastes were not extravagant. Although she liked pretty dresses and to have her hair "fixed" in the beauty shop, she was uninterested in luxuries. Her attitude toward the acquisition of money was equally conservative. She wanted sufficient quantities to meet her needs, but was not interested in stockpiling it for its own sake. Garry was not extravagant either, but he always feared the emergency that might occur and saved money compulsively to take care of any eventuality. Garry's caution and conservatism made him an excellent manager for family business affairs. Consequently, in 1920 when their father, in ill health, made a new will to replace one he had lost, he appointed Garry as executor.

When Edwin McCurdy Boring died on June 22, 1920, Alice received $1,000 in addition to her quarter share of the total estate. The total inventory was appraised at $40,357.89. Garry meticulously cared for the financial distribution, handled the interminable correspondence, and kept accurate records.[57] In one of many letters, Alice wrote to Garry acknowledging receipt of a check for $2,350, "probably the biggest check I have ever or shall ever receive in my life."[58]

Garry, although much younger than Alice, referred to her, as did the rest of the family, as "the Kid." Perhaps her newly acquired security allowed "the Kid" the freedom to act on her inclination to leave a vaguely unpleasant situation at Wellesley.

Discouraged with Wellesley, bored with routine, and saturated with family concerns, Boring became interested when an opportunity surfaced to return to China to teach biology in a proposed new institution, Peking (later called Yenching) University. Wellesley College had developed a special association with Yenching. As a Wellesley faculty member and one with a special interest in China, Boring was able to watch Yenching's development. Through her former colleagues and friends, she was aware of the trials and triumphs involved in the establishment of the new university. When Dean Alice Frame of Peking University suggested to Boring that "it would be a great help to them if Wellesley would lend...[her] to them for two years to teach biology," she saw a chance to leave Wellesley without burning any bridges.[59] If, as seemed likely, Wellesley agreed to give her a two-year leave of absence, she would have an opportunity to teach and do research in her beloved China without jeopardizing her security. Making a career in China still had not occurred to her or to those on the China Medical Board who would employ her. They planned to hire her only until biologist Nathaniel Gist Gee, who previously was committed to a three-year contract with the China Medical Board, could become permanent head of the department.[60]

The initial steps in the formation of the University occurred before Boring arrived in China to teach at the premedical school. Intense negotiations had occurred between 1916 and 1918 to establish a federated university forged from four separate entities. The largest of these institutions was Huei Wen (called Peking University in English) a school established in 1870 by the Methodist Mission in China. Western Christians, of course, were unpopular in those pre-Boxer Rebellion days and students were induced to attend the small primary school that was to develop into this university only by "letting it be understood that the school closed each day with a bowl of rice."[61] The "rice Christian" approach was effective, the school flourished, and in 1890 received a certificate of incorporation as a university.[62]

The second institution to contribute to the establishment of Yenching was a men's college, North China Union College located at Dengzhou, thirteen miles east of Beijing. It represented the Congregational Church through its American Board Mission, the Presbyterian Church through its Mission, and the British Congregational Church through its London Mission. The seeds of a possible merger appeared as early as 1901 in the correspondence of the President of the North China College to the Secretary of the American Board in Boston, in which he suggested establishing a union theological seminary in Beijing. He snidely noted that he hesitated to include the Methodists in the effort, for "they are very denominational in their work and produce men of quite a different type from our own. . . ."[63]

The North China Union Woman's College, like its men's counterpart, was a constituent college in the North China Educational Union. This college had the earliest origin of the three, developing from a girls' school, the Bridgman Academy, established in 1864. The Boxer Rebellion took an especially heavy toll on this school. Luella Miner, who became principal of the Academy in 1901, wrote that "the storm of 1900 swept away all of its buildings and a third of the pupils laid down their lives for the Master."[64] In 1905, the Woman's Board of Missions of the Interior provided funds for building and equipping the original college building, thus producing a pioneer attempt to provide a college education for women in China.[65]

The School of Theology, itself a composite institution, constituted the final ingredient to be merged into the reconstituted university. At the time that it was incorporated into Yenching it represented two separate unions in theological education in which five different missions participated.[66]

Once the principle of union had been accepted, the Methodists and of the Presbyterian-Congregational group became mired in petty disputes. The spirit of Christian good will appeared notably lacking as negotiations toward the union continued. Disagreement over name, location, and almost everything else made the consummation of the union seem unlikely. It was not until John Leighton Stuart (1876–1962) agreed to accept the presidency in 1918 that the petty disagreements between the two institutions were hushed. "Immediately," wrote Stuart, "I began to realize how much more intense were the divergencies between the two groups than I had expected."[67]

Graduates and supporters of the Methodist and of the Presbyterian-Congregational college could not agree on a name for the new university. Methodist graduates of Huei Wen (Peking University) threatened to repudiate their alma mater if the new institution was not named Huei Wen. The Presbyterian-Congregational graduates agreed to approve any name *except* Huei Wen, and promised, if this name was accepted, to "dramatically pile their diplomas on the Tungchow campus and let the bonfire symbolize the destruction for all of them of their alma mater." A completely different factor made it impossible to use the English, Peking University for the institution. A government university known in both English and Chinese as Peking University had been founded and was attaining both a national and international reputation. Therefore, it seemed "ridiculous" to arrogate to "their obscure little college" a name that "rightfully belonged to the Chinese who were making it the intellectual dynamo of their nation."[68]

After many emotional and vituperative sessions with neither side relenting, Stuart suggested that the decision be placed in the hands of an impartial commission of foreigners and Chinese. However, both sides refused the compromise suggested by the commission. Finally, when it looked as if the entire concept of union would be scrapped, Dr. Lowry of the Methodist group "with tears streaming down his face said that he had enough of commissions, that to scrap the idea of union was unthinkable and that as perhaps the one who had been most obdurate he would begin by throwing all of his cards on the table." From this point on, the seemingly impossible disagreements began to be resolved. Dr. Cheng Chin Yi, an outstanding Chinese Christian leader, suggested Yenching, "a glamorous word meaning capital [sic] of the ancient state of Yen and regarded by all Chinese as a poetic allusion to Peking."[69]

When Stuart was informed of the availability of some attractive property five miles from Beijing in "the celebrated Western Hills," the group purchased the property. Since ancient temples and palaces were already clustered in the area, they agreed to maintain architectural harmony by using an adaptation of Chinese architecture for the academic buildings. In keeping with the older buildings, "graceful curves and gorgeous coloring were designed for the exteriors...." They even recreated the landscaping of the garden of an ancient Manchu prince. By constructing the main structures of reinforced concrete and equipping them with modern lighting, heating, and plumbing, they avoided the inconveniences of the older buildings. Stuart saw the combination of the old and the new as symbolic of the mission of the university, "preserving all that was valuable in China's cultural heritage" with modern western technologies and ideas.[70]

Peking Union Medical College Resident Director, Henry Houghton, developed a special interest in Yenching, because of its potential to supply a premedical education to future Peking Union Medical College students. Occasioned by the need to rethink the premedical portion of the PUMC program, Dr. Paul Monroe, who served as a consultant on premedical education in China, recommended that PUMC's premedical program be phased out gradually and taken over by Peking University (soon to be Yenching).

Convinced that the departments of the medical school proper received preferential treatment, premedical teachers at PUMC complained that: "their teaching hours are so heavy that they do not have time for necessary reading, to say nothing of research work, particularly in the department of physics and chemistry. The situation is not so difficult in the department of biology."[71] Monroe recommended that the China Medical Board extend aid to Yenching, so that it could eventually eliminate the inequality by taking over premedical education for PUMC.[72] This proposal, which eventually had an enormous impact on Boring's future, created some anxieties among the existing premedical staff at PUMC. Houghton discussed "individually with the heads of the science departments" their attitudes toward remaining in China for an additional term, recognizing that Yenching would soon take over the premedical work.[73]

Although Boring realized that two or three years did not constitute a lifetime, she knew they could seem interminable if she was unhappy. If the Chinese experience did not offer the opportunity to grow professionally, she was uninterested. She did not want to be like "poor Miss Lane," who "has been trying to teach with nothing to teach with...; I am no such heroine as that!"[74] To avoid this frustration she wanted to make absolutely certain that she understood every aspect of the situation before she made any kind of a commitment. She received mixed signals from Roger S. Greene (by then a director of the China Medical Board), and Alice Browne Frame (dean of the Women's College). Greene envisioned a new university of excellence, although he was unclear as to how this goal was to be accomplished. On the other hand, Frame had only given Boring a "simple hint that maybe Wellesley would lend me to her for two years to teach the girls some biology."[75] Boring did not find the latter possibility appealing.

In order to clarify her understanding, Boring asked questions. If she did not understand the answers, she asked the same questions again. Although she queried everybody who would listen, it was Greene who bore the brunt of the assault. Patient at first, he was eventually annoyed by Boring's dogged persistence as she pressed him unmercifully for additional information. On November 10, 1922, he replied to a letter in which she had reiterated many of her previous questions which he thought he had answered. Obviously peeved, he wrote that he was sorry that his "letter of October 21 was apparently so incomplete and obscure to you." He promised to "try to do better this time."[76]

Boring, too, agonized over the questions. She, after all, was about to make a major change in her life, and, as she told Greene, she would not go unless she could receive assurance on several pivotal issues, including the relationship between the biology department at Yenching University and PUMC, the acquisition and disposition of equipment, the relationship between the women's department and the rest of the university, the association between the faculties of the two institutions, and salaries. Boring recognized the premedical division of PUMC as an ephemeral institution to be closed as soon as adequate alternative arrangements could be made. Therefore, she pushed Greene to clarify the relationship between PUMC and the science department at Yenching University. Proper, precise Greene responded that the two schools cooperated by sharing faculty and dividing up the students, with the elementary courses taught at Yenching and the more advanced ones at the medical college.[77]

Greene's answer did not satisfy Boring. Possibly, her "doubting Thomas" attitude was fueled by her years at PUMC, where there was a large gap between the salaries of the professors at the premedical school and the medical school, and the premedical faculty were overworked. Although Greene explained the current situation, she could not, from his description, "get a clear idea of what is to be done with the premedical classes in the future." This future interested Boring mightily, for she presumed to be a part of it. Never one to mince words, Boring diagnosed Greene's unwillingness or inability to successfully answer her questions as feeling his way, because he could not "turn any one department to P.U. until it has proved itself capable of preparing students adequately for the Medical School."[78] Stung by her bluntness, Greene proceeded to answer her questions explicitly, but obviously defensively. In a subsequent letter, he made it apparent that the premedical school at PUMC would not close until after the new university could competently offer a superb background in the pure sciences. He did not expect the new university to gain this stature until after it moved into its new buildings outside of Beijing, probably during the fall of 1924.[79]

Although Boring could cope with crude living conditions, low salaries, and heavy class loads, she found the idea of teaching biology without adequate equipment unthinkable. "Poor Miss Lane" with the nonexistent equipment haunted her every time she thought of the new position. She remembered the fine microscopes, well-prepared slides, and sophisticated equipment that she had used at PUMC. If Yenching University was to take over the premedical program, then it should inherit the equipment as well. In her early letter of inquiry to Greene, she questioned the disposition of the equipment. "I can not go out there unless I have something to work with...."[80] Greene's answer was hardly reassuring, for he admitted that "no equipment from our pre-medical school has been transferred to Peking University [Yenching] as yet...."[81] Remembering all of the microscopes and slides that she had collected during her first trip, she confessed to Greene that what she "really [was] getting at" was who was going to get the good equipment?[82]

The distressed Greene thought he had given Boring all of the information she had requested, and yet she persisted in asking what seemed to be the same questions.[83] In the meantime, Boring fired further specific questions to both Houghton, Director of the Peking Union Medical College, and Henry Winters Luce, of the New York office of Peking University.[84] Luce turned Boring's letter over to Stuart, who came to the rescue. Although his reply was far more general than Greene's, he was able to satisfy Boring whereas Greene could not. The diplomatic, dignified, and poised Stuart exuded confidence in both his person and on paper. While the University remained in Beijing, he assured her, Yenching would have full use of PUMC's equipment. Although Greene had said essentially the same thing, it was Stuart whose assurances she accepted that "we are to take over their Pre-Medical School and that this session and next session while we expect to be in the city, we have the full use of their equipment."[85]

Reassured by Stuart's positive answers, Boring accepted his explanation that until they moved to the new site the science departments of both institutions would have single departmental chairs. He said classes would be convened in the new buildings by 1924–1925, at which time no new students would be admitted to the premedical school at PUMC, although students in the two upper classes would finish their work in the city.[86]

After receiving Stuart's letter, Boring expressed her pleasure to him. "You have answered many of my numerous questions in a very satisfactory way." She admitted that "some of the problems involved seem to be less difficult than I had feared."[87] In her acceptance of his views, Boring first manifested the admiration for Stuart that she sustained throughout their lifelong association.[88]

Many of the specifics that Boring persistently requested were really not provided until after she had already been offered and accepted the position. Houghton reported to Greene that for the academic year 1923–1924 five courses would be taught in the department of biology of the PUMC premedical school: elementary biology, invertebrate zoology, vertebrate zoology, embryology, and heredity and evolution. The premedical staff included Aura E. Severinghaus, Edna Wolf, an additional foreign assistant or instructor, and a Chinese assistant. The courses to be offered at Yenching by Boring, her assistant Y.T. Chen, and a third person trained in botany would be: biology; zoology; botany; histology; and yeast, molds, and bacteria.[89]

Boring suspected that the women's college was being treated unfairly in the equipment distribution. Speculating that the men, not the women, would inherit the PUMC equipment, she suggested that men and women should share both the equipment and faculty members.[90] Although Greene did not disapprove of her suggestion, he appeared vague about the relationship between the Women's College and the rest of the University. "I presume," he replied, "that the women's college courses are being taught both in the University and in the Women's College buildings for the elementary students." Greene admitted that he did not know of any advanced women students. If such existed, he presumed that there were very few of them, and he had no objection to incorporating them into the pre-medical school to complete their education.[91]

The issue of Boring's relationship to the existing biology faculty at PUMC was difficult to resolve. During the period of negotiations, Greene and Stuart both recommended a single administrative chair for the biology departments of PUMC and Yenching. Although Stuart's ultimate goal was to secure Gee for the position, both he and Greene agreed that Boring was well-qualified to administer both departments on an interim basis.[92]

Houghton's reaction to Boring was unclear, for Greene essentially hired her without Houghton's express approval. Apologizing to Houghton for the omission, Greene explained that Yenching "could hardly do better than ask Miss Boring to take charge of the teaching of biology for two years." He also suggested that she should not be expected to teach under anyone with less experience than she, thus effectively denying the joint chairmanship to the younger and less experienced Aura Severinghaus, Dean of the Biology Department at PUMC.[93] Greene implied, but did not explicitly state, that Boring should be the head of the departments at both Yenching and PUMC.[94] To Greene's relief, Houghton praised Boring as "an unusually capable and stimulating teacher," and expressed his hope that she would accept the position for two or three years. He, however, remained silent about the headship of the combined departments.[95]

In the meantime, Boring wrote Luce with the letter forwarded to Stuart, specifically inquiring about the status of Severinghaus and Edna M. Wolf of the PUMC biology department.[96] In Stuart's answer, he indicated that the biology staff of both institutions would be under Boring's direction. If she accepted "our invitation," Stuart wrote, he would solicit her opinion about Severinghaus's suitability.[97]

Thus, it came as a shock when, after Boring had officially accepted the position, she received a letter from Peking University's senior biology teacher, Anna Lane, stating that "Mr. Severinghaus is taking over the headship of the Biology Department" for PUMC and Yenching which "is what I [Boring] thought I was doing."[98] Astonished and dismayed that even after (or perhaps because of) her meticulous questioning of every detail of the position something had gone amiss, she sought an explanation. Both Greene and Stuart had indicated that she was to be the combined head, so it must have been Henry Houghton who balked. Why, Boring asked Stuart, "would Dr. Houghton have done this when he knew your negotiations with me are pending?" Certainly, she did "not want to be petty and spoil everything,"... but she, nevertheless, insisted that professionally she could not work "under a man so much younger and less experienced than I am." Hurt by Houghton's rejection, she still recognized the importance of cordial relations between the two institutions and proposed an alternative. She suggested that Severinghaus become the head at PUMC and she at Yenching so that they could "coordinate and cooperate." Although she would have preferred the arrangement that Stuart had proffered because it would place Yenching in a stronger position, she was willing to accept the alternative after being assured that "Severinghouse [sic] is a fine fellow and wants to do everything to help us."[99]

Boring's proposed compromise was one that Houghton and others also had considered and were willing to accept. They agreed that although the two institutions would cooperate during the coming year, the administration of the biology departments would be entirely independent.[100] On March 4, 1923, the official memorandum from Beijing arrived, and Boring agreed to the terms it proposed, writing that, "on the whole," she was "much encouraged by it."[101]

Although salary was not of primary importance to Boring, she wrote Henry Luce that her experience with mission salaries indicated that they were disconcertingly low. Since "I have never been a missionary," she suspected that it might be difficult to live on such a pittance.[102] Apologizing for the low salaries, Stuart reported that the scale was "780 gold at a fixed rate of two to one" with lodging and travel in both directions included.[103]

Salaries and other obstacles notwithstanding, Boring was tempted to accept the position if offered from the first time she heard of the possibility. After she was certain that Wellesley would hold her position, she did not entertain seriously the possibility of not going. The chance to "build up a first class biology department" was too intriguing to ignore. Idealistically, she mused that "it would seem like a bit of a real contribution to civilization as opposed to teaching in America."[104]

Notes

1. Marjory Eggleston, Secretary to Wallace Buttrick, CMB Secretary, 25 July 1918, Rockefeller Archive Center.
2. For a discussion of the relationship between the West and non-western countries, see Donna Haraway, "Teddy Bear Patriarchy. Taxidermy in the Garden of Eden," in *Primate Visions*, pp. 26–58.
3. Mary Brown Bullock, *An American Transplant. The Rockefeller Foundation and Peking Union Medical College* (Berkeley: Univ. of Calif. Press, 1980), p. 2.
4. Wolfgang Franke, *China and the West*, trans. R.A. Wilson (Columbia, S.C.: University of South Carolina Press, 1967), p. 29.
5. Ibid, pp. 48–49.
6. J. Mason Gentzler, *Changing China: Readings in the History of China from the Opium War to the Present* (New York: Praeger Publishers, 1977), p. 32.
7. Because the leader of the Taipings, Hung Hsiu-ch'uan, (1814–1864) professed Christianity and forbade opium smoking, westerners felt that the rebellion's success might insure the penetration of western ideas into China. They conveniently ignored the nature of his Christianity. Having learned in a vision that he was the younger brother of Jesus Christ, Hung demanded a fanatical loyalty from his troops. As the troops swarmed into conquered areas, they slaughtered those who refused to surrender. Gentzler, *Changing China*, pp. 43–44.
8. Ibid., pp. 43–46.

9. Jonathan D. Spence, *The Gate of Heavenly Peace: The Chinese and Their Revolution 1895–1980* (Harmondsworth, Middlesex, England: Penguin Books Ltd., 1982).

10. Sun Yat Sen was born near Guangzhou to an impoverished peasant family and went to Hawaii, where his brother had become a successful business-man. He attended school in Hawaii, but returned to China to study western medicine, first under an American doctor and then with the British in Hong Kong. Sun's experiences with the West persuaded him that western scientific and industrial skills could be useful in China. Spence, *The Gate of Heavenly Peace*, pp. 44–46.

11. Ibid., pp. 115–16.

12. Ibid., pp. 130–31.

13. Ibid., p. 135.

14. William R. Hutchison, *Errand to the World: American Protestant Thought and Foreign Missions* (Chicago: University of Chicago Press, 1987), p. 123.

15. John Z. Bowers, *Western Medicine in a Chinese Palace: Peking Union Medical College, 1917–1951* (The Josiah Macy, Jr. Foundation, n.d.), p. 33.

16. Ibid., p. 4.

17. Ibid., p. 6.

18. James C. Thomson, Jr., *While China Faced West: American Reformers in Nationalist China, 1928–1937* (Cambridge, MA: Harvard University Press, 1969), p. 4.

19. John D. Rockefeller's support for "scientific medicine" in any context was ironic, for the only kind of medicine in which he had confidence was the homeopathic variety. Consequently, Gates's ability to convince Rockefeller to support "scientific medicine" was a testament to persuasiveness.

20. This commission consisted of Harry Pratt Judson, president of the University of Chicago, Francis W. Peabody of the Harvard Medical School, and Roger S. Greene, then of the U.S. Consular Service. Three commissions in all were involved: the Burton Commission (1909), the First China Medical Commission (1914), and the Second China Medical Commission (1915).

21. Roger S. Greene, "The Rockefeller Foundation in China," *Asia: Journal of the American Asiatic Association* 19, 11 (Nov. 1919), 1117–1124. Rockefeller Archive Collection, CMB, Inc., Box 62, Folder 435.

22. Flexner's report affected different constituencies variously. It had definite gender and racial implications which, as will be seen, were transported to China.

23. Robert Arnove, *Philanthropy and Cultural Imperialism: The Foundations at Home and Abroad.* Boston: G.K. Hall, 1980.

24. Bowers, *Western Medicine in a Chinese Palace*, pp. 41–43.

25. Ibid., p. 43.

26. Ibid., p. 54.

27. Medical Missions of the Rockefeller Institute, Rockefeller Archive Center, CMB S11, B7, #88.

28. Ibid., p. 55.
29. Bullock, *An American Transplant*, p. 41.
30. Bowers, *Western Medicine in a Chinese Palace*, p. 35.
31. E. Richard Brown, *Rockefeller Medicine Men: Medicine and Capitalism in America*, (Berkeley: Univ. of California Press, 1979), p. 4.
32. *Dedication Ceremonies and Medical Conference: Peking Union Medical College, September 15–22, 1921* (Beijing: PUMC, 1922), pp. 63–64.
33. Charles W. Young, "Peking Union Medical College, Requirements," Rockefeller Archive Collection, CMB, Inc., Box 126, Folder 912.
34. Bullock, *An American Transplant*, p. 15.
35. H.P. Judson to J.D. Rockefeller, Jr., 5-17-14, dr. 6, CMC-HPJ). Report of the Commission, 601A-CMB, Vol. VIII, pp. 7–9). Rockefeller Archive Center, p. 548.
36. Charles W. Young, "Peking Union Medical College, Requirements," Rockefeller Archive Collection, CMB, Inc., Box 126, Folder 912.
37. Boring to Pearl, 31 March 1920, American Philosophical Society Library.
38. Hutchison, *Errand to the World*, pp. 102–103.
39. Faculty Members, Rockefeller Archive Center, RG 1, Series 601, Box 25, Folder 235.
40. H. Barchet to Henry S. Houghton, 13 Aug. 1920, Rockefeller Archive Center, CMB, Inc., Box 73, Folder 512; Roger S. Greene to R.M. Pearce, 14 Dec. 1920, CMB, Inc., Box 73, Folder 517; Houghton to George E. Vincent, Esq., 23 Sept. 1920, CMB, Inc., Box 73, Folder 517.
41. Roger Greene, CMB, Inc., Box 62, Folder 435, p. 1117.
42. McLean to A.M. Dunlop, 9 April 1919, Rockefeller Archive Center, CMB, Inc., Box 73, Folder 517.
43. Greene explained that "while it is true that the Chinese people are in some respects very conservative, present conditions in China having caused such a complete break with old school traditions that the taking of the additional step involved in co-education in a high-grade professional school does not seem so revolutionary to many Chinese as it does to some of us." Greene, "Rockefeller Foundation in China," p. 1121.
44. Report, Rockefeller Archive Center, CMB, Inc., Box 73, Folder 511.
45. Arthur J. Brown to North China Mission No. 301, Shantung Mission, No. 399, and University Council of the Shantung Christian University, Rockefeller Archive Center, No. 50, #88, CMB S 11, B7.
46. Ibid.
47. Minutes Administrative Board, May 25, 1920; May 28, 1950 [sic], Rockefeller Archive Center, CMB, Inc., Box 511.
48. *Dedication Ceremonies and Medical Conference: Peking Union Medical College, September 15–22, 1921* (Beijing, PUMC, 1922), p. 54.
49. Bullock, *An American Transplant*, p. 19.
50. *Dedication Ceremonies and Medical Conference*, p. 51.
51. Greene, Diary, Rockefeller Archive Center, CMB, Inc., Box 62, Folder 437.

52. Greene. Diary, Rockefeller Archive Center. 12 July 1920. CMB Inc. Box 62, Folder 438, p. 259.

53. Alice M. Boring to Raymond Pearl, 31 March 1920, American Philosophical Society Library.

54. Boring to Pearl, 21 October 1920, American Philosophical Society Library.

55. Marian E. Hubbard, "Report to Wellesley President, Ellen F. Pendleton," 9 June 1921, President's Office Files, Wellesley College; Rossiter, *Women Scientists in America: Struggles and Strategies to 1940*, pp. 23–24.

56. Edwin Garrigues Boring. *Edwin Garrigues Boring* (Worcester, MA: Clark University Press, 1952), pp. 28–29.

57. Edwin McCurdy Boring, Last Will and Testament, City and County of Philadelphia, 1920.

58. A.M. Boring to E.G. Boring, 10 February 1922, Pusey Collection, Harvard University, HUG 4229.25.5.

59. Boring to Greene, 18 Oct. 1922, Rockefeller Archive Center, CMB, Inc., Box 126, Folder 913, 27 April 1922. Dean Frame was the wife of Reverend Murray Scott Frame, Dean, Department of History, Yenching University. She was born 29 October 1878 in Harpoot, Turkey, and attended Mt. Holyoke College.

60. In his position, Gee promoted science teaching in preparatory schools and encouraged students to consider medicine as a career. John Leighton Stuart to Boring, 15 Dec. 1922, Special Collection Archives, Yale Divinity School.

61. Howard S. Galt, *History of Yenching University* (Unpublished ms.), p. 2.

62. Ibid, p. 3.

63. Ibid., p. 20.

64. Ibid., p. 46.

65. Ibid.

66. Ibid., p. 8.

67. John Leighton Stuart, *Fifty Years in China* (New York: Random House, Inc., n.d.), p. 50.

68. Ibid., pp. 51–53.

69. Ibid., p. 53.

70. Ibid., p. 56.

71. Report, Rockefeller Archive Center, CMB, Inc., Box 62, Folder 438, 12 July 1920.

72. Report, China Medical Board, CMB Vol. XII, Rockefeller Archive Center, RG 1, Series 601, Box 24, Item 233, 12 April 1922. On March 13, 1922, the CMB resolved "that the proposed gradual transfer of PRE-MEDICAL WORK from the Peking Union Medical College to PEKING (YENCHING) UNIVERSITY be, and it is hereby approved in principle, and that the officers of the China Medical Board and of the Peking Union Medical College be requested to submit definite proposals to the China Medical Board, so far as co-operation on the part of this Board is involved." Ibid.

73. Houghton, Journal for December, 1921, Rockefeller Archive Center, CMB, Inc., Box 62, Folder 438, Jan. 1922.
74. Boring to Greene, 3 Nov. 1922, Rockefeller Archive Center, CMB, Inc., Box 15, Folder 103.
75. Ibid.
76. Greene to Boring, 10 Nov. 1922, Rockefeller Archive Center, CMB, Inc., Box 15, Folder 103.
77. Greene to Boring, 21 Oct. 1922, Rockefeller Archive Center, CMB, Inc., Box 15, Folder 103.
78. Boring to Greene, 3 Nov. 1922, Rockefeller Archive Center, CMB, Inc., Box 15, Folder 103.
79. Greene to Boring, 10 Nov. 1922, Rockefeller Archive Center, CMB, Inc., Box 15, Folder 103.
80. Boring to Greene, 18 Oct. 1922, Rockefeller Archive Center, CMB, Inc., Box 15, Folder 103.
81. Greene to Boring, 21 Oct. 1922, Rockefeller Archive Center, CMB, Inc., Box 15, Folder 103.
82. Ibid.
83. Greene to Boring, 10 Nov. 1922, Rockefeller Archive Center, CMB, Inc., Box 15, Folder 103.
84. Houghton to Greene, 21 Nov. 1922, Rockefeller Archive Center, CMB, Inc., Box 15, Folder 103; Boring to Henry W. Luce, 11 Dec. 1922, Special Collection Archives, Yale Divinity School. Henry Winters Luce was the father of Henry Robinson Luce who managed the Time-Life-Fortune magazine empire; Boring to Luce, 11 Dec. 1922, Special Collection Archives, Yale Divinity School.
85. J. Leighton Stuart to Boring, 15 Dec. 1922, Special Collection Archives, Yale Divinity School.
86. Ibid.
87. Boring To Stuart, 17 Dec. 1922, Special Collection Archives, Yale Divinity School.
88. Ibid. Boring's respect for Stuart was shared by many. In a Memorial Edition of the *Yenching University Alumni Bulletin*, Margaret Speer expressed this feeling when she wrote, "I have thought with new admiration of what Leighton accomplished and have wondered how he did it. With daily experience of the difficulties of getting a small faculty to work together with any sort of harmony, I think with astonishment and immense admiration of the way he kept a much larger group of many nationalities together, and usually happily together—often differing often disagreeing, of course, even wrangling, but somehow always moving together, with the maximum of sympathy and understanding and the minimum of pettiness." Margaret Speer, "An Appreciation Memorial Service Honoring John Leighton Stuart, the Late Chancellor of Yenching University, Peiping, China (Hong Kong: Yenching University Alumni Association, Dec. 1963).

89. Houghton to Greene, 16 Jan. 1923, Rockefeller Archive Center. This report contains a listing of all of the equipment of the department of biology at Yenching and for PUMC.

90. Boring to Greene, 18 Oct. 1922, Rockefeller Archive Center, CMB, Inc., Box 15, Folder 103.

91. Greene to Boring, 21 Oct. 1922, Rockefeller Archive Center, CMB, Inc., Box 15, Folder 103.

92. The previous head of the PUMC biology department, Charles W. Packard, planned to return to the U.S. after his tour was completed, and, consequently, was not a part of the considerations. Houghton to Greene, 21 Nov. 1922, Rockefeller Archive Center, CMB, Inc., Box 15, Folder 103.

93. Greene to Houghton, 21 Oct. 1922, Rockefeller Archive Center, CMB, Inc., Box 15, Folder 103.

94. Ibid.

95. Houghton to Greene, 21 Nov. 1922, Rockefeller Archive Center, CMB, Inc., Box 15, Folder 103.

96. Boring to Luce, 11 Dec. 1922, Special Collection Archives, Yale Divinity School.

97. Stuart to Boring, 15 Dec. 1922, Special Collection Archives, Yale Divinity School.

98. Boring to Stuart, 11 Jan. 1923, Special Collection Archives, Yale Divinity School.

99. Ibid.

100. Greene to Boring, 24 Feb. 1923, Rockefeller Archive Center, CMB, Inc., Box 15, Folder 103.

101. Boring to Greene, 4 March 1923, Rockefeller Archive Center, CMB, Inc., Box 15, Folder 103.

102. Boring to Luce, 11 Dec. 1922, Special Collection Archives, Yale Divinity School.

103. Stuart to Boring, 15 Dec. 1922, Special Collection Archives, Yale Divinity School.

104. Boring to Greene, 18 Oct. 1922, Rockefeller Archive Center, CMB, Inc., Box 15, Folder 103.

Chapter 3
The Career Choice

When Boring appeared in Beijing in 1923, politics pushed both teaching and research into the background. Her arrival was sandwiched between two major periods of student demonstrations (1919 and 1925) superimposed on a civil war between competing warlords. Already biased against western imperialistic aims in China, she blamed the West for the bitter power struggles between warlords as well as for China's economic woes.

The earlier of the student demonstrations began on May 4, 1919, when Boring was in China for the first time. Chinese students were outraged when a report of the final Versailles treaty agreements appeared in a Beijing newspaper on May 1, 1919.[1] The treaty, which granted special privileges for the Japanese in return for much-needed loans, humiliated the Chinese. The students blamed the unfortunate Versailles decisions on their representatives to the Convention, claiming that they had sabotaged the national interests by their ineffective protests.[2] Although western countries feared Japan's growing power, they reluctantly accepted Japanese demands, preferring not to breach the unequal treaties system won after the Opium Wars,[3] and wanting to assure Japan's support as an ally against the encroachment of Asian communism.[4]

In protest, on the afternoon of May 4, approximately three thousand students from thirteen colleges and universities in the Beijing area convened at the Gate of Heavenly Peace on the southern edge of the Forbidden City. The incensed students shouted nationalistic and anti-Japanese slogans and waved banners to protest treaty provisions. The incident escalated to riot proportions. Although the immediate results of the movement appeared inconsequential, in the long run the May Fourth Movement represented a break with the past and presaged the events that attracted some Chinese toward the pragmatism of the United States and Britain and others towards Marxism.

The second major round of demonstrations began on May 30, 1925. A peaceful demonstration protesting the killing of a Chinese worker by a Japanese foreman in a Japanese cotton mill with striking Chinese workers escalated when the English police of the international concession killed ten and wounded fifty unarmed Chinese demonstrators in Shanghai. Although the movement attracted a wide following that resulted in a renewal of commitment to worker solidarity, the peasantry did not enter into these demonstrations. The anti-imperialistic and specifically anti-Japanese and anti-British emphases did not appeal to their grievances.[5]

On arriving in China, Boring was swept into Chinese educational and political affairs and neglected to inform her family of her safe arrival. Their first news came from "Miss Pendleton" (Ellen F. Pendleton, president of Wellesley College), who quoted a cable from the Presbyterian Board in a letter to Lydia Boring, reporting the "safe arrival Alice Boring Shanghai."[6] After this lapse in family communication, Alice wrote regularly. During her first heady experience with the politics and ideals of her Chinese associates, she eagerly attempted to explain the controversy's parameters to friends and relatives in the United States. Remembering the distorted press accounts she had encountered at home, she tried to clarify the record. She had not yet grasped the complexities of the situation, but operated with the certainty of a novice.

Since the May 4, 1919 incident, anti-imperialistic demonstrations erupted periodically, and in the spring and summer of 1924 threatened to be especially disruptive in Beijing. Students protesting the unfairness of extraterritoriality and unequal treaties were swept into the vortex of the controversy. Deserting their classrooms, they distributed anti-imperialist fliers, demonstrated in the streets, and delivered earnest harangues on street corners. As enthusiastic as any of the Chinese students, Boring busied herself with correcting English on handbills, encouraging student demonstrators, cleaning laboratories, and preparing orders for the next year. Accepting the student explanation that it was impossible both to study and agitate, she agreed that agitation was more important. Extraterritoriality and unequal treaties were abominations that made her seethe with indignation.[7]

Fearing that her own country would stand by the other "Powers," Boring asked her family "what the newspapers [in the United States] are saying about China." In spite of the disturbing reports, she hoped that the United States would "do something about making the other Powers see justice and sense." Her own role in exporting the students' idealism and

China's cause consisted of sending local reports home. Hoping to inspire her friends and relatives in the United States to sympathize with the students, she sent student fliers, and a copy of the *Peking Leader Supplement* filled with statements from Beijing "urging the Legation to take some action to do away with present injustices in China."[8] Her offended sense of Quaker fair play called for the "Great Powers" to make amends.

Recognizing that the students were not experienced demonstrators and many of their antics appeared to be "somewhat inconsequential," Boring noted that they effectively got the attention of the foreigners and the Chinese in the cities. "It reminds me," Boring wrote,

> of the old Women's Suffrage days. They go out in squads to lecture on the streets, they paste pictures and posters everywhere. They have new handbills every day to distribute on the streets. They have parades and banners, they have put placards on all the trolley cars and many of the rickshas, they have brought about a boycott on all British and Japanese banknotes, and are trying to effect one on British and Japanese goods. The British and Japanese shipping in the ports is all stopped by workmen's strikes. They are trying to bring about a general cessation of all work for one day, as a day of mourning.[9]

The more staid members of the community criticized the faculty members who actively helped the students. They considered it undignified for faculty members to respond to the beck and call of students. Boring retorted that she did not "think that sort of dignity is worth anything to civilization."[10] She gloried in her own luck to stumble upon "a concrete unjust situation that needs to be righted. ..." Her life had been radically transformed from what she perceived as the dreariness and boredom of Wellesley. The excitement of the time completely obliterated any desire that she might have had to set up facilities to continue research left behind in the United States. Totally caught up in the tide of events, she explained that "it takes me back to the days of the War,"

> when the U. of Maine boys were all excited and trying to decide what was right to do, and starting off full of glorious ideals. Youth has power and any group of people who does not trust youth at all, will soon be useless itself."[11]

During this time, Boring began to moderate her negative position on missionaries and on Christianity in general. She decided that her negative perception of Christian dogma and rules of conduct had obscured Christianity's virtues. She reported that "the Christian groups in China are at present almost unanimously against their own imperialistic and capitalistic classes." For the first time, she reported, "I have seen Christianity make an issue out of" something "worth making a fuss about." She pointed out that Christians and Chinese stood together in protesting "a case of international injustice...." They were not concerned with "theory or doctrine—like divinity or immortality." Nor were they fettered by a "set of conduct rules, like whether you should drink or smoke...." The entire concept was "thrilling," and she found it "inspiring to be a part of such a group."[12]

After the exhilaration of the demonstrations, Boring appreciated the opportunity for a vacation. Before she arrived at Yenching, Boring had met a young woman teacher, Alnah James, on the steamship President Madison as they crossed the Pacific Ocean to take up new posts at Yenching. She, James, and another woman, Dora Demiere, proposed to visit the vast northern expanse of Mongolia.

Henry Fairchild Osborn was president of the American Museum of Natural History and a professor at Columbia University. Osborn and his wife were also on the President Madison with Boring and James. The Osborns described some startling sights from Mongolia: a giant extinct rhinoceros with one "bone as large as the body of a man," two dinosaur eggs broken in half showing "the delicate bones of embryonic dinosaurs," and an "ancient long-sought ancestor of the fossil giant-horned dinosaur found years before in Montana." Osborn's enthusiastic prediction that Mongolia would prove to be the homeland of primitive humans added to the excitement.[13] Osborn, who was in his late sixties at the time, was on his way to join Roy Chapman Andrews and his expedition. In addition to Osborn and Andrews, the famous Swedish explorer of Tibet, Sven Hedin, and Jesuit paleontologist-philosopher-theologian, Teilhard de Chardin were in Beijing during Boring and James's first year. Everywhere they went, people discussed the expedition.

Consequently, when Boring had an opportunity to go to Mongolia the following summer, she accepted immediately. Ignoring the warning by the legation that "the United States government can give you no protection," the three women joined a Dr. and Mrs. Ingram who also were planning a Mongolian trip.[14] Warnings of remnants of a defeated warlord army turned bandits prowling the Mongolian plateau failed to discourage them, for they heard that the bandits were interested only in the rich caravans going back and forth between Kalgan and Urga.[15]

Dora, Alnah, and their Chinese servant, Shin Ling, left early and met Alice and the Ingram party at the Swedish Mission at Gulchaggan. Torrential rains, gummy mud, yellow-robed Lama priests, dirty inns, and friendly bandits all added to the challenge of arriving at their destination. When the sun finally appeared, the lush smooth grass, sweet-smelling honeysuckle, blue larkspur, white Queen Anne's lace, and yellow mustard were unpredictably spectacular. When they arrived at the simple mission, 5,000–6,000 feet above sea level, they met the Mission head, Miss Wiklund, a hospitable hostess. Although Gulchaggan served as their headquarters, they pushed north onto the edge of the Gobi [Desert] staying at Mongol settlements and sharing the native diet of mutton, cheese, and tea.[16]

Mongolia allowed Boring to exercise her characteristic spirit of freedom and nonconformity. The vast landscape, she marvelled, has

no fields no fences—every line goes on as far as you can see. Best of all, there are no times at which anything must be done; we go into our tent when it is dark, we talk till we are tired, we sleep till we wake, we lie in bed until the little Mongol girl brings us cereal, coffee and bread, we eat as much as we want, then we either get up or stay in bed as the spirit moves.[17]

During the last week of her Mongolian vacation, Boring wrote to her family about her new adventures, including being lost on horseback on the plains—"an awful feeling."[18] Miss Wiklund warned the three women never to get out of sight of the mission, because the deceptively flat-appearing terrain actually was rolling and filled with hollows and crevasses. Wiklund admonished them as they mounted their ponies to remember that "there are no landmarks here in Gulchaggan except the mission."[19] Attempting to heed her warning, they kept the mission in sight as they rode toward an interesting hill. It was much farther than they had anticipated, but the ride seemed well worth the effort when they found an obu (shrine) covered with prayers printed on pieces of paper. Intrigued, they did not start back until the sun began to set, and found, to their dismay, that they were unable to see the mission.[20]

After wandering in circles, Boring and her two companions found a Chinese-speaking Buddhist priest who explained that their home mission was seven miles away.[21] Boring remained with one priest, while another, accompanied by one of her companions, rode her horse back to the mission.

I do not know which situation was the more exciting—hers or mine. She started off in the pouring rain in the pitch dark with a strange Lama priest as a guide not sure whether he really understood where she wanted to go or whether he would take her there if he did know. I went into the little house of one of the priests to keep dry, knowing that I should have to wait there at least a couple of hours, and knowing that no women are allowed in these temples and that these Lama priests are the most dissolute and diseased persons as a rule on the face of the earth.[22]

In spite of the situation, "I was not a bit afraid and I received the utmost courtesy." The priests "admired all my clothes, especially my radium-faced watch," and "asked how old I was."[23]

Even though the vacation had been wonderful, Boring, anxious for mail, was ready to return to Beijing. The situation that she encountered served as a learning experience. Throughout her life, she tended to simplify, condense, and categorize complex events into two categories, one "right" and the other "wrong." Once she made up her mind, it sometimes took an avalanche of information to convince her to modify her ideas. When she first returned to China from the United States, she viewed the riots in Beijing as a confrontation between "good" (the Chinese) and "evil" (the western powers and Japan). She failed to recognize that the Chinese did not share a unanimity of vision for their country—that seething factionalism sliced into her idealized homogeneity. Stubborn though she was, when strongly confronted with new data, she eventually would respond to it.

It was a shock after the freedom and the easy pace of the Mongolian holiday to be thrust back into the realities of the increasingly unstable political situation in Beijing. Confronted with confusing signals, Boring began a long process of modifying her simplistic preconceptions. A civil war was in progress with the warlords of various provinces jockeying for position.[24] Wu Pei Fu with the support of Cao Kun and Feng Yu Xiang became powerful enough to prepare to unify China forcibly.

As it happened, Wu Pei Fu needed to prepare for war, as an old adversary, Zhang Zuo Lin, was reorganizing and consolidating his army. Wu's plans to attack before Zhang completed his military reorganization were thwarted because of his supporter Feng Yu Xiang's defection. Feng and his army occupied Beijing on October 22, 1924, forced President Cao Kun to resign on November 2, and changed Wu's status from the most powerful warlord in China to that of a fugitive.[25]

Boring described the situation as "thrilling, but not really dangerous...."[26] Marching troops, picturesque carts and camel trains loaded with provisions, and delayed mail service reminded her that she was in a potential war zone. Nevertheless, she assured brother Garry in a delayed birthday message on September 28, 1924, that news reports magnified the danger, exaggerated the inconvenience, and sensationalized the events.[27]

Political developments were to Boring's liking. Pleased that the former military leader, Wu Pei Fu, was deported to central China, and the "rickshaw boy" president (Cao Kun) whom "Wu put into power" was removed, she had great hopes for the new cabinet, which included Foreign Minister Wang C.T. and a "new general," Feng Yu Xiang, who would share the political power pending the election of a new president.[28]

Optimistic Alice was convinced that the new assemblage of officers would be successful.

> I know Daddy would have bet on this combination, I have enough Boring in me to make me thrill over the possibilities of reform in the present situation. But some people whom I respect very much, such as Dr. Stuart are pessimistic as to the outcome.[29]

The ascension of Feng Yu Xiang to power was one source of Boring's optimism. In 1914, he was baptized in the Methodist Episcopal Church, his Christianity making him unique among the warlords. Although cynics accused him of converting in order to ingratiate himself with foreign imperialists and to control his troops by using pseudo-Christian symbolism, his record advocating reform impressed Boring.[30] Unimpressed by Feng's piety, others substituted the epithet "the Betraying General," for his common title, "the Christian General," citing, among other incidents, his betrayal of Wu Pei Fu. Boring, however, was impressed that he had "married one of our Yenching girls last year...."[31]

Even in the unlikely possibility that the fighting did reach Beijing, Boring believed that foreigners would be safe, partially because she was convinced that Christian Feng would prevail. She assured her brother that the disagreements between rival warlords were different in nature from the disputes between the Chinese and the "Great Powers," so "do not worry whatever sensational stuff may appear in the American papers."[32] Boring insisted that her hope for China went further than faith in any one regime. "The Chinese," she explained, "have no real fighting instincts, and they will probably be the nation which inaugurates peace in the world."[33]

During the period of intense political activity, Boring wrote to her family that she did little biology. She assured them that a change would soon occur. "Wait until next year," she wrote,

> "when I have a real lab and we are out of this restless city life, and I am living in my piece of the Prince's Garden with a view of a lotus pond and camel bridge and the Chinese spirit of repose is not spoiled by all this foreign push."[34]

Alice was more candid about her goals with her brother than with the rest of the family. Lydia encouraged secrecy by implying that Alice was a deserter to family and tradition. Family considerations aside, she chided, Alice should return to the United States for the benefit of her career. "Ly keeps harping on research," Alice confided to Garry. Alice explained that she was "as likely to accomplish research here as at Wellesley or some similar place where . . . [she] should be likely to land in America." Still, it bothered Alice that Lydia was intransigent on the subject, and she hoped to persuade her to reconsider by encouraging a visit to China in 1926. Even if Ly remained unconvinced, Alice assured Garry she would not "let any sentimental feelings on the part of the family, that is, Ly, determine . . . [her] future."[35]

Although Boring did not make the final decision about that future until 1928, in 1924 she made her intentions clear to her brother. She told him that she expected to remain in China unless "something unexpected turns up to spoil the situation here." A decision must be made "this year" in order to plan both for living quarters and for future departmental personnel. Boring's Quaker background with its emphasis on humanitarian service influenced her decision. Thus, she could write of China that "here is something that needs to be done that I can do and enjoy doing; therefore life is congenial."[36]

Life for Boring, however, consisted of more than personal decisions and concerns about the state of China and the world. A personal anecdote provides a clue to her sense of humor, as well as to her relationship to those around her. She entitled her adventure, "The Power of a Vision" or "How Little Alice held a meeting to save Mongolia." Reminding her family that she had been cared for by Swedish missionaries during her Mongolian vacation of 1924, she, as a polite response, invited Miss Wiklund, "the one who did most for us, to come stay with me whenever she might come to Peking." Wiklund accepted the invitation, visited for two weeks in November, and proposed to return in the spring. As a good hostess, Boring "helped her with clothes and tailors and baggage and how to get to places, and had a dinner in her honor."

Boring's attempts to be helpful apparently had succeeded beyond her wildest dreams, because after Miss Wiklund returned to Mongolia she

> got a most remarkable letter from her [Wiklund] pouring out her heart to me saying she never had been so kindly treated, that she had a vision and knew that I was to help her with some big plans which were gradually maturing in her mind.[37]

The "big plans" involved Boring soliciting friends for money for the mission. A distinctly nervous Boring protested that her friends were not financially able to help. After explaining that she would do nothing to help raise money,

I invited her to stay with me while in Peking. Nothing more until about June 1, when a note arrived saying she would appear early in June. On June 8, I returned from my morning's work to find that she had arrived.[38]

Wiklund found Boring's unwillingness to arrange the requested money-raising meeting inconceivable, for "I was in her vision, so I had to do it." After trying unsuccessfully to find other people to host the "meeting," Boring gave up. Her soft-hearted side relented, for "you can not be rude to a guest in your own house." Reluctantly, she agreed to host the gathering and provide tea and cake "if I did not have to invite the people, and if no mention of raising money was made." After she helped make the guest list from those who had been in Mongolia, Boring ended up inviting the guests to a "little farewell tea for Miss Wiklund who was on her way to America." Boring still adamantly refused to allow money to be mentioned, but again was thwarted when "a kind man" asked "Miss Wiklund directly what she was going to do in America!!" Obviously, Wiklund explained her money-raising mission! Boring asked, "did you ever see any poor innocent mortal more relentlessly pursued by fate! And she [Miss Wiklund] of course believes that I was simply fulfilling her vision !!!"[39]

Unexpected and sometimes humorous encounters, heterogeneous peoples, and idealistic struggles (she continued to support the students in their disputes with the "Great Powers") characterized Boring's life in 1923–1924. She thrived on experiences ranging from Miss Wiklund to Buddhist monks and from anti-imperialist demonstrations to internal warlord politics and battles. In her own mind she knew that she was where she belonged and began to develop plans for serious involvement in teaching, living, and research at Yenching.

Yenching administrators were willing to offer Boring a permanent appointment in 1925, but she hesitated. She was not yet ready to resign her Wellesley post. The cautious Alice took precedence over the adventurous one in this case. In order to remain in China for the extra year (Wellesley had only loaned her for two years), Boring had to request an extension of her leave of absence, a request granted by Wellesley President Pendleton. She confided to Garry that she planned to remain an extra year at Yenching, teach at Wellesley for the year 1927–1928, and then return to China. By retaining her Visiting Professor title at Yenching, she could teach an additional year for Wellesley before severing the relationship. Boring found several practical reasons for remaining connected with Wellesley, even though she did not expect to enjoy the teaching. Doing so meant a "decent salary for a change" and Lydia's attitude continued to make her reluctant to make the announcement.

Garry and Kat not only were reconciled to Alice's career in China, but appeared enthusiastic about it. "I am so happy and proud over her," wrote Kat.[40] Garry underlined his support as he reiterated that "for the hundredth time I say that one needs to be where his capacities have scope and thine have had scope in Peking and that seems to me to be where thee needs to be."[41] Alice remained confident that Lydia would modify her violent and vocal opposition after a visit to China and would understand her sister's love for the place. Allowing Ly time to visit and become converted supplied another reason for Alice to delay her announcement.

The possibility that she could be replaced by a Chinese professor also delayed Alice's ultimate decision. Although she sympathized with one of Yenching's major goals, to hire Chinese professors whenever possible, the conservative part of Alice did not want to burn Wellesley bridges until she was sure of her Yenching position. Yenching policy decreed that whenever a competent Chinese professor could be found, he or she was to be hired over the American or European counterpart. This contingency represented the only way in which Boring thought she might lose her job. If a Chinese appeared "as well qualified as I am to head up the department," she might need to resign.

Growing Chinese nationalism influenced the course of mission education. In order to survive, Yenching, as other mission schools, had to register according to government regulations and operate under a Chinese pattern with as many Chinese faculty members and administrators as possible. If they failed to comply, President Stuart recognized that they faced the kind of opposition that ultimately would force them to close. The good relationship fostered by Stuart between the Chinese and westerners convinced Boring that even if a well-qualified Chinese biology faculty member appeared, her job would probably be secure, for they could put the department "on the Committee basis" keeping both professors and alternating the chairmanship.[42]

The new regulations issued by the Ministry of Education for the registration of Christian schools were less restrictive than the ones they replaced because of the sympathies of the framer. This man, a Christian and a long-time official in the Ministry of Education, offered to teach at Yenching at a modest salary while retaining his ministry connection.[43] Although some of the missionary faculty members were anxious over the increased representation of Chinese professors on the faculty and Board of Managers, Boring agreed with Stuart that there was little to fear for Yenching's future as long as the Chinese had a "genuine and wide-spread" understanding of "our attitude on nationalistic aspirations."[44]

The possibility of being replaced by a Chinese professor did arise. Yenching had the opportunity to hire a fine Chinese biologist, Cornell-trained C.F. Wu, who had three years of teaching experience at Fuzhou University. Although Boring considered resigning, she first discussed the possibility with Stuart. He and Dean William Hung both assured her that they would "rather not have Wu come at all if it meant my departure." The choice was unnecessary, for Wu was hired as an Associate Professor and Boring remained.[45]

The building progress on the new Yenching campus seemed interminably slow even after the philosophical questions about the nature of the buildings (Chinese or western style) had been settled. Boring's past behavior would have predicted impatience at the delay. However, after her year in China, she no longer exhibited the frenetic need for immediacy and certainty evident in her earlier correspondence with Greene and Luce. Although the renovation on her Yenching house was scheduled to be completed in 1925, she calmly accepted the news that it would not be ready until the summer of 1926. The building program for the whole University was equally sluggish. Even the probability that the University would remain in Beijing until the summer of 1926 did not disturb her overly.

Although the delay in moving meant that she might not come home in the summer of 1927 as planned, Boring remarked philosophically that the extra time would give her one more year's "gold income to accumulate for my trip home through Suez."[46]

Since her inheritance served as a buffer against shortages, Boring was not overly disturbed by the meager missionary salary. The money that allowed her to feel relaxed about her future came from her parents' estate, as meticulously administered by her brother.[47] Her principal was secure, and she had no need to borrow on it to take care of current expenses or to furnish her new house. Her emergency fund of $1,000 in a Beijing bank would cover additional furnishings or a trip home.[48]

Since everything Boring had been working toward since her return to China would reach a climax when she was scheduled to return home in 1927, she definitely did not want to be gone for that year. The time of "making do," borrowing equipment, and living in adequate but not ideal quarters was about to end. Returning to Wellesley when she was needed in Yenching to move equipment from the old laboratory to the new, inventory apparatus, order and catalogue materials and supplies, and organize the department seemed inconceivable. The proprietary interest that she had developed about the department's operation made her unwilling to leave until she was convinced that the department would

function smoothly without her. "After I have planned all those laboratories and storerooms, I want to move in and see things working in them
before I leave."[49]

When Boring first came to Yenching, she recognized the possibility of
losing her job to Nathaniel Gist Gee (1876–1937). South Carolina
native Gist (he seldom used the Nathaniel) Gee had taught biology and
worked in China for many years. His position from 1922–1927 was that
of premedical advisor for the Rockefeller Foundation's China Medical
Board. The Board was interested in funding only those projects that
were directly related to producing medical students. Gee was more
interested in promoting science education generally, and occasionally
used subterfuge to secure funding to aid the schools. He creatively
developed a fellowship program that would benefit both. In 1922, President Stuart had indicated that he wanted Gee to head the biology
department at Yenching. Since he had several years remaining on his
contract with the CMB he was unavailable for the position in 1922.
By 1927 the original goal of convincing Gee to take over the biology
department seemed unattainable, as he had received a permanent
appointment with the Rockefeller Foundation.[50] Hiring Boring originally was a temporary expedient, but shortly after she arrived both she
and Stuart knew that she belonged. "Tactfully," Stuart quizzed her
about future plans. With the premedical school closed at PUMC, and
Yenching taking over the function of the premedical school, he vitally
needed strong faculty members who were willing to work on missionary
salaries. Thus, barring unforeseen circumstances, her position seemed
secure. "It is fate," she wrote.

> I belong here. I know how to get along with this crowd. I understand their
> standards and evaluations in life and they understand mine and this is true of
> both Chinese and foreigners. I shall not become as good a scientist out here as I
> might have in America, but I am a much better developed human being, and I
> always was a better teacher and that is what is needed in China in the present
> stage of her science.[51]

Boring had established a reputation at Yenching as a "gifted, experienced
and capable teacher," who was very much in demand. According to one
of her colleagues, she was popular among both faculty and students,
"entering into all sorts of faculty and student companionships and jol-
lity, yet maintaining her dignity."[52] Therefore, it seemed inevitable that
the Yenching administration wanted her to return after her furlough.
Expressing their confidence in her abilities, they allowed her to select a
house, "which they would not do for a temporary person."[53]

II

During the time when Boring was making her career decision (1924–1926), internal and external politics continually wrenched Yenching. Antiforeign sentiment swelled after the Shanghai confrontation of May 30, 1925. The original incident inspired a wave of sympathy strikes, riots, boycotts of British and Japanese goods, and the destruction of their factories all over the country. It seemed it would be only a matter of time before the special privileges and protection of foreigners would be withdrawn. Although Boring and many of the other Yenching faculty members supported abolition of these privileges, the way in which the much-needed reform was to be accomplished caused concern. An underground group of the intelligentsia centered at the Beijing National University was "passionately convinced that there . . . [was] no hope for China in any peaceful reforms, [and] that a wild crash . . . [was] the only way out."[54]

The antiforeign sentiment and the strife generated by competing warlords, although essentially separate sources of dissension, became inextricably intertwined. Stuart did not consider the civil strife "wholly deplorable," for it seemed to represent "a healthy revolt against the aggression of certain too rapacious war-lords. . . ."[55]

An encounter between rival warlords Zhang Zuo Lin and Feng Xu Xiang turned into a violent confrontation involving students in the Beijing area. In order to keep Zhang of Manchuria from landing, Feng, who had steadily been gaining public confidence, mined the sea approaches to Beijing. The infuriated Japanese interpreted this move as an incursion on their rightful sphere and demanded that the harbor be cleared. The warlord confrontation then became merged with foreign imperialistic concerns. Boring described the beginning of the outbreak in a letter to her family.

> The trouble began at the Taku fort, at the entrance to the harbor of Tientsin. As usual two warlords are fighting each other, and the one who held the fort was afraid that boats coming into the harbor might be bringing ammunition for the other. So the harbor was declared closed and a Jap boat which insisted on coming in was fired on. Of course there is a treaty which arranges for keeping this harbor open for foreigners.[56]

The insensitive "Great Powers" issued a forty-eight-hour ultimatum that allowed China only this amount of time to assure free passage for boats into the harbor. Boring considered this course "the most stupid piece of folly imaginable." Just when time was beginning to heal the wounds of the Shanghai affair of the previous May, foreigners arrogantly asserted themselves again. Patriotic Chinese and "fair minded" westerners suggested a conference to consider the "Unequal Treaties" situation dispassionately. However, the inconvenience of the immediate situation took precedence over the long-range benefits of restraint. Most foreigners, claimed Boring, were more concerned with the disruption of mail service than in fighting wrongs. Helpless China came to terms and the harbor was opened "BUT the Chinese do not forget either injuries or kindnesses, and dear knows how far this blot on American goodwill in China may extend."[57]

In retribution, student demonstrators infiltrated by outside agitators marched on the residence of the ineffectual Chinese Chief Executive and jeered at his bodyguard. A skirmish resulted as the bodyguard tried to keep the demonstrators from entering.

> The soldiers shot one volley in the air and instead of waiting to see if that would scatter the crowd as our students insist it was already doing, they fired into the crowd and kept on firing. One of our Yenching girls was killed on the spot, two more girls and four men are badly injured in the hospital. Many more were hit with the buts [sic] of rifles or tramped over in the crush.[58]

The killing was indiscriminate. One girl described the shooting of two men who were walking beside her. One man, agonizing under the excruciating pain of his wound begged her to "step on him and end his misery...."[59]

This "massacre" resulted in a student strike. Boring insisted that 90% of the students wanted to return to regular class work, but 10%, the agitators, "have been able to keep the rest on a 'patriotic strike' all week." She claimed that the problem was exacerbated by the situation in the government schools where lack of money caused them to close after the Chinese New Year. The students at the government universities were "jealous" of the foreign universities that remained open, and were "only too glad of an opportunity to get our students out of work."[60] Boring, prodded by Stuart, understood that the "red influence" at the National University was an important factor in their action.

Looking back on her first experience with student agitators in 1924, Boring found her attitude had changed by 1926. In the early encounter, she viewed the striking students as naive heros, idealistically fighting to right the injustices imposed by the "Great Powers." However, by 1926 she saw them as dupes of a small number of radical students from the government institutions who were being paid to spread radical ideas and to stir up trouble in order to instigate a revolution. Although the group of radical students at Yenching remained small, its influence far exceeded its numbers. After the massacre, the Yenching radicals led a succession of student meetings at which they insisted on a general week of mourning for the slaughtered students.

Furthermore, the radicals agitated for a general work stoppage for the remainder of the year, so that the students could organize the country against the government. Boring was not even slightly tolerant of such an agenda. The government, "a poor weak thing," that hardly anyone wants in power only remains because "no other leaders come forward who appear any stronger or more patriotic. However, "the ninety percent sane students" were outshouted, outmaneuvered, and generally overwhelmed by the minority who called them traitors and cowards. The National University students threatened to come "and wail under our windows if we held classes." It took five days before the majority, led by the female students, recognized that they did have a choice.[61]

On Friday morning the entire body of women students had a mass meeting, decided to boycott joint committee meetings, and voted to go back to work immediately. The chairman of the joint committee received a telephone call from the president of the Women's Student Association who announced simply that the women had seceded and were returning to work. The men followed, prompting Boring to conclude that "the girls have certainly shown more sanity and courage than the men."[62]

The week of the strike left Boring drained. "It has been a horrible week. One has felt so helpless to do anything." During this time, faculty members worked on their own problems and tried "to talk sense to any students with whom . . . [they] thought . . . [they] had any influence." Coercion, which "does not work with the modern generation in America," would work "even less in China."

Boring noted a potential respite in the struggle between warlords Feng and Zhang. General Feng "has really retired and started for Europe to prove his peaceful intentions." However, Feng's "retirement" and the retreat of the "Kuo Min Chun, the People's Army" to the northwest would leave Beijing in control of Zhang Zuo Lin's soldiers, "who are mostly exbandits!" Assuring her family that foreigners were not in danger, she noted, however, that the Chinese in Beijing were "genuinely frightened." The city itself was chaotic, with the streets overburdened with carts and rickshaws carrying trunks of valuables on their way to bank vaults to be stored, shops closed with doors nailed tightly shut, and frightened people milling around. What would life be like, she wondered, "to know once more what to expect to happen the next day?"[63]

The lives of Boring's siblings seemed remote, although they attempted to keep their lives connected through letters. In Cambridge, the family's youngest, Edwin, and his wife, Lucy, were raising their three young children: [their youngest daughter was not born until 1931]; handling the family's financial affairs; and struggling with the problems facing a young academic.[64] Sensible Katharine and her husband Howard Rondthaler, a minister in the Moravian church at Winston-Salem, North Carolina, lived a simple life, raising their four children with a small amount of money. Lydia, living in Philadelphia, showed no interest in getting married and little in her school-teaching career. Her "irresponsibility" disturbed both Edwin and Katharine. To the annoyance of family members, Ly resigned her teaching job at the suggestion of her friend, Helen Fogg, who insisted that she had plenty of money for the two of them.[65]

Although Alice attempted to keep abreast of family happenings in the United States and to keep them informed of her activities, she was most directly concerned with the events in and around Beijing. By December 1925, the Faculty Executive Committee recommended that the academic year be terminated on May 31, 1926, allowing the move to the new campus to be initiated in early June. Preparing for this move, watching as the forces of warlords Zhang Zuo Lin and Feng Yu Xiang fought around Beijing, and teaching her students in the cramped temporary quarters in Beijing left little time and energy to focus on family problems.

During this chaotic period, Boring participated in a memorable occasion, the funeral of Sun Yat Sen. She wrote that

> you will probably all see pictures in the Sunday papers and movies of Sun Yat Sen's funeral, but I have seen the real thing. The whole thing has been one of the most thrilling events I have ever witnessed, next probably to the Armistice celebration in the Forbidden City of Peking in 1918. Some of the biggest, most vital forces in the present-day world came into conflict over this funeral, foreign against Chinese, anti-christian against christian, radical against conservative, communism against imperialism. The seething excitement over his sickness, death and burial show the place he has held in China. Everybody agrees that he has been honest, most people think that he has worked for an ideal, even when they admit that he used dubious means to his end.[66]

From her position on the steps of the PUMC anatomy building, she watched as a vested choir of twelve men singing "Alleluia" marched out the door. Following in solemn procession came two Chinese ministers, Dr. Timothy Tingtang Lew, Dean of the Yenching Theological School, and Dr. Y.Y. Tsu, Director of Religious Work at PUMC. Following the Director of Religious Work, ten Guomintang pallbearers carried the simple wooden coffin covered with the emblem of the Guomintang's radical wing, a red flag with a white sun on a blue field, into the Auditorium for the ceremony.[67]

Christians, conservative nationalists, and Guomintang leftists all claimed Sun as their own. He courted the West, persuaded that western scientific and industrial skills could be useful in China's rebirth. Sun also was a strong nationalist and his Guomintang issued a manifesto in 1924, castigating warlords and capitalists for replacing the Manchus as oppressors. Leftists claimed him as well, for when he was unable to obtain support from the western powers or Japan, he formed alliances with the Soviet Union. The Chinese Communist Party had been founded in 1921, with most of its early members urban intellectuals. Sun agreed to pursue a United Front Strategy with the Chinese Communists, a decision that coincided with the Comintern's goals.[68] In the process, the Guomintang was reorganized along Marxist-Leninist lines with one branch becoming increasingly radical.[69] During the last years of his life, Sun attempted to unify the factions that threatened to subvert attempts to achieve a truly nationalistic state. However, the diverse elements were unable to unite even during his final sickness.

Although the Peking Union Medical College Hospital was recognized as the best hospital in China, Guomintang members became incensed when western doctors explained that they could not cure Sun's liver cancer. Criticizing foreigners and foreign medicine, they took him away to be treated by Chinese medics. "Of course, he died anyhow," Boring wrote. She recognized that it was fortunate he did not die in the PUMC hospital, for the Guomintang would have blamed his death on foreigners.[70]

Boring noted that Sun was a hero to the students and they thronged around the anatomy building. As the procession began

> at first the students started to cheer and then they realized the inappropriateness of this and took off their hats in solemn silence until the coffin was within the auditorium. . . . After the procession entered, the gates were closed by the police. So far no trouble. Then various guests invited to the service began to arrive late, and the students got restless. If others could go in, why not they? Sun had been the friend of the common people. So they began storming the gate. I heard afterwards that this was a critical moment for the P.U.M.C. authorities. The Kuo Min Tang had made so much trouble during the preceding days that they thought this was the beginning of a riot.[71]

Sun's family, the government, and the Guomintang had finally agreed upon a compromise on what had been a controversial subject—the type of funeral that Sun should have. His body would be embalmed at the anatomy building, the family would hold a private Christian service in the College Chapel, and the body would be transferred to a building in the Central Park where it would lie in state for one week.[72]

Leslie Severinghaus, who provided the Sunday music for the regular services held in the Peking Union Medical College, planned the funeral service music. Bliss Wiant, who "frequently played and cared for the treasured pipe organ at the PUMC chapel," opened the service with the somber strains of Chopin's Funeral March.[73] The mood was maintained by the male Quartette's selections of "Abide with Me," "Beautiful Words of Life," and "Peace Perfect Peace."[74]

As Boring watched, throngs of students filled the street between the anatomy building and the Chapel where the service was taking place. They mobbed the fluted tile-roofed building flanked by mythical guardian creatures and clung to every window area, hoping for "a peep through the closed panelled apertures, for any small glimpse of what went on inside." After the Postlude, Felix Mendelssohn's "Consolation," the front doors opened and the Guomintang pallbearers who had sat through the hour-long Christian service "rather than let his body be carried by such awful persons as Christians," began the trek to Central Park.[75]

From her vantage point on the anatomy building's steps, Boring observed that promptly at 11:00 a.m. Mrs. Sun got into a carriage draped in black that immediately followed the coffin carried by several relays of Guomintang leaders.[76] On the walk to the park, student members "ran and struggled, each group with its own college banner," trying to be at the head of the procession. As Boring moved through the people-thronged streets, she was "a bit worried" as she recognized members of the Yenching Women's College being swept along with the masses.[77]

"A strange disorderly unorganized procession" it was, but deeply moving to Boring. The affair was truly democratic, for "there they were all of them claiming a share in him, Christians, antichristians, foreigners, anti-foreigners, Russian radicals, Chinese radicals, Chinese conservatives, students, officials." The amalgam of people and ideas might have been the basis for a broader understanding, but, as Boring lamented, "the pity of it all was that in all claiming a share in him they did not see that they might do all of this in harmony, but fell to struggling among themselves." The irony of the situation was that Sun blended many of the characteristics within himself. Although a Christian he was still the leader of the Guomintang. The Guomintang would not acknowledge his Christianity, and the Anglican Church refused to let their choir sing at his funeral because he was the leader of the Guomintang.[78]

Reflecting on Sun's life, Boring recalled the arguments of Harry Ward of the Union Theological Seminary on Social Reconstruction. Ward had pointed out, and Boring agreed, the Christian Church was guilty of a flagrant failure to carry out the real principles of Christianity in modern society. She was intrigued by his remarks that some of the Soviet leaders had shown more real religion in their careers than many so-called Christians.[79] However, the two Guomintang factions, conservatives in Nanjing (led by Chiang Kai Shek) and leftists in Wuhan also lacked tolerance.

The power joust around Beijing became more urgent as the time to move to the new Yenching campus approached. Many Americans and other westerners feared the dangerous atmosphere and fled to safer territory.

In spite of the military situation, the move to the new campus began according to schedule. As announced, the spring term ended on the last day of May, 1926, and students and faculty members scurried to prepare for relocation. Unforeseen tensions dominated the move. Under the best of circumstances, transporting scientific apparatus, library books, furniture, and equipment fifteen miles into already completed quarters would have been a formidable task. Given incomplete buildings; non-functioning electrical, water, and telephone systems; and a more than usually unstable political environment, accomplishment of the move seemed almost miraculous.

The summer's move and the prospects of an exciting, but difficult, school year encouraged Boring to take a two-week camping vacation to relax and regroup her personal resources. Hiking, camping, paddling in mountain streams, and wearing audaciously comfortable knickers rejuvenated her. By moving into the hills beyond Beijing, she was able to strip away everyday operational concerns and reconsider her reasons for being in China. As it happened, this renewal was especially important, for the events of the first year of occupancy, 1926–1927, made the future of the fledgling campus uncertain.

The inconvenience of teaching in an atmosphere punctuated by the continuous "click, click" of the stone-mason's hammers and crowded temporary quarters seemed insignificant compared to the advantage of ample grounds, a magnificent mountain view, and country fresh air. An additional annoyance occurred as rival warlords Zhang Zuo Lin and Feng Yu Xiang battled over the control of Beijing, and soldiers from both sides periodically swarmed across the campus. This problem was eliminated when money was raised to construct an eight-foot high barrier wall.

In the summer of 1926 Boring moved into her new house. In spite of minor inconveniences and undaunted by the thought of beginning school in new, unfinished quarters, she rejoiced that it was "going to be a wonderful year, but a hard one. . . ."[80]

The challenges of that "wonderful year" were even more intense than Boring had anticipated. The political conflict accelerated to such a degree that impulsive western responses threatened the entire foreign presence in China. Yenching, Boring reassured her family, remained relatively safe. The new wall discouraged convenient trespassing and since neither Zhang Zuo Lin nor Feng Yu Xiang had a specific grievance against the University, they were insulated from actual violence. However, as foreigners in another's land, Yenching's American and British faculty members were influenced by their governments' response to local events. The "Great Powers" blindly insisted upon privileges inherited from the Boxer Rebellion and inflexibly refused to recognize new realities.

Thus, when the factionalized Guomintang entered Nanjing on March 24, 1927, Britain and the United States responded by bombarding the city from gunboats. Antiforeign repercussions were extensive, resulting in a mass foreign exodus and the closing of many foreign institutions. Brand-new Yenching's future was also in jeopardy. For a short time even Boring's faith was shaken, but Stuart effectively encouraged Yenching faculty and staff, insisting that the wave of "hate, violence, misunderstanding, lawlessness, and fear" was transitory.[81] The worst of the excesses lasted only a few weeks, and by April 7, 1927, Boring assured her family that the strengthened moderates under Chiang Kai Shek would assure future stability. She expected that the only battle to come close to Beijing would be a confrontation between Zhang Zuo Lin and Feng Yu Xiang. Convinced that Feng would win, she dismissed his "Red" tendencies in favor of his stands for "law and order and Christian principles."[82]

Rallying behind Stuart, the foreign faculty voted unanimously to "stick by the university and keep classes going." Boring predicted that the Chinese faculty and students would "pull Yenching through this crisis" and praised the "remarkable spirit of goodwill" that strengthened the university's position, and made it preeminent among other Christian institutions.[83]

As the situation stabilized, the westerners who had fled in panic began to trickle back, pretending that they had been on vacation. Nevertheless, the situation throughout 1927 remained precarious.[84]

Before the onset of the 1927 emergency, Alice had suggested to Garry that if Lydia visited China her opposition to Alice's Chinese career would evaporate. Therefore, she induced him to convince Ly to visit China before Alice's furlough in the United States. Alice knew that this year at home would be more satisfactory to "both of us" if Lydia knew beforehand "how I live out here." To make Lydia's Chinese vacation enjoyable, Alice proposed to invite Ly's friend, Helen Fogg, as Lydia's traveling companion.[85]

In spite of his own skepticism, Garry convinced Lydia to plan the trip for 1927–1928. However, in the summer of 1927, the political situation was sufficiently unstable as to merit reconsideration. When Lydia asked his opinion about the trip, Garry advised against it. However, he assured Alice that his counsel was meaningless, for "she [Lydia] never takes my advice anyhow." From letters and newspaper reports that he received, Garry concluded that there was no surety that the "row" would have settled down by fall when Ly and Helen were scheduled to arrive. He was not as optimistic as Alice that Ly would get a "kick" from "preserving Chinese unity and national aspirations by hiding in a dark hole while the unofficered northern rear guard collects pianos and diamond rings."[86]

The situation during the autumn of 1927 would not have alleviated Garry's anxiety. In one of the interminable regional wars, Yenching was again in the midst of an area of fighting. The governor of Shanxi attacked the forces of Zhang Zuo Lin, invaded the Beijing region, and drew the battle line near the campus. University personnel were awakened one night by the noise of heavy firing and a night sky bright with exploding shells. Before complete panic occurred, firing ceased; it was traced to a fire on a munitions car of a nearby train.[87]

Although the threat of war lurked beyond Yenching's new wall, the threat of imminent attack faded as the autumn slipped into winter. China seemed sufficiently safe to make Lydia's visit a possibility. As Alice considered the visit, she decided that including Helen was an inspired idea. Ly would have a more enjoyable trip, and Alice would not feel obliged to leave her numerous academic and social responsibilities at the new university to entertain her.

Full of her wonderful solution, Alice wrote to Lydia. Never diplomatic, Alice explained directly why she wanted Helen to come—to contribute to Lydia's good time. Helen's feelings were hurt, and psychologist Garry pleaded with Alice to rephrase her invitation so that Helen would feel wanted for her own sake. How, he asked Alice, "could one go virtually as a guest, even if a paying guest, unless welcomed for one's own sake?" Helen eventually agreed to accompany Lydia, and Garry encouraged Alice to "make a special point of welcoming Helen when she comes or even by mail before she comes."[88]

When Lydia and Helen arrived, they encountered another war. In the spring of 1928, Japan invaded and occupied Shandong. The fighting bordered on massacre, and incensed Chinese vowed retribution. The students at Yenching were swept by a wave of nationalism. The Japanese attack on Shandong occurred as the Nationalist army under Chiang Kai Shek was pushing northward in quest of Beijing. Although the Japanese temporarily blocked Chiang's path, they soon retired sufficiently to allow his advance toward the city.

During this time, Lydia and Helen were touring China. Garry noted that reports of Ly's trip around Tientsin "sounded most unwarlike." He expressed hope that "she doesn't miss the war altogether," but loved Alice's image of them all "hiding behind the Great Wall."[89]

In June as the sisters and Helen were attempting to make arrangements for the trip home, Zhang Zuo Lin retreated to his capitol in Manchuria where he allegedly was assassinated by a bomb explosion aboard his train. Zhang's departure eliminated the need for battles around Beijing, and it was soon occupied by Chiang Kai Shek's Nationalist government.

The Chinese vacation, with all of its excitement did not seem to change Lydia's mind about the suitability of a career in China for Alice. However, they seem to have arrived at an unspoken truce and Lydia became less vocal about her opposition. Perhaps she finally truly realized that Alice was not going to move back to the United States and that she might as well accept reality.

Notes

1. Jonathan D. Spence, *The Gate of Heavenly Peace. The Chinese and Their Revolution 1895–1980* (Harmondsworth, Middlesex, England: Penguin Books Ltd., 1982). p. 153.
2. The students ignored the fact that the Chinese delegates had refused to sign the treaty.
3. As a result of China's defeat in the Opium Wars in 1842, it was forced to negotiate an unfavorable treaty with Great Britain (and during the next two years equally unpalatable ones with France and the United States). These crippling indemnities ("unequal treaties") and special privileges to western nations and their citizens ("extraterritoriality") stimulated the protests from the Chinese that Boring referred to.
4. Military Intelligence Division. Declassified NND740058 3-26-86. China, 15 Sept. 1920, National Archives; China, 14 Jan. 1918, Letter to Major Barrows, National Archives.
5. Spence, *The Gate of Heavenly Peace*, pp. 222–23.
6. Lydia T. Boring to Family, 10 Sept. 1923, Pusey Archive Center, Harvard University, HUG 4229.25.5, 1923–1924; Edwin was disturbed as Boring family members were expected to keep the others informed of their where-

abouts at all times. Edwin G. Boring to Alice M. Boring, 5 Oct. 1923, Pusey Archive Center, Harvard University, HUG 4229.25.5, 1923–1924.

7. A.M. Boring to Family, 14 June 1924, Special Collection Archives, Yale Divinity School.

8. Ibid.

9. Ibid.

10. Ibid.

11. Ibid.

12. Ibid.

13. Alnah James Johnston, *The Footprints of the Pheasant in the Snow* (Portland, Maine: Anthoensen Press, 1978), pp. 15–17.

14. Ibid., pp. 100–101.

15. Ibid., p. 101.

16. A.M. Boring to Family, 1 Sept. 1924, Special Collection Archives, Yale Divinity School.

17. A.M. Boring to Family, 22 Aug. 1924, Special Collection Archives, Yale Divinity School.

18. A.M. Boring to Family, 1 Sept. 1924, Special Collection Archives, Yale Divinity School.

19. Johnston, *The Footprints of the Pheasant in the Snow*, p. 123.

20. Ibid., p. 124.

21. A.M. Boring to Family, 1 Sept. 1924, Special Collection Archives, Yale Divinity School.

22. Ibid.

23. Ibid.

24. James E. Sheridan, *Chinese Warlord, the Career of Feng Yu-hsiang* (Stanford, CA: Stanford University Press, 1966), p. 124 ff.

25. Ibid., p. 135.

26. A.M. Boring to Family, 24 Oct. 1924, Special Collection Archives, Yale Divinity School.

27. A.M. Boring to E.G. Boring, 28 Sept. 1924, Pusey Archive Collection, Harvard Univ., Boring Family Correspondence.

28. A.M. Boring to Family, 9 Nov. 1924, Special Collection Archives, Yale Divinity School.

29. Ibid.

30. Sheridan, *Chinese Warlord*, pp. 52–53.

31. Ibid; A.M. Boring to Family, 24 Oct. 1924, Special Collection Archives, Yale Divinity School.

32. A.M. Boring to E.G. Boring, 28 Sept. 1924, Pusey Archive Collection, Harvard University, Boring Family Correspondence.

33. A.M. Boring to Raymond Pearl, 28 Oct. 1924, American Philosophical Society Library.

34. A.M. Boring to Family, 9 Nov. 1924, Special Collection Archives, Yale Divinity School.

35. A.M. Boring to E.G. Boring, 28 Sept. 1924, Pusey Archive Collection, Harvard University, Boring Family Correspondence.

36. A.M. Boring to E.G. Boring, 28 Sept. 1924, Pusey Archive Collection, Harvard University, Boring Family Correspondence.

37. A.M. Boring to Family, 14 June 1925, Special Collection Archives, Yale Divinity School.

38. Ibid.

39. Ibid.

40. K.G. Boring to E.G. Boring, 13 June 1925, Pusey Archive Collection, Harvard University, Rondthaler Family Correspondence, Box 511, Folder 1139.

41. E.G. Boring to A.M. Boring, 4 Nov. 1925, Pusey Archive Collection, Harvard University, Boring Family Correspondence.

42. A.M. Boring to E.G. Boring, 26 July 1925, Pusey Archive Collection, Harvard University, Boring Family Correspondence; J. Leighton Stuart, Report to Board of Trustees, 9 Dec. 1925, Stuart Papers, Yale University, RG11, Folder 5460.

43. Stuart, Report to Board of Trustees, 9 Dec. 1925.

44. Ibid.

45. A.M. Boring to E.G. Boring, 18 Aug. 1925. Pusey Archive Collection, Harvard University, Boring Family Correspondence.

46. Alice M. Boring to E.G. Boring, 10 April 1925, Pusey Archive Collection, Harvard University, Boring Family Correspondence.

47. Ibid.

48. A.M. Boring to E.G. Boring, 25 May 1925, Pusey Archive Collection, Harvard University, Boring Family Correspondence.

49. A.M. Boring to E.G. Boring, 26 July 1925, Pusey Archive Collection, Harvard University, Boring Family Correspondence.

50. Gee's job with the China Medical Board was not finished and, when it was, "his wife wants to go back to South Carolina so the possibilities of getting him are slim." A.M. Boring to E.G. Boring, 26 July 1925, Pusey Archive Collection, Harvard University, Boring Family Correspondence.

51. A.M. Boring to E.G. Boring 18 Aug. 1925, Pusey Archive Collection, Harvard University, Boring Family Correspondence. Gee's term was due to expire in 1926. Roger Greene praised his services as advisor on premedical education, presuming that he was mostly responsible for the improvement of science teaching in China's colleges. Greene reported that it was largely because of Gee's work that "it has seemed safe to close the pre-medical school at P.U.M.C. this year...." Because of his excellent work, Greene proposed that Gee's appointment be extended and modified. Boring need not have been concerned about Gee as competition for her position. Greene to George E. Vincent, 22 July 1925, Rockefeller Archive Center, CMB, S1II, B81.

52. Richard H. Ritter to Ogilvie, 4 Oct. 1987.

53. A.M. Boring to E.G. Boring, 26 July 1925, Pusey Archive Collection, Harvard University, Boring Family Correspondence.

54. J. Leighton Stuart, Report to Board of Trustees, Stuart Papers, Yale University, RG11, Folder 5460, 9 Dec. 1925.

55. Ibid.

56. A.M. Boring to Family, 21 March 1926, Special Collection Archives, Yale Divinity School. See also Greene to Marjorie Eggleston, 19 November 1925, Rockefeller Archive Center, CMB, S1 II, B81.

57. Ibid.

58. A.M. Boring to Family, 28 March 1926, Special Collection Archives, Yale Divinity School.

59. A.M. Boring to Family, 21 March 1926, Special Collection Archives, Yale Divinity School; Jonathan D. Spence, *The Gate of Heavenly Peace The Chinese and Their Revolution 1895–1980* (New York: Penguin Books, 1982), pp. 231–32.

60. A.M. Boring to Family, 21 March 1926, Special Collection Archives, Yale Divinity School.

61. Ibid.

62. Ibid.

63. Ibid.

64. Edwin Garrigues Boring, "Edwin Garrigues Boring" (Worcester, MA: Clark University Press, 1952). Reprinted from *A History of Psychology in Autobiography*, Vol. IV, Pusey Archive Collection, Harvard University, HUG 4229 10, pp 34–36. Originally intending to become an engineer, a field in which, by his own admission, he was only mediocre, Edwin began his academic preparation at Cornell. In order to satisfy an elective requirement, he enrolled in a psychology class taught by Edward B. Titchener (1867–1927). Fascinated both by the subject matter and Titchener's approach, Edwin decided to pursue graduate work in psychology. He met his future wife, Lucy M. Day, while in the Ph.D. program at Cornell. Lucy, too, was a psychology graduate student and received her Ph.D. in 1912, two years before Edwin received his. After serving in World War I and teaching at Clark University, Edwin began teaching at Harvard. During the time in which Alice was considering a Chinese career, he was attempting to reform Harvard's psychology department, then a captive of the philosophy department.

65. E.G. Boring to K.G. Boring, 10 April 1926, Pusey Archive Collection, Harvard University, Rondthaler Family Correspondence, HUG 4229.5, Folder 1139, Box 51.

66. Alice M. Boring, "The Funeral of Sun Yat Sen," *Bryn Mawr Alumnae Bulletin*, 5 (Oct. 1925), 16–18. Although Boring writes that there were ten pallbearers, the program lists sixteen.

67. Ibid.

68. C. Martin Wilbur, *Sun Yat-Sen, Frustrated Patriot* (New York: Columbia University Press, 1976), pp. 222–224.

69. Spence, *The Gate of Heavenly Peace*, p. 204.

70. Boring, "The Funeral of Sun Yat Sen."

71. Ibid.

72. Ibid.

73. Mildred Wiant to Clifford Choquette, 4 April 1988.

74. Severinghaus to Choquette, 27 February 1988; Order of Service, Private Funeral of Sun Yat Sen, Peking Union Medical College Chapel, Peking, China, March Nineteenth, Nineteen Hundred and Twenty-Five, Fourteenth Year of the Republic of China at ten o'clock.

75. Severinghaus to Choquette, 27 February 1988.

76. Ibid.

77. Ibid.

78. Ibid.

79. Ibid.

80. Alice M. Boring to E.G. Boring, 18 Aug. 1926, Pusey Archive Collection, Harvard University, Boring Family Correspondence.

81. Howard S. Galt, *History of Yenching University* (unpublished ms.), p. 183.

82. A.M. Boring to Family and Grace [Boynton], 7 April 1927, Special Collection Archives, Yale Divinity School.

83. Ibid.

84. E.G. Boring to A.M. Boring, 8 June 1927, Pusey Archive Collection, Harvard University, Boring Family Correspondence.

85. A.M. Boring to E.G. Boring, 18 August 1926, Pusey Archive Collection, Harvard University, Boring Family Correspondence.

86. E.G. Boring to A.M. Boring, 8 June 1927.

87. A.M. Boring to Family and Grace, 7 April 1927.

88. E.G. Boring to A.M. Boring, 9 Jan. 1928, Pusey Archive Collection, Harvard University, Boring Family Correspondence.

89. E.G. Boring to A.M. Boring, 22 May 1928, Pusey Archive Collection, Harvard University, Boring Family Correspondence.

Chapter 4
From Laboratory Biology to Field Natural History

By the end of the spring semester, 1928, Boring had run out of excuses to postpone her furlough. Lydia had made her visit and was ready to return home. The political situation around Beijing was relatively stable and she no longer feared for the fledgling Yenching's existence. If she postponed her leave until the following year, she would miss the long-deferred formal opening of Yenching scheduled for the fall of 1929.

Still somewhat reluctantly, Alice began the long trek home in the summer of 1928. She chose to scrimp and endure some discomfort in order to go through Russia and Germany rather than the more direct, but less interesting, Pacific route.

Boring knew that the political calm had spawned a new exuberance throughout Yenching's student body. The students claimed that there should be a new Yenching to match the new spirit of Chinese unity, a view that Boring enthusiastically shared. At the beginning of the Fall semester 1928–1929 when Boring was in the United States, she would have learned that new students were greeted enthusiastically by a welcoming committee at the University gate. To emphasize their optimism, students waved colorful banners, chanted nationalistic slogans, and tacked party propaganda posters to convenient trees and buildings.[1]

The year that Boring would miss promised to be very different from the past one. Although the previous year had been exciting, the emphasis had been on survival and maintenance. Necessity had forced the subordination of educational and research objectives to political realities. That year, 1928, on the other hand, promised stability and the opportunity to improve Yenching's academic potential. Alice consoled herself for her absence by thinking of her plans for the furlough—plans that would result in a new career direction beneficial both to her and to Yenching.

Philadelphia was the site of these new plans. Alice had previously confided to Garry that she hoped to placate Lydia by spending her furlough with her and still use the time to advantage by studying at the University of Pennsylvania. She was not especially anxious to encounter her old research associates, for she had decided to move from laboratory to field biology and was reluctant to discuss the change with her former colleagues. To them, experimental genetics and cytology were the exciting biological frontiers, and Boring was convinced that they would not approve of her shift to the less glamorous area of taxonomy. For that reason she failed to visit her old friend and colleague, Dr. Pearl, did not inform him of the change in her research focus until August 1929, as she was "steaming across the Pacific back to China after my year in America."[2]

Demanding teaching and student advising schedules and a lack of dedication to experimental science together with a fascination with the variety of Chinese herpetofauna suggested a research shift. Unlike experimental biology, taxonomic research could be undertaken sporadically as time constraints allowed. In studying Chinese reptiles and amphibians, Boring was engaging in a less competitive form of research than in her previous experimental work and could expect that her contributions would transcend the mere exportation of American science. Boring's new research was of immediate practical benefit to the Chinese. The probability of discovering information inaccessible to most western biologists made up for any inadequacies she might have felt about her own research abilities.

At the same time she avoided the experimental biologists, Boring sought the advice and opinions of herpetologists Clifford H. Pope and G.K. Noble of the American Museum of Natural History. Boring had met Pope in China and supported him in his work on Chinese reptiles and amphibians. She advised him about conditions in the country, provided sources for equipment and supplies, and put him in touch with individuals who could assist them. The friendly collegial relationship that they had established continued when Boring returned to the United States. Accustomed to staring at a parade of darkly stained chromosomes in the cell nuclei of animals, Boring found it confusing to look at the entire animal with its scales, teeth, and sense organs. She asked many questions. How do taxonomists arrive at relationships? What tools do they use and how do they use them? Although before she left China, Boring had embarked upon a "teach yourself" program, she wanted more information and she wanted it from experts Pope and Noble. Boring also corresponded with Albert Hazen Wright of Cornell, who was then the leading authority on the life histories of North American frogs. He sent her his papers and answered questions. He accepted Boring's most famous student Liu Cheng Chao for the Cornell graduate program, and Liu received his Ph.D. in 1934 from that university.

Boring corresponded with these men while she worked "hard at anatomy and animal distribution" at the University of Pennsylvania.[3] From them she received reprints of papers, explanations of terms, and unlimited access to the facilities of the American Museum.

When Noble sent her a reprint of his work on the phylogeny of the Salienta, "a landmark in Amphibian work," Boring expressed her pleasure. No one, she explained, "can do much in Amphibia without it as a foundation, so I especially value it."[4] Later, she requested and received his help in interpreting the paper. During the process of learning about amphibians and reptiles, Boring gave a "Journal Club" report for the zoology department at the University of Pennsylvania in which she reported on Noble's paper. As she made distribution maps to illustrate her talk, she required clarification from Noble on several points. Almost apologetically she indicated that the answers to her questions were no doubt to be found "somewhere in your papers," but that she seemed to have missed them. Noble's reply made it clear that both he and Boring agreed that he was the teacher and she the student. Noble answered with a hint of chiding that, indeed, "all of the above facts except the statement concerning *Tylototriton*" were to be found in his paper.[5] The relationship between Pope and Noble, and Boring was not one-sided, however. At Boring's request, Pope agreed to write a paper on "Field Amphibia Problems." In order to produce this work, he requested access to Boring's extensive collection of data cards but hesitated to ask her to expose them to the vagaries of the mail system. Generous as always, Boring wrote that she would "be an ungrateful wretch to both you and Dr. Noble" if she "refused after all of your hospitality."[6] Her philosophy of sharing data emerged, as she explained that she was "of the opinion that nothing is too valuable to use by any one who can get any use or pleasure out of it." She felt the same way about wanting her data to be properly used as she did about using her "great grandfather's spoons every day in China instead of leaving them in a safety vault in America as my sister advised."[7] Pope used Boring's data cards to finish his paper and sent it to her before she returned to China. On July 12, 1929, he informed her that he was sending the promised manuscript. He asked her to make major suggestions if needed, proofread it for typographical errors, and "publish it where or whenever you wish, or ... scrap it."[8]

Boring considered herself more competent in amphibian than in reptilian taxonomy. She had advised science educator-biologist Nathaniel Gist Gee on his "Amphibian List" and had received "a nice appreciative letter from him" for her help. However, Gee had compiled a list of reptiles that also needed attention, and Boring asked Pope if he had "time to do anything for his [Gee's] reptile list." Although she would have preferred to check the materials herself, she did not feel competent to do so. She wanted to increase her confidence in her own ability to recognize subtle differences between species and subspecies of Chinese reptiles and planned study time in the American Museum to accomplish this end.

Boring had scheduled time in the month of May, 1929, to visit the "snake room" of the American Museum. One year in the United States hardly seemed adequate for all of the things she wanted to do, so she was forced to compress, to postpone, and to eliminate certain activities. Family obligations, speaking engagements, business affairs, and social events all vied for her limited research time. Therefore, reluctantly, she informed Pope that her "snake trip" to New York would have to be postponed until June, "as I seem to have many engagements already for May." Working in the narrow-aisled, high-shelved herpetology range could be stifling in hot weather, and Boring did not look forward to the experience. She asked Pope if the snake rooms would be "ferociously" hot in June. She hoped that the Chinese snakes could be gathered together in one place "which can be made endurable by an electric fan."[9] On Sunday, June 9, 1929, Boring arrived in New York and began to work in the Museum the next day.

By the time she was ready to leave for China, Boring not only had improved her knowledge of Chinese reptiles, but had worked up a "complete check list of all the Amphibia ever recorded from any part of China. ..." From the range maps that she made, she discovered that some specimens were Indian forms which "have moved up" while others were "Siberian forms which have moved down." She was now prepared to present her findings at a biological conference to be held at Yenching in conjunction with the university's formal opening.[10]

The information that she gained and the contacts she made, strengthened Boring's ability to do taxonomic and distributional research when she returned to China, making her a greater asset to Yenching professionally. However, she used her time in the United States to help Yenching in other ways as well. Constant fund-raising efforts were required for the university's survival. The *Peking News*, an irregularly appearing publication, helped the fund-raising effort. By reminding people of Yenching's mission through human interest articles, funds were collected between formal campaigns. Yenching Executive Secretary John Wannamaker asked Boring to contribute to this magazine. Her contribution "hit the nail...completely on the head." President Stuart's assistant asked Boring to send a photograph so that "the letter may possess not only force and vigor, but also the requisite beauty...."[11] Boring's enthusiasm for her university was infectious and she seldom allowed an opportunity to pass to act as its advocate.

Although Boring often seemed to to court adversarial relationships and eschew the preferred Quaker style of consensus building, nevertheless, her Quaker idealism sometimes emerged at an opportune moment. She was able to defuse a potential crisis between Yenching's missionary and scholarly factions. During her furlough, rumors were rife about the establishment of a Harvard-Yenching Institute for Oriental studies from the proceeds of the Charles Martin Hall Estate. Hall, the inventor of an aluminum manufacturing process, proposed to found an institute with the purpose of promoting Sinological studies at Harvard and in China, at Yenching and other centers. The actual form the institute would take was unclear. Brother Garry, exposed as he was to the Harvard gossip, passed on his information to Alice, who, in turn, relayed it to Stuart. Rumor indicated that of a total of nine Trustees, three would be from the Hall Estate, three from Harvard, and three from Yenching.[12] The scholarly factions and the missionary factions disagreed about the purpose of the institute. Garry engaged in some "covert priming" of missionary Lucius C. Porter, so that he would not alienate the Hall faction.[13] Blunt Alice appreciated Garry's efforts at diplomacy, which "is not my forte as thee knows!" More than diplomacy might be needed, for "J.W. a Hall trustee" would unfortunately arrive at Yenching's formal opening at the same time as the missionary trustees.[14] Alice kept Stuart informed of the situation, and suggested "that a scholarly rather than pious atmosphere will be more advantageous." Stuart, she knew, was a master diplomat and, although he would be wedged between the various factions, would keep the peace if it could be kept.[15]

Several items of personal business had to be completed before Boring could return to China. Garry, always the dependable businessman, agreed to take care of papers in Alice's safety deposit box.[16] A persistent back problem had annoyed her while she was in China, and she was determined to have it corrected before she returned. "My ilio-sacral joint is not cured," she complained to Garry. She had heard of the ideal doctor in Boston, an osteopathic surgeon, and asked Garry to have his wife, Lucy, make her an appointment. With her back improved, business taken care of, Ly mollified, and her research completed, most of the necessary accomplishments of the leave were taken care of.[17]

When Boring had a box of books sent to the Yenching New York office from Wellesley, her China decision seemed irrevocable. As long as the books were at Wellesley, she had not severed all of her ties. But when the books arrived in New York en route to China, even Lydia would have had to accept the inevitable—Alice would make her career in China.[18]

Boring's apology to Pearl for failing to visit him during her leave confirmed her new research commitment. She wrote that, "I fully intended to be in Baltimore at some time during the year and see you for auld lang syne and the joy of again watching a brilliant mind work...." She explained that she still held "that you and Thomas H. Morgan can settle more stimulating ideas in ten minutes than any other two persons who have ever crossed my horizons."[19] She admitted to Pearl that she had inaugurated a new project involving the herpetofauna of China. Of her changed interests she wrote, "I do not know where it is going to land me," but "I hope it will mean that I can spend my vacations exploring interesting mountains and deserts in all sorts of exciting places in China."[20]

Boring need not have been apprehensive about Pearl's reaction to her changed interests. He assured her that taxonomy was indeed respectable. "What nonsense is this about my not approving of taxonomic work? Quite the contrary! I am coming to believe it is the only kind of biological work that has any permanent or real value." He claimed he had been "strongly tempted to take it up ... and may even yet." Another advantage, he proposed, was that "it is pleasant and tends to keep you out in the open air." After his gentle teasing, he wrote that "quite seriously I think you have done a very wise thing in turning your energies in this direction, especially considering the fact that you are working out there in China."[21]

Boring must have felt gratified by Pearl's response. Her taxonomic work at the American Museum had immediate results, for she had completed her Chinese Amphibian check list with bibliography and notes on distribution in time for the Yenching fall biology conference held in conjunction with Yenching's formal opening. She wrote Noble that she and N. Gist Gee were presenting the paper together and expected to publish it in the Peking Natural History Society's journal, the *Peking Natural History Bulletin*, which she edited.[22] Noble, pleased with her results, was especially complimentary about her success in interesting her students in amphibian studies.[23]

As she sailed across the Pacific Ocean in mid-August, 1929, Boring looked forward to using the new laboratories she had helped to design, reacquainting herself with her favorite students, and further integrating herself into the Yenching "inner circle" dominated by Leighton Stuart. The uncertainty surrounding her future resolved, she anticipated the long-deferred formal opening of the University.

In addition to transmitting general information to those at Yenching, Boring personally became involved in organizing the biology section of the Group Conferences for Papers and Discussion. Long hours of reading and working in the laboratories at the University of Pennsylvania, braving the combination of stifling heat and the smell of alcohol preservative, and corresponding with colleagues back at Yenching prepared her well for her direct part in the formal opening. The correspondence led to a smooth program in the biology section, and the research culminated in the excellent paper that she produced in conjunction with Gee.

The clear North China autumn with its warm days and crisp nights was ideal for the opening. Reveling in the glorious September and October days, Boring was pleased to show off her Yenching at its best to foreign visitors. These visitors included members of the Board of Trustees and representatives from ten institutions. Perhaps a bit nervous as she observed delegates from the Presbyterian and Methodist Episcopal Mission Boards sitting close to the representatives of Columbia University, the Carnegie Foundation, and Harvard University, she marveled at Stuart's ability to smooth over differences before they surfaced. Local institutions sent their representatives who mingled with the foreign emissaries. Activities ranging from religious services to sports exhibitions, musical concerts and plays to banquets and receptions were carefully designed to have a wide appeal.[24]

The four-day program was itself a combination of the sacred and the secular. Good-luck beasts watched over the buildings and decorated the flower and tree-laden grounds. God was praised, benefactors honored, and Sun Yat Sen's role in the establishment of the "New China" acknowledged.[25]

In a series of conferences that began on Monday, September 30, and continued through Tuesday, scholars and students from China and foreign countries presented and discussed papers on Chinese culture, philosophy, social sciences and natural science. Boring sent the program from the biology conference to Noble and was gratified when he congratulated her "on the number of students whom you are interesting in the study of Amphibia."[26] In fact, her program at Yenching became one of two major centers in China for the study of amphibians and reptiles.[27]

The opening events climaxed with an extended academic procession and the official transfer of the facility from the Trustees to the University itself. Franklin Warner, President of the Board of Trustees, presented Fu Lei Chuan, Chancellor of the University, with a golden key symbolizing the transfer of the buildings constructed through the efforts of the Trustees to the academic head of the University. On October 1, 1929, after three years of use, Yenching was officially opened.[28]

II

After the optimism spawned by the opening and generated by the relatively stable Chinese political situation, Boring expected an era of accomplishment undisturbed by outside events. The future looked bright, and she could get on with her job—to teach young Chinese students biology and to work on the taxonomy and distribution of reptiles and amphibians. Once more, however, the world outside of Yenching had a different idea. The interference, this time, was not from riots or warring factions, but from the effects of the world-wide depression.

A mission institution such as Yenching must work constantly to assure an adequate financial base. During the second decade of the twentieth century, its success reflected the exuberance born of economic prosperity in the United States. With the end of the post-war depression in 1922, spectacular profits on real estate and stock speculation seduced buyers into thinking that the Bull Market would continue forever. Prosperous people were convinced easily to share their wealth with the developing university outside of Beijing. Stuart summarized the results of the campaign of October 1927 to May 1928, reporting that they had aggregated a total of $500,000 for the campaign objectives, provided a small surplus, and collected an additional $176,623 for unspecified needs. One million dollars was added to the endowment funds during 1928 for the Harvard-Yenching Institute from the Hall Estate, and an additional half million dollars was to be held in trust for Yenching University by the Harvard-Yenching Institute Trustees to be used in strengthening undergraduate studies with special reference to Chinese and related studies.[29]

Less than a month after the opening, Yenching officials suffered the aftershock of "Black Tuesday," October 29, 1929. A jingle current in the United States could also have been applied to Yenching University.

> Mellon pulled the whistle
> Hoover rang the bell
> Wall Street gave the signal
> And the country went to hell

Soon, the business of teaching and running the university had to be secondary to treasure hunting.

Reluctantly, Boring, was drawn into the great search for money since in the fall of 1930, she became acting dean of the College of Natural Sciences. She enjoyed presiding over curricular changes, scheduling classes, and correlating the activities of the different science departments. However, she was far from enthusiastic about the activities necessary to raise money.[30] During her early years in China, Boring had demonstrated her repugnance to asking her friends for money when a missionary, Miss Wiklund, coerced her into giving a party and inviting her friends in order to solicit money to support her cause.

As dean, Boring was required to address questions of morale and money, but was unable to understand the nature of the demands placed on Leighton Stuart as president. Not only was he responsible for maintaining morale, but also for raising money from an economically pressed constituency. During 1929, after the stock market crash, he had spent a considerable amount of time fund raising in the United States. Boring claimed his absence had a disastrous effect on Yenching's *esprit de corps*. She pleaded with Chairman Franklin Warner not to require Stuart to take another long leave of absence within the next two or three years, for on his return he was faced with the need to perform miracles. "It is the kind of thing," wrote Boring, "which you can not make sense of in New York, that makes it imperative that President Stuart be not called to America to raise money in the nearby future."[31]

To Alice Boring, the attractive, personable Leighton Stuart was invincible. If "everybody" had confidence in Stuart's ability to forestall conflict, Alice led the "everybody." Ever since his initial reassurances to her about Yenching, she was one of his most ardent supporters. The confidence he exuded about things Chinese came from his background and experience.[32]

Stuart was positioned at the vortex of what Boring characterized as a "fine group of people" at Yenching. Handsome, convivial, and charismatic, Stuart was idolized by female Yenching faculty and staff members. Hoping to be drawn into the inner orbit, they sometimes resorted to negative campaign tactics, including depreciating the accomplishments of their colleagues. More than once, Stuart's actual or imagined favoritism disrupted the tranquility of the Yenching faculty. The one who detected coolness or aloofness in his manner was devastated. The favored one basked in the sun of his approval. English teacher Grace Boynton expressed the feelings of many faculty members as she wrote of Stuart's presence at graduation. While admiring the spirit of his terminally ill wife who "told her husband that no matter what her condition was she wished him to be present and to give the graduates their diplomas himself," Boynton was especially "full of sympathy for Dr. Stuart who is widely and deeply beloved." After Mrs. Stuart's death, the dream of a potential romance complicated professional relationships at Yenching.[33]

Boring was a member of Stuart's fan club, and her admiration for him sometimes tinted her relationship with others. A rift over Stuart between contemplative Grace Boynton and outspoken Alice Boring made both of them, particularly Boynton, uncomfortable. Boynton and Boring lived together in 1934. Distinguished Chinese writer, Bing Xin, recalled that while Boynton was on leave, Boring had become accustomed to having Sunday dinner with Stuart. When Boynton returned and appeared on these occasions, Boring asked her to leave, hurting sensitive Boynton's feelings.[34] The situation escalated until the two women could hardly be in the same room with the other. Boring, in her outspoken way, thought she had cleared the air in September 1934 by asking Boynton to move out. Boynton did not see it as "clearing the air," and nursed hurt feelings for years.

Psychologist brother Garry commended Alice on her courage to confront the issue, assuring her that her approach was healthier than the "more cowardly" mental kind of adjustment practiced by Boynton. "I congratulate thee on having so definitely met the problem."[35]

As Garry recognized, Grace and Alice had two very different personalities. Grace was introspective, with her feelings often breaking the surface. Her wounds, real or imaginary, festered, making it difficult for her to forgive or forget. As she replayed events, she often concluded that the slights she perceived were deserved—some flaw in her basic makeup. Acceptance by Stuart, which meant acceptance by Alice (a part of Stuart's "inner circle"), was vitally important, yet seemingly unattainable. Alice, on the other hand, looked outside of herself for answers and was more likely to become angry and respond with an unconsidered pronouncement, but just as unexpectedly reconsider her response and forget the incident. To associates who knew her less than intimately, Alice's inclination to pronounce judgment immediately was annoying. To those who knew her as a friend, her good intentions usually outweighed her impulsiveness. Boring and Boynton knew each other intimately for much of their professional lives, yet their different ways of viewing the world made a real friendship difficult.

To those associates who knew Alice superficially, her black and white treatment of issues and her dogmatic way of making pronouncements suggested a domineering person determined to influence the course of events. The reactions of the "Friday lunch" bunch at Yenching illustrates the effect Boring could have on companions. Margaret Speer, who joined the Yenching English faculty in 1926, recalled her impressions of Boring amid her colleagues.

> Alice Boring and Grace Boynton, who was a Wellesley woman about ten years older than I, a member of the English Department, invited two young Chinese members of the faculty and Augusta Wagner and me to have lunch with them every Friday. "Friday Lunch" became an accepted institution on the campus. As far as we were concerned it was just lovely. We were young, new members of the faculty. The two Chinese were a young biology teacher who was Alice Boring's protege and who came out the same time I did after having gone to Vassar; and Yang Ping, a brilliant poet who had been Grace Boynton's protege.[36]

As "Friday Lunch" expanded to include more people, Boring's assurance sometimes generated conflict among her less powerful colleagues.

> Every Friday we went to lunch. Every Friday, Alice Boring told us what she thought the University ought to do. We didn't always agree. We wrote a poem about her once, something about the power behind the power behind the power behind the throne.[37]

Few associates outwardly challenged her opinions, partly because of her favored position with Stuart. The slightly snide view of some of the "lunch bunch" people seems to conflict with that of other colleagues who stressed her helpfulness and good nature. The young professor, Harold Shadick, thought of her "as one of the more dynamic older faculty members (I was 23 when I began teaching history in 1925) who was kind, socially to juniors."[38]

Although her colleagues envied or disparaged Boring's influence on Stuart, he, himself apparently was immune to criticism. As Boring indicated, his successful balancing of factions was respected by most of Yenching's faculty and staff. Her claim that the University functioned poorly in his absence had support from many colleagues. In spite of faculty misgivings, Stuart was "called to America to raise money." He reported to his uneasy staff that "it is with great reluctance that I have felt it my duty to respond to another summons from the Trustees to visit America." The only apparent solution to the University's Depression-caused financial woes was to increase the "as yet very limited endowment funds. . . ."[39]

Boring was unable to understand the crucial importance of fund raising to Yenching's very existence. She objected strongly when Gee and Stuart encouraged her to solicit friends for money. Rather than risk alienating her scientist friends by asking for money, she recommended her practice of sending out reprints from Yenching's science department to establish good public relations which could, in the long run, produce some contributions.[40] However, Gee and Stuart had more tangible goals than good public relations in mind. When Gee persisted and asked her to send him the names of the scientists to whom she sent the reprints, Boring retorted that "they none of them have any money and will feel that I have betrayed them, if you ask them for any."[41]

It seemed as if a drastic reduction would be necessary in the budget of the College of Natural Sciences. Stuart recommended to the Executive Secreatry of the Board of Trustees in New York, B.A. Garside, that such cuts be postponed and that the budget remain as proposed for 1932–1933 with the understanding that reductions deemed necessary would be made in the following year's budget. He justified maintaining the budget as proposed on the grounds that excellent work was emerging from the college and that this work "is itself an asset of no slight value." Also, he proclaimed, it is difficult to rebuild a staff "secured with great effort" and if, "as we are hoping, we shall have our complete endowment in future, it would be a pity to let any individuals go whom we should want to keep with us."[42]

In her Christmas letter of 1934, Boring referred to the specter of the Depression that invaded all of their enterprises. To compensate for the lack of money coming in from the United States, Stuart launched a million dollar endowment campaign in China. "Everybody threw cold water on it [the plan]; what never had been done, never could; Chinese would not give, could not give, etc." She accepted Stuart's view that if "China would not come to our rescue in this extremity," we must have failed to make Yenching sufficiently valuable and "might as well quit." Official China contributed to Yenching's rescue, hosting a Yenching reception in Nanjing sponsored by Chiang Kai Shek and Wang Ching Wei. Official approval might not mean money, but it was still gratifying. "I keep wondering why these government officials are doing all this for us." They remained supportive even after "we have refused to admit some of their sons when they have not come up to standard...." Even more devastatingly, "we have conscientiously flunked them out when they have not kept up to standard after they were in."[43]

Boring attributed the success to Stuart. "Has he worked magic on them?" He worked the same kind of magic "on most of us who belong to Yenching, so that we work and play, eat and sleep for Yenching." He clearly had worked his magic on Boring. Hints of hero worship skip through her letters. This admiration was reciprocated, as Stuart gave

Alice additional responsibilities. One can only speculate about an incipient romance between the two. Alice's obvious anger at Grace Boynton when her presence interfered with her "alone time" with Stuart, brother Garry's teasing of Alice about Stuart, and her students' undocumented awareness that there was a special relationship between the two suggest that, if not a full-blown romance, their relationship was more than just that of good friends. Boring's relationship with the handsome widower Stuart orbited around Yenching, yet her students and colleagues were convinced that they had a mutual romantic interest. Students recalled the two walking hand in hand across the bridge on the Yenching campus. Grace Boynton certainly would not have been so jealous of Boring's favored position with Stuart if she had not believed that Alice was involved with Stuart in a way in which she was not and would have liked to have been. Alice, herself, would not have been so upset with Grace had she not wanted to keep Stuart all to herself. It was Alice to whom Stuart chose to confide his dreams and not the volatile Boynton. Cornell Professor Harold Shadick was Boring's colleague at Yenching for sixteen years but, since he taught history, philosophy, and literature they had little opportunity for academic contacts. He was, however, aware of the close relationship between Boring and Stuart, noting that

> after the death of Mrs. Aline Stuart in 1926, she became, in effect, social secretary and hostess to Leighton Stuart. She was his companion on frequent horse rides. She arranged for Nellie and me to use his horses several times in 1927 when we were courting. Later we once saw how efficiently she managed a camping trip when we were invited to make a foursome for a weekend at a temple in the hills.[44]

Boring's Christmas letter explained that the "good feelings" inspired by Stuart resulted in the Yenching people "being held up to the Chinese public as highly commendable educators, gentlemen, and scholars, and it is a very pleasant experience!" Because of Stuart's great tact, Boring concluded that there was no longer "much basis for talk about anti-foreign feeling in China." Yenching's blend of thirty-five foreigners out of a faculty and staff of somewhat more than a hundred seemed a prime example of true integration.[45]

During the time of the great financial crisis, Boring had not only consolidated her position as a trusted faculty member and competent administrator, but also had matured in her commitment to Yenching. When she examined her own change in feeling during these years, she admitted that in 1918 she came to China "as an adventure, ..." with "a decided anti-missionary bias...." However, as she observed the commitment of Roger Greene, Henry Houghton, Lucius Porter and, above all, Leighton

Stuart, she became transformed "into the most loyal supporter of the kind of work which Yenching stands for. . . ." Her year as acting dean made the problems of Yenching "the stuff my life is made of. . . ." She suggested that her "conservative Quaker ancestry, her scientific training, and a new spirit found at Yenching. . . ." balanced "each other in the analysis."[46]

The balance, however, had to be internal for external events were again chaotic. Precarious finances represented only one aspect of the uncertainty of the early 1930s. The era of peace that surrounded the Formal Opening and which suffused the entire university with a spirit of optimism and progress was short lived. Chiang's transformation from a warlord among warlords to a warlord over warlords seemed to presage a true nationalism. His was not a government of consensus, however, and intrigue constantly threatened his position. Alliances and counteralliances resulted in a precarious peace in the autumn of 1930.

Teased again by the prospect of peace, Boring nevertheless was not surprised when it did not occur. The revolt of 1930 that established Chiang's power had little effect on the University, but a new series of events involved it profoundly. This time the problem did not directly concern competing warlords nor the regime's communist opponents. Japan had methodically infiltrated many Chinese institutions, but on September 18, 1931, a crisis occurred; Japan invaded Moukden. Incensed students demanded strong action on the part of the Nationalist government. Instead, the government of Beijing, with the blessings of the Nanjing government, decided not to resist. Chiang did not even declare war on Japan, but took his case to the League of Nations in Geneva. Meanwhile, Japan continued to encroach on the northeastern area and soon occupied all of Manchuria. The League seemed to be singularly ineffective. It issued verbal protests and set up an investigative commission headed by Lord Lytton. His 1933 report advised a compromise with Japan. Many of the Chinese intelligentsia were disgusted with the vacillating, weak response of the Nanjing government.[47] China became a victim of the Japanese long before Pearl Harbor (1941) when the United States became involved in the war.

As the Yenching students gathered their protest forces, Boring must have felt dismay at what seemed certain to be yet another academic disruption. At first, the students worked within the framework of the Peking Students' Union. However, this organization was rent by factionalism and strife so they decided to proceed independently. They organized mass meetings, boycotts of Japanese goods, a student "Resistance to Japan" committee, student lecture bands, and *The Torch*, a publication to provide a medium for information and agitation through which students could express their outrage.

Faculty members also became involved. The Chinese faculty members with the sympathy, although without the direct participation, of their foreign colleagues organized a resistance movement that cooperated with the students. The participants met weekly and published the minutes of these meetings in the *University Bulletin*.

After the invasion, many university students who fled from Manchuria made their way to Beijing. Yenching responded by admitting them on a special basis, and, by the end of November, twenty-six men and four women refugee students had been admitted.[48]

The Yenching students still were not satisfied that they had done enough. The Nanjing government's lame and halting response to their patriotic activities was unacceptable to the passionate students. They proposed to startle the government into hearing their case by a mass migration of the entire student body to present a petition directly. Faculty members, although sympathizing with the students' feelings, opposed the march. They could not help remembering that it was Chiang who had brought some measure of stability to the country. Of course, they would have preferred him to have acted decisively against the Japanese, but many still were convinced that his regime was far better than the alternatives.[49] Boring's sympathies were with the students as usual. However, later she met Chiang's wife, Soong Mei Ling, "a Wellesley girl of the class of 1917," at a Wellesley reunion in Beijing. Madame Chiang's simple, sincere, and direct manner when "we got her started talking about what the government is doing and planning for the common people of China," convinced Boring as well as her colleagues that, as one said, "either that woman is a colossal hypocrite or else I shall have to change my mind completely about the Generalissimo and the government."[50] When Madame Chiang explained that college graduates were helping in the reconstruction, working on salaries of $30.00 a month, Boring was inspired by this spirit of "sacrifice and patriotism, and service to the people." It seemed that Chiang was providing a nucleus to build on for the future, and that eventually he would "reduce chaos to order."[51]

The faculty members who supported Chiang at the time of the Japanese invasion, strongly expressed their opposition to the students' petition. The students felt betrayed, and a faculty-student confrontation was precipitated. When the students again voted to go to Nanjing, Chancellor Wu Lei Chuan (1870–1944) resigned because he had failed to dissuade the rash students. Wu's resignation was not what the students had hoped to accomplish and faculty-student negotiations resulted in a compromise. Both sides agreed to work toward a "Patriotic Week" observed by both faculty and students. Those students who felt it necessary could go to

Nanjing with their petition and the University would not forcibly prevent them from doing so. However, all students were encouraged to remain at Yenching and to participate in "Patriotic Week." When three-fourths of the students participated, Chancellor Wu withdrew his resignation. Even though "Patriotic Week" did not produce tangible results it was important in healing the student-faculty rift, and student-faculty solidarity strengthened the general morale of the University.

After "Patriotic Week," Stuart left for his fund raising trip to the United States—the trip that Boring so opposed. During his absence, Japan became bolder and invaded Shanghai. Both students and faculty members were horrified, but powerless, as they recalled the devastating losses in the Nineteenth Army. At long distance, Edwin Boring expressed his dismay at the events. "Lord, I get so angry about the Japanese these days. If I read the papers it throws me all off emotionally for the rest of the day." He, like the students, wanted to do something. "I want Hoover to start an economic Boycott or do something wild, all in my practical inexperience of these things."[52]

The academic year ended in June 1932, without additional incident. Although the fall term began without problems, in January 1933, Japan occupied Jehol, penetrated into Chahar and convinced the princes of Inner Mongolia to sever their alliance with Nanjing. Incensed by Chiang's lack of action, Yenching students organized a protest strike. The students finally agreed to return to classes, take the deferred examinations of the previous semester, and begin their new courses in the spring. The faculty for its part agreed to support the students in their patriotic activities.

It became more and more difficult for students to concentrate on academics as they observed a foreign power engulfing their country one piece at a time. Only very single-minded ones kept their attention fully focused on the dissection of the dogfish or on Chinese history during the Ming Dynasty. The Japanese incursions made them wonder whether they would ever have an opportunity to use their theoretical knowledge. Sociology student Zhang Shu Yi confessed that she and many of her fellow students were more involved with the underground than school work.[53]

While she was involved in the anti-Japanese underground activities, Ruth Hung (Beasley) "had the challenge" of Boring's classes. She quickly was disillusioned from her belief that she would have an easier time because of Boring's friendship with her parents, William and Rhoda Hung. In spite of Boring's "constant pushings and scolding," Ruth neglected her studies—particularly Dr. Wilson's chemistry class—and joined other students in underground activities.[54] When she thought about it, Boring knew that the political situation obsessed all patriotic young Chinese students. However, she could not understand why they were not equally preoccupied with their studies.

Although the political and military problems continued to mount, in the fall of 1934, when Boring composed her Christmas letter, the future seemed rosy. How could she seem less than optimistic when she viewed the massed chrysanthemums and strolled the Western Hills with their leaves turning to bronze, orange, and gold? How could she feel discouraged when she could take a weekend trip with the Peking Natural History Society to the caves where the "Peking Man," *Sinanthropus pekinensis,* was discovered? The specter of the relentless Japanese army gobbling up cities and towns and infiltrating educational institutions seemed far away at this time.

> Faculty morale remained high in spite of financial hardships. If ever democracy was practised, it is at Yenching. If ever there was a faculty where there are as many different opinions as there are individuals, it is at Yenching. And yet we seem to belong to an integrated whole.[55]

When she examined her own college, Boring found it healthy. It "is full to overflowing as it was last year." The large numbers made it possible to be selective about the quality of applicants for admission. Nobody who was "conditioned in Mathematics" was admitted and "the leaning towards Chemistry and Premedicine continues as last year."[56] In spite of her heavy advisement load (110 premedical advisees), Boring claimed that her work schedule of 1934 was "the pleasantest I have ever had."[57]

Yenching students were not nearly as complacent as Boring over the events of 1933 and 1934. Once again Chiang Kai Shek had acquiesced to Japanese demands and signed the Truce of Tangu, simply a recognition of Japan's accomplished feat in Inner Mongolia. The students once more were dismayed at the central government's impotence or disinterest. Although they were in the middle of their pre-examination reviews, they demanded the suspension of academic work to engage in patriotic activities. Initially, most of the faculty members, while sympathizing with the student frustration, wanted classes to continue. They agreed to be lenient in special cases when students had specific projects that they wanted to work on. This approach was too mild for the Yenching activists who, with students from other universities, planned a widespread protest. They met on the evening of December 8, 1935, to finalize their plans to stay away from classes the next day and proposed to play a prominent part in the scheduled protest demonstrations. Although most faculty members bowed to the inevitable, Boring considered the mounds of material she wanted to cover in her course, did not understand the depth of student commitment to the protest, and announced that her class would meet as usual. Although premedical student Wu Jie Ping and some of his class-mates stayed away, most students reluctantly appeared for class, remem-bering Boring's influence on PUMC admissions. As she, as usual, cast her eyes around the classroom before beginning her lecture, she saw Pro-fessor of Biology C.F. Wu standing in the doorway. Wu took her aside and convinced her that her attempt to hold class was a mistake. Once she absorbed the gravity of the situation, she dismissed class and her pre-medical students joined the others in the demonstration.[58] Boring's repu-tation as a student advocate was tarnished somewhat over this incident. The news that Miss Boring opposed the students' patriotism spread quickly from the biology department to the other areas of the university. Zhang Shu Yi of the sociology department recalled student displeasure with her stance. Although after Professor Wu described the realities of the situation, Boring recognized her own tunnel vision, it took time for the students to forgive.[59]

Boring viewed the entire situation as a misunderstanding. As she per-ceived the problem, faculty and students were at odds with each other over the continuation of class work, yet cooperated in patriotic activities. She would have found the very idea that the students would think her unpatriotic appalling! After all, she had been an advocate for their posi-tions, and those of the Chinese in general, many times in the past. She opposed the activities only because she thought her students and China itself would suffer in the long run if the students did not tend to their studies.

After Black Thursday, times of tranquility were sparse in China. The Yenching community developed its own social structure, struggled to maintain itself financially, and speculated about the future under Japan's shadow. Boring became more flexible when confronted with ideas that challenged her previously held ones. It clearly was not possible for her to insist that her students put their studies before their political activities.

II

As the country and the University suffered from the effects of the Depres-sion and Japanese incursions, Alice took her own advice and continued to work at teaching and research. Although Boring regretted any negative effect her move from genetics to taxonomy might have on her relationships with Morgan, Pearl, Conklin, and other former colleagues in experimental biology, she experienced no other remorse about her decision. Exploring organic diversity through the relatively unknown Chinese fauna proved intellectually challenging, socially gratifying, and logistically possible.

Boring encountered a taxonomy that differed from the early stages of naming and describing organisms. After Carolus Linnaeus (1707–1778) systematized the study by providing tools and rules for naming plants and animals, standard categories were established, and a universal system developed that transcended linguistic and nationalistic boundaries. To Linnaeus, the "higher" categories, those above the species, were devised for convenience and were not indicative of relationships. He considered the species, on the other hand, real and immutable, although he later recognized some difficulties with this view. As theories of evolution flourished, the old idea of fixed species began to be reconsidered. In this new phase, naming became less important than determining relationships. A preoccupation with phylogeny led taxonomists to focus on the relationship between the higher categories rather than between individual species. They searched for ancestral forms and "missing links" in order to support an evolutionary hypothesis. It was not long before those who searched for new phyla, order, families, or genera were disappointed. A common reaction to this dearth of new possibilities was to split the older categories. Although in some cases, the splitting was justified, in others it merely led to the disintegration of natural categories.[60]

In both of the early phases, the collectors emphasized the individual—the "type" specimen. The type species was defined as the single species upon which a genus was based. Collectors concentrated upon obtaining a single specimen, the holotype, considered "the type" by the original author of the species. A new vocabulary developed around this concept.[61] By the time Boring became involved in taxonomy, interest had again reverted to the study of local fauna, but with a different emphasis. The old typological concept, the idea of a fixed species, had been replaced by a dynamic concept in which the study of variation within populations and the slight variations between adjacent populations were seen to provide the key to understanding speciation. It no longer was significant merely to collect types and paratypes. Long series of specimens from each locality were needed, so that slight variations between individuals could be documented and analyzed quantitatively.

To collect these long series of specimens, museums and universities launched expeditions to many parts of the United States and to remote parts of the world. In zoology departments and museums all over the

United States, a spirit of expectation surfaced toward the end of the winter. Museum and university personnel rummaged through store-rooms littered with the debris of expeditions past. The old spirit stoves were cleaned, cooking gear with the remains of last year's beans were scraped and washed, tent stakes were counted and missing ones replaced with wire coat hangers, and sleeping bags and tents were hung out to air. Groups of potential collectors poured over range maps and superimposed little circles for different named species on outline maps of their proposed collecting area. Expendable supplies were collected: formalin to preserve the "herps;" cotton bats, wires, and arsenic for study skins of mammals and birds; traps to collect mammals; guns and ammunition to collect birds; individualized "snake sticks" bent to perfection from old auto-mobile antennae. When the collectors returned with their specimens, they analyzed their carefully kept field notebooks and catalogues, sent the skulls or skeletons of some of their prizes to a "bug" room tenanted by dermestid beetles with a taste for decaying flesh, and carefully labeled their study skins or bottled reptiles and amphibians.

Once the specimens were prepared, the taxonomists were ready to analyze the long series presented by the collectors. Specimens were arranged according to locality, and standard measurements were taken with dial calipers. Measurements were compiled, suggesting the range of individual variation within a specific geographic locality and making comparisons with other localities possible. By comparing long series from contiguous collecting sites, taxonomists could determine whether vari-ants belonged to different species or were only subspecifically different.[62]

Taxonomists of the late nineteenth and early twentieth century postu-lated that the differences between the subspecies and species represented a compounding of numerous small variations. They also concluded that much local and geographic variation was closely correlated with the envir-onment. This explanation led to a conflict with the geneticists in the early part of the twentieth century.

In 1900, Gregor Mendel's (1822–1884) long ignored classic paper (1866) on the results of crossing garden peas was independently discov-ered by several individuals. The rediscovery of Mendel's paper and the increased understanding of cell processes sparked an interest in heredity that minimized the role of the environment. Because of the nature of some of the genetic material chosen, the early conclusions of the geneti-cists differed drastically from those of the students of natural populations. Consequently, during the first twenty-five years of the twentieth century, conflict occurred between the naturalist taxonomist and the experimental biologist.

Although by the time Boring changed her research interests from genetics to taxonomy the problem generally had been resolved, many of the experimentalists remained hostile to the taxonomists. Thomas Hunt Morgan's selection of the fruit fly, *Drosophila melanogaster,* as a suitable subject for genetic research and the demonstration that even a very small selective advantage of a new allele or allelic combination would eventually result in a genetic transformation of populations helped bring the two groups together. Three animal geneticists who were originally trained as taxonomists, Richard Goldschmidt, Francis Bertody Sumner, and Theodosius Dobzhansky, introduced the population concept of the taxonomists into genetics. This change convinced the many taxonomists to interpret the slight observed variations as small mutations.[63]

The new taxonomic outlook, combined with imperialistic political and economic phenomena, provided opportunities for reconnaissance missions to parts of the world not well-known to western science. The reasons for taxonomy's popularity were not all scientific. Classification demanded exploration and collection. Museum expeditions to remote areas of the globe offered opportunities, under the guise of scientific legitimacy, to demonstrate the dominance of man—western man—over the dwindling natural environment. The same motivation inspired the cultural imperialism of the western cultures.[64]

To early twentieth-century taxonomists, Asia was uncharted ground. In the first two decades of the century, explorers garnered financial support, braved physical hardships and political turmoil, to proudly present new specimens to their museums.[65] Roy Chapman Andrews (1884–1960) of the American Museum of Natural History led two of these early expeditions. Although satisfied with his earlier limited accomplishments, he developed a more ambitious program for a third expedition. By bringing together biologists from many different areas and correlating their expertise, he hoped to solve some puzzling problems, particularly those bearing on human evolution.

This third expedition was the best equipped, in terms of supplies, conveyances, and personnel, of any ever sent out by a museum. Dodge Brothers motor cars fed by gasoline carried in leaking cans by camels and medicated by spare parts of all conceivable varieties were used to explore the Gobi desert for the first time. The discovery of dinosaur eggs, traces of Paleolithic and Eolithic humans, and mammalian fossils contemporaneous with dinosaurs all provided data to extend knowledge boundaries.[66] Some of these discoveries resulted from good fortune, others from the "well-prepared mind." On a scorching hot July 15 in 1923, a member of the expedition, George Olsen, reported that he had found some fossil eggs. The prospect strained the credulity of the members of the party, since Olsen was working on a Cretaceous deposit which was too early for large birds. Dismissing the find as nothing but a sandstone concretion or other geological phenomenon, they were astonished when they found three partly broken, elongated objects, eight inches long by seven inches in circumference. They all agreed that the reddish-brown, rugose objects were indeed eggs. Previously, it had only been assumed that dinosaurs laid eggs, but after viewing the discovery they were convinced that they indeed had discovered dinosaur eggs. The blown sand that gently buried the eggs protected them. Fragile skeletons of embryonic dinosaurs peaked out of cracked eggs, and skulls of baby dinosaurs which had met their fate shortly after hatching were found nearby.[67]

Although the major thrust of the Third Asiatic Expedition, 1920–1930, was an expedition to Mongolia, it also included a survey of Chinese fish, amphibians, and reptiles. In 1921, Clifford H. Pope, an American Museum of Natural History herpetologist, arrived, at first unable to speak Chinese. Since Mongolian winters with temperatures dropping to forty or fifty degrees below zero effectively stopped the numbers of reptiles and amphibians available for study in this area, Pope remained in China to make a herpetological and ichthyological survey of many of its provinces. His work resulted in the largest collections of fish, reptiles, and amphibians ever made in China.[68]

Boring helped Pope as he worked on his survey. Recognizing that cooperation was the basis of success in taxonomic work, she provided him with specimens and data. He, in turn, loaned her specimens from the collections of the American Museum. Such an exchange insured that each could examine types, topotypes, and paratypes and contribute significantly to understanding the geographic distribution of species and subspecies in China.[69]

China yielded an abundance of reptiles and amphibians. For example, there was the rare skink, *Eumeces pekinensis*, that nested in colonies on open hillsides and laid its eggs under a stone where the female stood sentinel and whose life cycle begged to be investigated. However, an animal did not have to be rare to be important to the taxonomists. The most common forms, *Rana nigromaculata,* found throughout China, the grass frog, *Rana amurensis*, and the common toad of northeastern Asia, *Bufo bufo asiaticus,* were as important to taxonomists as the rarer varieties, for their specific and subspecific status were unclear, necessitating procuring long series to study problems of relationship and distribution. Snakes, including the small pit-viper, and numerous water snakes populated most parts of China. The docile red-banded black snake, *Dinodon rufozona-*

tum, was semi-aquatic, and Pope described capturing a specimen by tying a frog to a long string and waiting patiently for the snake to return. The snake's greed caused it to vanish into the collector's bag. Long after Pope left China, Boring continued to work on many of these fascinating creatures. She was most intrigued by the amphibians. A wealth of frogs, toads, and salamanders were available for the observing.

During the early twentieth century, many foreign taxonomists established their reputations by collecting and classifying previously unidentified specimens. This trend encouraged young Chinese students to choose this route. Although modern taxonomy appeared as a western innovation, traditional Chinese naturalists practiced collecting and naming plants and animals. Confucius himself provided a mandate to his disciples to learn the names of herbs, trees, birds, and animals. Herbals and *materia medica* emphasizing the practical and aesthetic use of plants, had been produced sporadically for many years. In China, the practical emphasis not only was apparent in the herbals but in other descriptive works on the culture of fishes, raising of birds, growing of oranges and tea, and identification of mosses and mushrooms.[70]

Perhaps because of their familiarity with traditional descriptive biology, modern Chinese students were comfortable with this field. Boring's colleague, internationally known entomologist C.F. Wu, exemplified the excellence of Chinese scholars in taxonomic areas. Boring, concentrating on vertebrates, and Wu, invertebrates, had no difficulty in convincing the brightest students to study their native fauna. After being introduced to the Linnaean system of classification, the International Rules of Nomenclature, concepts of type specimens, definitions of species and subspecies, and improved techniques of systematic collecting, Chinese students were prepared to join their teachers in studying and interpreting the complexity of their land.[71]

Finding funds for taxonomic research required ingenuity and persistence. The obvious source, the Rockefeller Foundation, funded only research connected with medicine or science teaching, and consistently refused to support research unconnected with either of these fields. Although Rockefeller adviser Gee was unsuccessful in his attempt to induce the Foundation to support taxonomic research, he was able to manipulate the system in an indirect way by providing money to biology teachers who did research in taxonomy, "without regard to these biologists' research interests."[72] A second foundation, The China Foundation for the Promotion of Education and Culture, funded by Boxer Indemnity monies returned by the United States government, did provide for direct funding for research and supported institutions studying the flora and fauna of China.

Taxonomists working in the Beijing area needed outlets for discussion and publication. An important association, the Peking Natural History Society, was formed in the fall of 1925 with Boring as one of the thirty-eight charter members. The new organization reflected the burgeoning interest in collecting, collating, and classifying that flourished during the heyday of the Third Asiatic Expedition. The organizers planned to foster the systematic study of China's flora and fauna by cooperating with existing scientific organizations. Specific groups such as the Fan Memorial Institute, the Chinese Geological Survey, the Rockefeller Foundation, and the Third Asiatic Expedition, all contributed members.[73] By the end of the first year the society's membership had grown to 109, largely through the efforts of secretary-treasurer Gist Gee who corresponded with interested people around China and the world.

Publication outlets for the Society's members were vital, but funding was difficult to attain. Gist Gee, who was especially interested in the project, asked Roger Greene to "bring this matter to the attention of someone who will be interested in seeing us start into the program. . . ." Scientists in China had no trouble in publishing short articles. *The China Journal of Arts and Sciences* and the *Lingnan Science Journal* were favored outlets. However, longer articles were difficult to place. Gee was convinced that if they could make a beginning by enticing wealthy individuals or organizations to support the project, "the China Foundation would look upon the matter with favor and probably see the program put through for a period of years."[74]

In spite of the funding difficulties, the Society's Council voted to produce two types of publications: technical bulletins on fauna and flora and educational booklets of a more popular nature. From these two ideas came the regular quarterly bulletin and the numerous handbooks published by the Society.

Boring took advantage of both the *Bulletin* and the handbook series to publish the results of her research. Between 1929 and 1950, she published twenty-one papers in the *Bulletin* and one handbook (1932). Although the Society's publications provided an important outlet for her research, the networking activities that it encouraged were even more important. Without contacts with other collectors, museums, and biologists, taxonomic research would have been impossible. Boring's taxonomic problems required examining every available specimen from every possible source. When she and her student C.C. Liu began to study *Kaloula*, an Indomalaysian genus of frogs, they found very confused records. Because of the cooperation of students in Nanjing and Taiku, Shanxi, records of biologists Leonhard Stejneger, Clifford Pope, Karl Schmidt and others, they were able to reinterpret Pope's assessment that records of *Kaloula* from central China represented a different species from *Kaloula* of northern China. By comparing specimens from the Yenching campus, from Taiku in Shanxi, from Nanjing, and by comparing these records with descriptions of materials from other authors, they concluded that all of the forms represented a single species. Networking made this new interpretation possible.

Boring and Liu, however, made a mistake when working with *Kaloula* that underscored to them the importance of observing specimens from throughout a species' range—possible only through networking. Liu turned over a stone outside of Mukden and found a male frog much larger and stouter than the typical *Kaloula*. Its voice was distinctive—a deep, loud croak, "somewhat like the starting of a locomotive, the separate croaks gradually speeding up with shorter intervals." After their kin was captured, the elusive frogs tantalized their stalker by croaking until he got within twenty feet of them and then becoming silent. Without the croak for guidance, he was unable to capture other specimens.[75] Boring had long preached the danger of naming a new species from a single specimen, but this time she ignored her own good advice and designated this individual a new species. After more specimens were located, they recognized that the vocal *Kaloula* was not a new species, but only after naming it *Kaloula manchuriensis*. Later Boring synonymized it with the common form, *K. borealis*.[76]

The species problem that intrigued biologists could be approached through a study of internal comparative anatomy as well as through a comparison of external variations. Boring and Li Hui Lin, a Yenching student who wrote his thesis under Professor J.C. Liu, became interested in the specific status of the Chinese amphioxus. This project also involved cooperation with collectors and institutions. Boring and Liu observed specimens ordered from Woods Hole, Massachusetts, of the European amphioxus, *Branchiostoma lanceolatum*, and the American, *Branchiostoma caribeum* and compared these forms to the Chinese form. Muscular characteristics (myotome number) as well as behavioral characteristics and external anatomical features provided the basis for the study. Although they were hampered by scarcity of material and inadequate reports in the literature, they tentatively concluded that the Chinese form represented a different species.[77]

Boring and her student Tso Kan Chang studied variation among Chinese Amphibia and were again reminded of the importance of institutional cooperation. They needed more specimens than they were able to collect themselves. To add to the number of specimens, they mounted expensive mini-expeditions to southern Jiangxi, Zhejiang, and Anhui provinces,[78] funded by the Rockefeller Foundation and the China Foundation at different times.[79] However, to complete their work, they exchanged material from many different sources, including "twenty-five Hongkong *Triturus sinensis* from Dr. Herklots and twenty-six Futsing and Chungan *Pachytriton* from Mr. Pope of the American Museum of Natural History and from Dr. T.H. Cheng of Fukien Christian University...."[80]

Compared to that of a botanist, a herpetologist's life was difficult. Exchanging herpetological specimens preserved in moist-cloth wrapped bags or breakable bottles was much more cumbersome than exchanging herbarium sheets, yet Boring and Chang managed to do so, as did other herpetologists. They supplied other institutions with specimens from their new collecting localities in return for other amphibians.

T.K. Chang's collecting trips in Zhejiang in 1930, 1931, and 1932; Anhui in 1933; and Jiangxi and South Zhejiang in 1935 produced new data. Boring and Chang's interpretation of these materials expanded the knowledge of amphibian distribution in these provinces. By compiling an annotated list of species, a table of species distribution, and distribution maps, the authors extended the data base, suggesting a need to reinterpret and reevaluate some of the earlier works.[81]

Although institutional cooperation was important in all of Boring's taxonomic works, it represented the essence of one paper published in the *Peking Natural History Bulletin*. Her "Survey of the Amphibia of North China" was based on the collection in the Musée Hoangho-Paiho of the Mission de Sanxian in Tianjin. Because the specimens were taken from critical localities, the collection proved important to unraveling specific relationships. Father Émile Licent, S.J., who made seventy-two collecting trips within a twenty-two-year period in the region between Siberia and the Yangtse Valley, deposited his specimens in the museum and invited Boring to study them.[82] By his invitation to Boring to study these specimens, Father Licent reflected his confidence in her knowledge of Chinese amphibia. Her research on these amphibians allowed her to gain a better understanding of the relationship between Chinese and European forms and the eastern distribution limits of Himalayan species. The result, an annotated list of species, a table of specimens collected from different localities, a range map, and a collection of references on North China Amphibia, represented an extension of knowledge of North China's amphibians. Boring's genetics background surfaced as she struck down species based on individual specimens or small groups of specimens, including her own *Kaloula manchuriensis*, in favor of acknowledging a wide range of variation within a single species.[83]

Her publications demonstrate that the bulk of Boring's research involved herpetological taxonomy, distribution, and faunal studies. However, her general curiosity led her in some surprising directions. When an oddity appeared, she became interested and encouraged her students to help in the interpretation. One such occurrence involved hermaphrodism in goats. When "two young abnormal goats were sent to the laboratory as having abnormal reproductive organs," she included her student, Y. Kao, in an anatomical and histological study which they published jointly.[84] Her inclusion of Kao illustrates Boring's willingness to allow her students to participate in her research.

Boring never was proprietory about her research and delighted in giving credit to deserving students. Research, to her, was a teaching tool, not an end in itself. Her comments to Lydia about the relative merits of teaching and research were reflected in her approach to both of these areas.

Beijing had an important visitor in 1925, Boring's old teacher and friend Edwin Grant Conklin. The Peking Natural History Society through Gee as secretary, invited Conklin to deliver a lecture in the PUMC auditorium. It was to stress science education, and included an outline of the purposes of the Marine Biological Laboratory at Woods Hole in order to inspire a similar enterprise in China. In addition to his lecture on the aims of biological training, he also spread his idea that the promotion of general biology would aid the development of human biology, *i.e.*, eugenics. It seems likely that Boring would have visited with him on this trip, but she did not record it. Notable for their omission from Boring's letters are references to two of her former teachers' interest in positive eugenics. Both Pearl and Conklin (as well as many other U.S. scientists) were interested in "improvement" of the races. In 1930, Conklin published a paper entitled "The Purposive Improvement of the Human Race" in *Human Biology and Racial Welfare*. Not until Hitler made such outrageous use of eugenics in the late 1930s did U.S. scientists back down. Given this climate of "improvement" and the fact that her former teachers were heavily involved in these ideas, there are no records of Boring's involvement in the eugenics movement.

Notes

1. Howard S. Galt, *History of Yenching University*, (Unpublished ms.) pp. 185–86.

2. A.M. Boring to Raymond Pearl, 19 Aug. 1929, American Philosophical Society Library.

3. A.M. Boring to G.K. Noble, 26 Feb. 1929, Archives, American Museum of Natural History, Dept. of Herpetology.

4. Ibid.

5. Noble to Boring, 2 May 1929, Archives, American Museum of Natural History, Dept. of Herpetology.

6. Boring to Clifford H. Pope, 10 Feb. 1929, Archives, American Museum of Natural History, Dept. of Herpetology.

7. Ibid.

8. Pope to Boring, 12 July 1929, Archives, American Museum of Natural History, Dept. of Herpetology.

9. Ibid.

10. A.M. Boring to E.G. Boring, 1 June 1929, Pusey Archive Collection, Harvard University, Boring Family Collection.

11. Assistant to President to Boring, 4 Oct. 1928, Special Collection Archives, Yale Divinity School.

12. E.G. Boring to A.M. Boring, 25 April 1929, Pusey Archive Collection, Harvard University, Boring Family Collection.

13. Porter was the first Dean of Men at Yenching and Professor of Philosophy. He was widely known as the campus "trouble shooter."

14. Possibly John Wannamaker.

15. A.M. Boring to E.G. Boring, 1 June 1929, Pusey Archive Collection, Harvard University, Boring Family Collection.

16. They included an income bond, Alice's will ("please send me my will as I forgot what I said"), a fire insurance policy ("has lapsed and should be destroyed"), a list of securities ("should be revised and revision given thee"), ground rent deeds, and "Peterson's notes." Always generous, Alice had loaned "Pete" money for his medical education. She refused to collect interest and "told him not to bother about trying to pay back the principal now while he is struggling to get a practice started and raise a family...." Instead, he was "to pay it back to me later when he is prosperous and I am an old lady no longer earning a salary."

17. Ibid.

18. Boring to Louise, 14 Oct. 1928, Special Collection Archives, Yale University.

19. A.M. Boring to Pearl, 19 Aug. 1929, American Philosophical Society Library.

20. Ibid.

21. Pearl to Boring, 27 Sept. 1929, American Philosophical Society Library.

22. Boring to Noble, 8 Oct. 1929, Archives, American Museum of Natural History, Dept. of Herpetology.

23. Noble to Boring, 12 Nov. 1929, Archives, American Museum of Natural History, Dept. of Herpetology.

24. Howard S. Galt, *History of Yenching University*, pp. 187–88. Galt noted that the following institutions sent prominent scholars and official representatives: "The National Ministry of Education. The Hopei Provincial Government. The Provincial Bureau of Education. The Peiping City Government. The Legations of Great Britain, America, France, Sweden, Norway, and Denmark. The China Foundation for Education and Culture. The Rockefeller Foundation. The Peking Union Medical College. The National Peking University. The National Normal University. The National University of Peiping. The National Tsing Hua University. The National Northeastern University. The National Hsi An University. Hankai University. Peiyang University. Cheelee University. The Central College, Wuchang. The West China Union University. The University of Nanking. Ginling College. Soochow University. St. John's University. Also from many missions, Christian middle schools, and other institutions." The following American universities sent representatives: "Columbia University. Princeton University. Auburn Theological Seminary. University of Chicago. Ohio State University. Wellesley College. The Presbyterian and the Methodist Episcopal Mission Boards."

25. Ibid., pp. 187–89.

26. G.K. Noble to Boring, 12 Nov. 1929, Archives American Museum of Natural History, Dept. of Herpetology.

27. Kraig Adler and E.R. Mi Zhao *Herpetology of China, Society for the Study of Amphibians and Reptiles*, 1993, p. 522.

28. Galt, *History of Yenching University*, p. 190.

29. Ibid, p. 217.

30. Report of the Registrar of the University, July 1928–July 1931, Rockefeller Foundation Archives, RG 1, Series 601, Box 41, Folder 342. In addition to the College of Natural Sciences, there was a College of Arts and Letters and a College of Public Affairs. As Dean, Boring worked under a new percentage grade correspondence established in October 1929. The University as a whole, Graduate Division, and the College of Natural Science all showed increases in the numbers of women enrolled. The ratio between men and women in 1928 was 3.29:1.00; 1929, 2.98:1; 1930, 2.53:1.00. In the graduate division, nine women were enrolled in 1928, eight in 1929, and ten in 1930. In the College of Natural Science, fifty-two women were enrolled in 1929 and seventy-one in 1930. Of the new freshmen enrolled in the College of Natural Science, sixteen were women in 1929 and thirty-two in 1930.

31. A.M. Boring to Franklin Warner, Chairman of the Board of Trustees, Yenching University, 17 Nov. 1930, Special Collection Archives, Yale Divinity School.

32. One of four boys of missionary parents, Stuart, born in Hangchow, China, did not even visit the United States until 1887 when he was eleven years old and his parents were on furlough. After this furlough, his parents returned

to China, leaving Leighton with his mother's relatives in Mobile, Alabama, to attend school. When Stuart was sixteen years old, he attended Pantops Academy in Charlottesville, Virginia. The following year, he entered Hampden-Sidney College as a sophomore. After graduating in 1896, he returned to Pantops to teach Greek and Latin for three years. In 1899 he entered Richmond's Union Theological Seminary and acquired a reputation as a scholar. Not surprisingly, given his background, he decided to enter the Presbyterian mission field as a teacher. On a mission fund-raising tour in the southern United States, he met Aline Rodd whom he married in New Orleans on November 17, 1904. In December of that year, Leighton and his bride left by steamboat for China. The couple joined his parents in Hangchow where he began his missionary work while attempting to master some of the elusive complexities of the Chinese language.

After three and one-half years in Hangchow, Stuart joined the faculty of the Nanking Theological Seminary. At the seminary, he gained administrative experience as head of the New Testament Department. He continued his scholarly work and published two works: *Essentials of New Testament Greek* (1916) and *The Greek-Chinese-English Dictionary of the New Testament* (1918). His reputation as a publishing scholar, an able administrator, and a successful fund-raiser led to his appointment as president of the embryonic Yenching.

33. Grace M. Boynton to Nehemiah Boynton, 30 May 1926 (Yenchiao Diary, Appendix).

34. Janet Smith Rhodes to Marilyn Bailey Ogilvie, 23 July 1987. Bing Xin to Ogilvie, Beijing, PRC, 20 July 1988.

35. Edwin G. Boring to Alice M. Boring, 28 Sept. 1934, Pusey Archive Collection, Harvard University, Boring Family Correspondence.

36. Margaret Bailey Speer, interview by Caroline Rittenhouse, 22 Sept. 1982, 7 June 1983. The Vassar biologist who participated in the "Friday Lunch" was "Fredericka Giang, who just died last spring. She married a biologist [Dr. Li Ty Chi], and they were members of the department." Bing Xin was one of the young Chinese women.

37. Ibid.

38. Harold Shadick to Cliff Choquette. 14 April 1989.

39. Stuart to Members of the Faculty, 4 March 1931, Yale University Archives, Stuart Papers, R.G. 11, Folder 5488. The Depression in the United States not only made it more difficult to raise endowment funds, but the monies raised produced less income. Since the securities in which endowment funds were invested declined in value, the rate of income was reduced correspondingly. The situation was not as serious during the early years of the Depression as it was during the later, because the exchange rate for the proceeds from the sale of American currency in China compensated somewhat for the reduced income; Howard S. Galt, *History of Yenching University*, p. 221.

40. A.M. Boring to Nathaniel Gist Gee and Stuart, 3 Dec. 1932, Special Collection Archives, Yale Divinity School.

41. A.M. Boring to Gee, 21 Feb. 1932, Special Collection Archives, Yale Divinity School.

42. Stuart to B.A. Garside, 24 Aug. 1932, Yale University Archives, Stuart Papers. The Foundation reconsidered its former actions, and decided to provide a single sum of $250,000 contingent upon matching funds and allowed the Trustees five years to collect it. Stuart's diligence and diplomacy were important factors in allowing the condition to be met by June 1934, thus providing an additional half million dollars for the endowment fund, the income of which was to be used for the support of the College of Natural Science. Galt, *History of Yenching*.

   "Borrowing from Peter to pay Paul" was one of the major techniques used to complete the match. In the minutes of the Trustees of September 26, 1932, it was reported that "in order to complete the Endowment Funds for Natural Science it has been necessary for the University to pour into that fund all gifts of every kind not definitely allocated elsewhere...." Minutes to Stuart and Galt, 26 Sept., 1932, Yale University Archives, Stuart Papers, 11/5499.

43. Ibid.

44. Harold Shadick to Cliff Choquette. 14 April 1989.

45. Ibid.

46. A.M. Boring to Franklin Warner, 17 Nov. 1930, Special Collection Archives, Yale Divinity School.

47. Galt, *History of Yenching University*, p. 196.

48. Ibid., pp. 197–99.

49. Ibid.

50. Ibid.

51. Ibid.

52. E.G. Boring to A.M. Boring, 2 Feb. 1932, Pusey Archive Collection, Harvard University, Boring Family Correspondence.

53. Zhang Shu Yi to Ogilvie, Beijing, 13 July 1988.

54. Ruth Hung Beasley to Clifford Choquette, 16 January 1988.

55. A.M. Boring to Friends, "A Christmas Letter," 15 Nov. 1934.

56. Ibid.

57. Ibid. From her description of her course load, "General Biology, Vertebrate Comparative Anatomy, and Histology;" her advising responsibilities, "direct problems on Anatomy and Amphibian Natural History for several seniors and graduate students; her research, "with Variation in Toads and Frogs, ..." her characterization of herself as "cultivating an attitude of leisure almost to the point of laziness," seems unjustified.

58. Wu Jie Ping to Ogilvie, Beijing, 13 July 1988.

59. Ibid.

60. Ernst Mayr, E. Gordon Linsley, and Robert L. Usinger, *Methods and Principles of Systematic Zoology* (New York: McGraw-Hill, 1953), pp. 8–9.

61. Paratypes were specimens supplementary to the holotype used by the original author; a topotype was a specimen from the type locality of a species; a neotype was a specimen selected to replace the holotype when the type specimen was lost or destroyed. Edward Theodore Schenk and John H. McMasters, *Procedure in Taxonomy, Including a Reprint of the International Rules of Zoological Nomenclature with Summaries of Opinions Rendered to the Present Date* (Stanford, CA: Stanford University Press, 1936), p. 7.

62. Whereas adjacent subspecies can interbreed, or potentially can do so if separated by geographic barriers, species are reproductively isolated from other populations. Natural populations, almost indistinguishable structurally, represent different species if they do not interbreed. On the other hand, two very differently appearing animals may only be subspecifically different because gradations occur along the range where interbreeding occurs.

63. Mayr, Linsley, and Usinger, *Methods and Principles of Systematic Zoology*, p. 12.

64. Donna Harraway, "Teddy Bear Patriarchy: Taxidermy in the Garden of Eden, New York City, 1908–1936," *Social Text* 5 (1984): 21–64.

65. Sven Hedin, Roy Chapman Andrews (3 Asiatic Expeditions), and numerous expeditions sponsored by the Smithsonian Institution added to the taxonomic knowledge of China.

66. *China Yearbook*, "The Third Asiatic Expedition," (1923, p. 431). A controversy arose in 1928 about the storage of Andrew's paleontological specimens in a "neutral" place for inspection. It was agreed that the cases could be stored in PUMC's Lockhart Hall. Roger Greene, Diary, 4 October 1928, Rockefeller Archive Center, Diary, 1927–1929.

67. Roy Chapman Andrews, *The New Conquest of Central Asia: A Narrative of the Explorations of the Central Asiatic Expeditions in Mongolia and China, 1921–1930.* (New York: The American Museum of Natural History), pp. 208–210.

68. Andrews, *The New Conquest of Central Asia; A Narrative of the Explorations of the Central Asiatic Expeditions in Mongolia and China, 1921–1930*; Clifford Hillhouse Pope, *The Reptiles of China: Turtles, Crocodilians, Snakes, Lizards* (New York: The American Museum of Natural History, 1935), Vol. 10.

69. Clifford Hillhouse Pope, *The Reptiles of China: Turtles, Crocodilians, Snakes, Lizards.* (New York: The American Museum of Natural History, 1935), pp. vi, 507.

70. C. Ping and H.H. Hu, "Biological Science," in *Symposium on Chinese Culture*, ed. Sophia H. Chen Zen (New York: Paragon Book Reprint Corp., 1969), pp. 194–95.

71. Chenfu F. Wu, a student of Gee, produced numerous publications, including a major monograph of Chinese insects. He was head of the biology department at Yenching and was offered, but refused, the dean-

ship of the College of Arts and Sciences. N. Gist Gee to Max Mason, 26 July 1929, Rockefeller Archive Center, RG 1, Series 601, Box 40, Folder 333.

72. William J. Haas, "Botany in Republican China: the Leading Role of Taxonomy," pp. 14–15; 22–23. An example of the Rockefeller Foundation's indirect support for taxonomic research can be seen in grants received by C.F. Wu toward preparing a monograph of Chinese insects. N. Gist Gee to W.S. Carter, 21 Sept. 1931, Rockefeller Archive Center. Boring also received help in connection with her studies of Chinese Amphibia. Gee to H.A. Spoehr, 27 March 1931, Rockefeller Archive Center, RG1, Series 601, Box 41, Folder 336.

73. The Peking Natural History Society was founded in the fall of 1925. The idea of such a society originated with Dr. Grabau of the Geological Society, Mr. Sohtsu King and Mr. N. Gist Gee. Dr. Grabau as the convener of the first meeting noted that "Its avowed object is the systematic study of the fauna and flora of China. . . . It is not the intention that this society shall in any way replace or duplicate the work done and planned by other scientific organizations of China. It is to provide an opportunity for the members of other organizations to meet together on common ground, to co-operate with them where it can, and to spread an interest in, and a love for, the work as widely as it may, not only in Peking, but throughout the length and breadth of China." Dr. Roy Chapman Andrews and Dr. Walter Granger of the Third Asiatic Expedition were among those who attended the first meeting. Alice M. Boring, "Early Days of the Peking Natural History Society," pp. 77–79.

74. Gee to Greene, 10 Dec. 1926, Rockefeller Archive Center, 1855 CMB Sl II B81. Gee did not obtain the support he had been seeking. On August 13, 1929, he wrote that "we have no journal which is properly financed out here for the publication of scientific papers." The *Bulletin* of the Peking Natural History Society remained dependent on membership fees, and it was virtually impossible to publish scientific papers with expensive plates. Gee to Mason, 13 August 1929, Rockefeller Archive Center, RG1, Series 601, Box 40, Folder 333.

75. A.M. Boring and C.C. Liu, "A New Species of Kaloula with a Discussion of the Genus in China," *Peking Natural History Bulletin*, 6 (1931–1932), pp. 19–24 (21–22).

76. A.M. Boring, "A Survey of the Amphibia of North China Based on the Collection by E. Licent S.J. in the Musee Hoangho-Paiho," *Peking Natural History Bulletin*, 10 (1935–1936), pp. 327–352 (345).

77. A.M. Boring and Hui-Lin Li, "Is the Chinese Amphioxus a Separate Species?" *Peking Natural History Bulletin* 6 (1931–32), pp. 9–18.

78. The transliteration common in Boring's time was Kiangsi, Chekiang, and Anhui.

79. The grants provided for four summers of collecting.

80. Tso-Kan Chang and A.M. Boring, "Studies in Variation among the Chinese Amphibia, *Peking Natural History Bulletin*, 9 (1934–1935), pp. 327–361 (327).

81. Chang and A.M. Boring, "A Survey of the Amphibia of Southeast China: An Analysis of the Basis of Species Distribution," *Peking Natural History Bulletin*, 10 (1935–1936), pp. 253–274 (273).

82. Pierre Teilhard de Chardin, S.J., spent twenty-five years in China and the Far East after arriving in 1923 to work in Pere Licent's research centers.

83. A.M. Boring, "A Survey of the Amphibia of North China." Two specimens of *Kaloula borealis*, borrowed from the American Museum, in exchange for specimens she had given to the museum, helped her in interpreting the material.

84. A.M. Boring and Y. Kao, "Two Hermaphrodite Goats," *Peking Natural History Bulletin* 11 (1936–1937), pp. 115–17.

Figure 1.   The Boring Family, 1907.
Courtesy of Katherine Hsu, M.D.

Figure 2.   Nettie Maria
Stevens, 1904.
Courtesy of the Carnegie
Institute of Washington

Figure 3.   Friends' Central School.
Courtesy of the Friends' Central School

Figure 4.   Bryn Mawr College, 1899.
Courtesy of Bryn Mawr College archives

Figure 5. Dr Stuart, late 1930s.
Courtesy of Dora Fugh Lee

Figure 6. Incarceration at Peiping (Beijing), 1941.
Courtesy of Dora Fugh Lee

Figure 7.   Dr Stuart, 1946.
Courtesy of Dora Fugh Lee

Figure 8.   Chou En Lai and Dr Stuart, Nankir, 1946.
Courtesy of Dora Fugh Lee

Figure 9. *Vibrissaphora boringii,* Sichuan Province, China.
Courtesy of Kraig Adler

Figure 10.   Pre-med students, Yenching University,
taken in front of Alice Boring's residence, Peking, 1932/3.
Courtesy of Katherine Hsu, M.D.

Figure 11.   Alice Boring and godson Li Shu Xin.
Courtesy of Katherine Hsu, M.D.

Figure 12.   Commencement at Yenching University, June 1939.
Courtesy of Edward Rondthaler III

Figure 13.   Peking University Medical College.
Photograph by Marilyn Bailey Ogilvie

Figure 14.   Lydia, Katharine
and Alice Boring, c. October
1950.
Courtesy of Edward Rondthaler III

Figure 15. Professor Lin Chang Shan, one of Boring's students, at the gate to Yenching University.
Photograph by Marilyn Bailey Ogilvie

Figure 16. Three former students in President Stuart's house at Yenching University. L to r, Jiang Lijin, Sun You Yun, Ye Dao Chun.
Photograph by Marilyn Bailey Ogilvie

Chapter 5
Teaching and Advising

Amphibian distribution, hermaphroditic goats, and calling frogs may have fascinated Boring, but she appreciated the enhancement of her own reputation or the addition of new data through research only when they served to make her a better teacher. Teaching always was her primary priority. Universally known as a hard task master, she was both knowledgable and conscientious. Successful survivors in Alice Boring's biology classes demonstrated understanding of biological principles, mastery of laboratory techniques, and command of communication skills. Sensitivity to their teacher's moods and values was also important to success. Caring and tolerant to a fault with her favorites, she could appear vindictive and short with those she considered lazy and unmotivated.

Many years after their last encounter with Boring, students retained clear recollections of both her teaching style and personality. Students meeting Boring for the first time considered her strict, demanding, and humorless. Only later did they realize that she behaved toward her favored students as if they were her children.[1] They were surprised when they recognized the softness beneath her crusty exterior. When eminent Beijing physician Wu Jie Ping was a freshman at Yenching in September 1933, he was warned that Boring's classes were impossibly difficult. To avoid any kind of confrontation, he conscientiously and unobtrusively worked on his lessons. However, misunderstanding an assignment, he and a friend brought themselves to Boring's attention by submitting a joint effort on what was to be an individual project on the dissection of the dogfish. Fearing reprisals, they were enormously relieved when she accepted their explanation that they had not intended to cheat.[2]

Favored students could always count on Boring's support. Tang Xi Xue, who admitted to being a Boring favorite, graded tests for her. She (Tan) found that another student favorite had completely missed a question. Boring looked at the "0" Tang had given the student, concluded that he had misunderstood the question, and gave him full credit.[3] When Laurence T. Wu was a sophomore at Yenching in 1935, he made an unimpressive score on his first comparative anatomy examination. Boring called him into her office, chastised him for his weak performance, and suggested ways that he might improve. He followed the advice of successful upper class students who explained how to write a successful Boring test[4] and produced a perfect second quiz. Boring again called him into her office, this time to congratulate him on his improvement. Wu quoted "an old Chinese saying" to pronounce his highest tribute to her as mentor and educator: "I thank her. My sons thank her."[5]

Boring could be especially understanding when a bright student had academic problems because of inadequate preparation. Since the early decision to make English the medium of instruction at PUMC, those students who had not had an early grounding in the language were at a disadvantage. Yenching students who had attended mission schools had a decided edge, for these schools provided excellent training from English-speaking teachers. Jin Ying Chang was almost devastated by his inadequate background in the language. After he received two "Fs" on two successive weekly quizzes in general biology, Boring requested a conference. Pleasantly surprised to find her kind and understanding, he, nevertheless, declined her offers of help, fearing it "might give her a bad impression." Jin worked especially hard, got full credit on the next quiz, and from that point on did very well, earning coveted "Es" from Boring.[6]

Hard working but academically less gifted students could expect the benefit of the doubt from Boring. She would not recommend the academically unqualified to PUMC, but would help them with alternative plans. Carefully monitoring student progress, she sent warning letters to those falling below the acceptable level. If a "worthy" student was faced with a letter from "Alice Boring, Premedical Advisor," with advice to "begin to plan either to drop medicine and take up some other subject or else enter some other medical school," Boring would provide recommendations to less demanding medical schools. If, on the other hand, she found the student "unworthy," she let him fend for himself.

Boring's biases were not based on academic achievements alone. A student who was especially personable, had a physician father, and was a male, might receive some special consideration. For example, Boring recommended one young man with a weak academic record, "a delightful person, always jolly and cheerful, liked by all his comrades," to the Admissions Committee of the National Medical College, Shanghai. It also helped that his father was a "well-known doctor in Peiping."[7] Zhou Hua Kang, who was head of the premedical group in his third year, reported that "we knew that some students whom she didn't like never got in! . . . I got the impression that she did write a good recommendation letter for me. That's why I got in."[8] He was impressed with her rigorous, uncompromising approach to scholarship. Still, he stressed that she was "very friendly."

Boring had the reputation for another type of favoritism—preferring men students over women. Even those women who admitted that they were among the elect, agreed. Fan Qi conceded that "she preferred her gentleman students over her lady students," but "still she likes us."[9] Two other women, Sun You Yun and Jiang Lijin, both acknowledged that Boring preferred men, but granted that she had been fair with them.[10] Nai Hsuan Chang Shen recalled that even though she and the other women students thought Boring a bit "more partial to the boys than to the girls," this bias was less important than her enthusiasm for her subject that inspired students of both sexes.[11] In retrospect, students remember Boring's teaching for this enthusiasm and for her relentless insistence on excellence.

The laboratory was the focus for Boring's teaching. She and other Yenching science teachers spent much of their time in laboratories and were keenly interested in problem-solving techniques in the classroom. In many of the smaller Chinese institutions laboratory work was almost unknown. Teachers taught from books, were ill prepared in their subjects, and did not know how to improve. Boring, as one of Yenching's science teachers participating in the Rockefeller "local fellowships" for young teachers from the provinces, helped these teachers see the importance of laboratory instruction. A teacher from a mission institution with little training could come to Yenching, be exposed to up-to-date laboratories, and improve (or initially acquire) laboratory skills.[12]

Boring demanded scrupulous honesty of her students in the laboratory. Woe quickly befell the student who attempted to approximate results without completing the exercise, cut corners, or juggle data to get correct results.[13] Prenursing student Wang Xiu Ying suspected that Boring would demand student perfection when the laboratory assistant printed instructions and terms on the blackboard in the "neatest of block letters." As Wang correctly assumed, the precision she demanded of her assistant extended to her students. Although it was painful at the time, Wang insisted that Boring-prepared students became successful nurses.[14]

Since Boring centered her teaching around the laboratory, the selection and training of assistants was especially important. When Professor of

Zoology Lin Chang Shan became Boring's junior laboratory assistant, he recognized that she trained her assistants as unrelentingly as she did her students in class. To prepare for a laboratory session, she called all of her assistants together, had them sit down beside her at the laboratory table, and proceeded to explain the purpose of the exercise. She would then interrogate the assistants to be certain they understood the material. Not until she was satisfied with each person's progress did she turn the meeting over to the senior assistant. Selection for this senior position was considered a great honor.[15] Although Boring used laboratory assistants in both general biology and comparative anatomy, she made all of the delicate preparations for the histology laboratories herself.[16]

The "very high standards" demanded in the laboratories convinced Liu Ming to change his major to sociology after one year![17] The long laboratories were especially difficult for varsity athletes. Boring approved of her students participating in athletics as long as sports did not interfere with academics. However, she was not willing to modify her standards to accommodate athletes' needs. Zhou Huang Kang, a varsity basketball player, could never perfect his drawings because he had to leave the laboratories by 4:00 p.m. for practices and games. He recalled that "all of the students in that class had their drawings exhibited with the exception of me. I didn't have time." Varsity volleyball player, Feng Chuan Yi, had similar experiences. He suspected from the amount of work required that Boring thought biology was his only class.[18] Lin Chi Wu, a physical education teacher, confirmed Boring's reputation for giving athletes a hard time. He strenuously avoided Boring's classes and laughingly recalled that he was engaged in so many sports that he did not "want to waste so much time studying."

Some students found Boring devoid of a sense of humor, but others claimed that she had a very keen one. Frederick F. Kao recalled her hearty laugh as she played on her own name, lecturing on some vertebrates who dug tunnels by "boring."[19] Wang Xiu Ying, however, found little humor in Boring's laboratory demeanor. Laboratories were serious occasions to be treated with diligence, precision, and solemnity.

Before Boring began the lecture sessions, she characteristically scanned the room, tugged at her dress or sweater, and put her glasses on and off. After this ritual, she began the session. A square mirror situated amid the clutter on her desk seemed anomalous for a woman who gave the impression of caring little for her appearance. During class, she invariably glanced in the mirror, took off her glasses, and unconsciously touched her face, providing a rare display of vanity that provoked muffled laughter among the students.[20] Boring's apparent lack of interest in style separated her from the brightly clad American women on the campus. She usually dressed in light blue or gray dresses. Fan Qi recalled seeing Boring in what she assumed was a new dress. After complimenting her, Fan learned that the "new" dress was the old one turned inside out."[21]

Unnerved Freshman students trembled to think they might appear stupid in front of Miss Boring. As students struggled to come up with answers to her questions, she would touch her lips with the chalk and wait expectantly for the response. If the answer was incorrect, she saw to it that they corrected the mistake, but did not ridicule them.[22]

High grades were difficult to earn in Boring's classes. She had been known to remark that a perfect score was possible only for God himself.[23] Her assignments challenged the best of students, sending them scurrying to the dictionary to understand new vocabulary.[24] They had to cope with two foreign languages, English and the scientific vocabulary. Boring insisted that her students use English rather than Chinese whenever possible, since English competency was essential for success at PUMC. She would chide them for speaking Chinese to each other. For her part, Boring never became proficient in Chinese.[25] She learned enough basics to communicate with servants, but even they knew as much or more English than she did Chinese. Boring's Chinese students were tolerant of her lack of understanding of their language, her sometimes foggy understanding of the political situation, and her imposition of unwanted western traditions upon them. They insisted that her sometimes high-handed methods were clearly motivated by love and by what she deemed to be the students' best interests.

Boring made certain that each biology student was invited to dinner at her house at least once a year, and students who were unable to go home for the Christmas and Easter holidays were invited as her dinner guests.[26] In inviting students home, she was following a Yenching custom, for faculty members often asked students to their houses. As Chien Liu recalled, one of the year's social highlights was to visit Boring at home.[27]

Boring presumed that many of her students would go to the United States to complete advanced degrees. To prepare them to be comfortable in a western atmosphere, she invited students in small groups to see, as Feng Chuan Yi reported, "whether we can use knives and forks."[28] Christmas was a time when transplanted western traditions such as caroling parties were especially encouraged. On Christmas Eve, after a party at Boring's house, Fan Qi recalled "caroling outside of every professor's house" after which "they invited us in for tea." At a Christmas concert, the students sang Handel's "Hallelujah Chorus."[29]

When she knew that students would be going to the United States to study, Boring gave them special tutoring in western customs. She was especially supportive of husband and wife Jin and Tang. Jin left China first, to work on his Ph.D. degree in the United States. His wife, Tang, remained in China for a short time before she could join him in San Francisco. Boring organized several "helping" sessions to prepare Tang for what she would encounter in the United States. She invited her to dinner, informed her about American customs, "even table manners...and she told me to have a happy life."[30]

Boring had advice for all of her students. In retrospect at least, students did not seem to resent her well-intentioned interference in their lives, though the advice could be rather far reaching! After Frederick Kao, who entered Yenching University as a freshman in 1938, decided to become a premedical major, Boring commanded him to "keep well, study hard, have plenty of fresh air and good exercise." He gracefully accepted the advice of this American woman who spoke only English to him, wondering "why a woman from a faraway foreign land cared so much about my education and livelihood." She was "honest, with foresight..." and one who "cared about me as I was, no proselytization, no sermons, just good sense as a professor treating a student, a perfect setting in any society."[31]

Boring did not confine her help and advice to her own students. Hou Ren Zhi, now Professor of Geography at Beijing University, explained his encounter with Boring as a history major. His major professor volunteered him to give a talk in English on the geographical Peking to the Peking Association of University Women. Never having given a talk in English, he was naturally panicked. As secretary of the organization, Boring came to see him about the presentation and Hou said he expected a different person from the one he actually encountered. "Her reputation [for strictness] had made a very deep impression on me. But she was so kind and encouraged me to go." Boring "treated me just like her own pupil." He noted that it was unexpected and unusual "for such a distinguished professor to come to see me—a young student." Hou agreed that it would have been hard to say "no" to Boring. "She's very energetic, you know!" When he went to give the talk Boring took him in her own car.

II

The number of students in the College of Natural Science increased yearly. Although an enlarged enrollment demonstrated the health of the department, it also meant more work for the faculty members.[32] The increased pressure made Boring more willing to leave Yenching in 1936 when she was scheduled for another furlough. She was ready to rest, see her family, and examine specimens at the American Museum.

Boring preferred to have her leave mapped out ahead of time, but the activities of her busy family made it impossible to make plans for the Thanksgiving and Christmas holidays.[33] Since the family would be scattered during the summer, she decided to base her activities in New York City and work at the American Museum of Natural History. Now that she had collected data on a wide variety of Chinese amphibians, she wanted to "check our Yenching-gathered data with what Mr. Pope obtained while on the Roy Chapman Andrew's Asiatic expedition...." She and Pope planned to collaborate on a book on Chinese amphibians.[34]

While she was in the United States, Boring was not confronted on a daily basis with the burgeoning aggression of the Japanese. However, in China, as the Japanese increased their encroachments, the fighting between the Guomintang and the Communists had escalated to the extent that the Chinese were unable to present a unified anti-Japanese front. This lack of unity inspired Beijing students to form the National Salvation Union in 1936, which was designed to end the fighting between the Guomintang and the Communists by presenting a united front against the Japanese.[35] Demonstrations in several major cities failed to convince the Guomintang to cooperate with the Union, and toward the end of November 1936, it arrested several Union members. Attempts at cooperation by Chiang Kai Shek's troops in the northwest in early December failed dismally. Chiang, who decided to direct the campaign against the Union personally, was arrested by his own troops. After intense negotiations, Chiang was released on the provision that he renounce the anti-Communist struggle and unite the country against the Japanese. The Communists reached an agreement with the Guomintang in the summer of 1937. They agreed to refrain from attempts to overthrow the Nationalist government, to place the Red Army troops under Guomintang supervision, to eliminate the name "soviet" for their Yanan stronghold, and to establish voting procedures in which non-Communists were eligible for office.

A Japanese attack gave impetus to the consummation of the agreement between Nationalists and Communists. Newly returned from her furlough, Boring was involved in the consequences of this attack.

On July 7, 1937, Japanese troops from the Tianjin Garrison attempted to take over the Marco Polo Railway Bridge which spanned the Yong Ting River. This bridge, fifteen miles southwest of Beijing, provided the key communications link with Wuhan and central China. The Japanese, expecting China to either surrender or offer to accommodate the invaders, were surprised when the Chinese did neither. Resisting fiercely, they forced the Japanese to bring in additional troops. With strengthened forces, other Japanese units occupied Beijing and Tianjin; in November, they launched a successful major attack on Shanghai and in December 1937, Nanjing fell. By August 1937, China and Japan were in a state of open, although undeclared, warfare.

The events of 1937 changed the nature of both Boring's research and personal life. She was directly involved in the aftermath of the Marco Polo Bridge incident and in the occupation of Beijing. While she and six other members of the Yenching faculty were on vacation at a mountain resort about seventy miles south of Beijing, they heard that the railroad had been bombed by the Japanese, cutting them off from Yenching.

Since crises had become a way of life for Boring and her colleagues, they were not overly alarmed by the initial report of the bombing. However, as their time away from Yenching stretched to three weeks "of utter isolation from contact with the outside world," concern escalated. The isolation that had seemed so desirable became frightening, for after the railway was cut, "we did not get a single letter or newspaper, and had no idea what might be happening to Peiping and Yenching."[36]

The American Consul at Hankou telegraphed the resort with what Boring considered ridiculous, inappropriate advice, strongly advising the vacationers to "go to a place of safety." Since, Boring insisted, "we were perfectly safe on the mountain," an incautious move from the resort might have proved more hazardous than remaining: "the country roads were thick with mud from the unusually heavy rains this summer, and the roads might be blocked by swift torrents."[37]

When they learned that Beijing was occupied, the group had little choice but to continue south to Hankou. "Utter desolation" was replaced by hope when they reluctantly "braved the wrath of the Consul whom ...[they] had disobeyed so many times, and asked him to send a radio message from the American gunboat in the harbor to the American Embassy in Peiping to ask if Yenching was really opening and what... [they] should do." Boring recorded that she would never "forget the day when the reply came: 'Yenching opening as usual. Return immediately via Canton and Hongkong.'"[38]

A blocked harbor at Ningpo and a crew strike at Tsingtao that nearly resulted in their transfer to a steamer that was later quarantined for cholera added excitement to the trip north. They were met by Lucius Porter, whose handsome familiar face and dramatic bearing were welcome as he marshalled them onto a special train car to Beijing, where busses took them directly to the Yenching campus. In spite of the tales of terror and "annoyances of transportation in the north," the trip went smoothly.[39]

An unharmed Yenching, exuding an atmosphere of "more peace and normality than anywhere we have been since we left our mountain seventy miles south of Peiping five weeks ago," welcomed Boring. Although day-to-day life proceeded with only minor incidents, a sense of foreboding hung over even the most ordinary activities. Anti-Japanese underground activities took precedence over studies for all but the most dedicated scholars.

After the swift Japanese victories, there were four possible areas in which Chinese could live: Japanese-occupied northern China under a Chinese regime (the home of Yenching); the Yangtze Valley area in central China, led by another puppet regime based in Nanjing (including much of the richest area in China); northwestern China with the expanded Communist base area at Yanan; and southwestern China, where political power centered in Chiang Kai Shek's wartime capital of Chongquing in Sichuan province.

Students from the unoccupied southern territories hesitated to return to school in the occupied area. When Stuart went south to Shanghai to encourage students to return to school, he found many people convinced that Yenching's administration was making unacceptable compromises with Japan in order to remain open. Using his best rhetoric, Stuart assured them otherwise.[40]

In spite of his distress with the fragmented, indecisive official reaction of the American government, Stuart was exhilarated "over the new spirit" of the Chinese. Finally, the many-factioned Chinese were pulling together against a common enemy. Stuart praised Chiang Kai Shek, who preferred "defeat, hardship, and danger to the easy life, with all the money he could want if he would accept a Japanese peace...."[41]

Boring and Stuart agreed that Yenching must be kept open as long as possible, for not to do so would be cowardly.[42] Neither of them tolerated views that they considered cowardly. To them, (perhaps unfairly) Grace Boynton fell into this category. While Alice and company were wending their way back from enforced mountain exile, Boynton had expressed the fear that cataclysms would erupt if Yenching was reopened. Relieved that her worst fears had not materialized, she "sent Leighton a little note" on September 17, 1937, "saying I am glad Yenching is open and sorry I have been such a Doubting Thomasine."[43]

Although the rift with Boynton in 1934 disturbed Boring, she never allowed it to disrupt her life. Her diverse interests allowed little time to contemplate one severed relationship, although she gratefully accepted an opportunity to mend the breech. When Grace told Alice that she wanted to remain friends and that her feelings of friendship were unchanged, Boring responded with, "that's beautiful," and suggested that they meet regularly. Boynton suspected that Boring "would soon get impatient with that routine." Although the conversation between Boynton and Boring removed some of the sting from the wounds, Alice and Grace never became close friends again.[44]

The quarrel with Boynton was the only major conflict Boring had with a friend. However, the easy companionship that she had enjoyed earlier with people seemed strained during this time. Others besides Boynton recalled her being "unwell" at this period. Ruth Hung Beasley overheard her parents, William and Rhoda Hung, talking earnestly with Boring although she could not understand what they were saying. They later explained to Ruth that she must overlook Miss Boring's brusqueness and remember that she was unwell.[45]

A feeling of being restrained also soured humors. One of Boring's favorite summer activities had been to leave Yenching for a summer wander, but it was no longer possible to travel any distance for a vacation. Because of her experience in the summer of 1937, instead of her usual travels during the vacation season of 1938 she planned to stay at her own house in the Prince's Garden and attempt to get a "vacation state of mind in the usual workaday environment."[46]

Most students entering Yenching University were only partly aware of the turmoil that the faculty members were undergoing. Frederick Kao entered Yenching the year after the Marco Polo Bridge incident. To him, his freshman year at Yenching was "one of the most stimulating" years of his life. In spite of the somewhat overwhelming atmosphere generated by large numbers of foreign faculty members and some foreign students, he thought he saw a prophesy for the future of the human race: "to mingle, to exchange ideas, and to learn differences, without counteraction— idealistic and futuristic ways to deal with the problems of the world." Kao later realized that during this time "the minds of all the American faculty members, including Miss Boring, must have been occupied with unpleasant thoughts. . . ." Nevertheless, the full teaching schedule was met, although "we students sensed that the faculty was worried about the future. . . . Yenching was a fragile place."[47]

Boring supplied the family with a personalized account "of the ups and downs of facts and feelings" on the Yenching campus to supplement "the very good China news which you are getting in your American newspapers (as I see from my regular Sunday *New York Times*)."[48] From July 7, the date of the bombing of the Marco Polo Bridge, they had been isolated. Notices were circulated occasionally on the campus "urging discretion as to what was said on buses to Peking, and no public meetings [were allowed] except on such innocuous subjects as science and religion."[49]

Boring explained that the campus had been, for the most part, exempt from a number of "petty tyrannies" perpetrated by the Japanese. When Stuart returned from one of his trips south, "full of confidence and courage," he convinced the faculty that the military situation was better than they had hoped and "that the Central Government does not consider us unpatriotic by staying here."[50]

Stuart did not mention the giant rift that had developed within the United Front. The apparent solidarity between the Communists and the Nationalists had begun to crumble seriously by 1938. During a period of calm as both Chinese and Japanese were recovering from bitter, bloody campaigns, the Communists and Nationalists began to clash with each other again. Although many western leaders, including Stuart, regarded Chiang Kai Shek as the heroic leader of a united Free China, others considered the Central Government to be rife with dissension, corruption, inefficiency, and political intimidation.

Stuart's insistence that Yenching faculty members must not participate in politics appeared to bear fruit. After one academic year in occupied territory, the university had not, according to Boring, "made any fundamental compromises in standards or freedom." This was possible, she stated, because of the policy of "our wise president" who bore "the brunt" of the "constant struggle." The official position of the university was that "as an educational institution we would take no part in any political matters and therefore have paid no attention to orders or invitations to join in 'victory parades' or mass meetings against the Chiang Kai Shek regime."[51]

An absent President Stuart never failed to unnerve Boring, for she was convinced that only he could successfully baffle Japanese militarists. Stuart defused potential conflicts and was able to persuade them not "to kill us or arrest too many of our students."[52] Stuart's position was paradoxical. To insure the safety of the Yenching students and faculty, he must remain at Yenching. The Chinese faculty members were especially dependent on his presence, for campus rumors prophesied their imminent arrest. As long as Stuart remained on campus plying the occupiers with flattery and good dinners, the Chinese remained relatively safe.[53] However, if Stuart stayed on campus he would be unable to marshal support from the unoccupied south, the United States, and Europe necessary to keep the campus operating. Consequently, his activities consisted of a delicate balancing act, leaving when absolutely necessary, staying whenever possible, and soothing the distraught as required.

Boring found suspect those who failed to commit themselves to Stuart's ideals. During one of the Friday lunch discussions Alice became "much exercised" because she perceived that Stuart's secretary, Doris, was not properly loyal. In the first place, Doris had tried to resign and return home the previous year, but Stuart had convinced her to stay. As tensions mounted she remained in a state of constant dread, expecting "something awful to happen every time her door opens." Boynton sympathized with Doris who knew "all about all the risks which Leighton takes so blithely for himself and for all the rest of us." Sarcastically, she noted that "Leighton hates to put pressure on a woman, but of course he does need a secretary." Boring took a different view of the situation. "Alice, who is naturally a very brave person, is furious with Doris for failing Leighton."[54]

Tensions from the external unknown were reflected in the ways in which friend reacted to friend. "At Friday Lunch everybody yapped at everybody else." Boynton sniped at Boring as she reflected on one of these lunches. "AMB told about the letters she is sending home by private hand; I marvelled that she takes the chance of getting helpless people into jeopardy."[55]

Grace Boynton's journals are her very personal reflections on events and cannot be accepted as "truth." On the other hand, they certainly represent how she felt in different situations, and since her reflections often center upon Boring and Stuart they explain what some people, at least, were thinking.

According to Boynton, the Yenching campus reverberated with rumors of a romance between Stuart and Alice Gregg, a "southern woman of aristocratic origin" from Shanghai whom Stuart invited to visit Yenching. Stuart "put her up at the house reserved for single women…just where eyes would be most curious and tongues would wag the fastest."[56] Boynton assumed that Gregg mistakenly "had taken wedding bells for granted." When it became evident that she was mistaken, Gregg plaintively told Boynton that she was "just" Stuart's "Shanghai sweetie." Boynton applied the Gregg incident to what she knew, or thought she knew, about Alice's experience with Stuart. Hearing Gregg's woes provoked Boynton to get "angry with Leighton all over again." It "dawned on Leighton" at the very end of the visit "that Alice Gregg had ideas, when I gather he sweetly explained that she shouldn't have them and he would come and see her in Shanghai just as soon as he could to demonstrate that all was forgiven."[57] Boynton was certain that during the Gregg visit Alice was "frantic," but Stuart "never seemed aware that AMB was green with jealousy."[58]

Stuart either ignored or was unaware of the furor generated on campus by the Gregg incident. He never neglected his university duties and was especially attentive to the "political situation" which was touch and go all summer." Yenching, "in general didn't like Alice Gregg who artlessly assumed the airs of a lady elect. . . . " Boynton, however, "liked her," and blamed Stuart, asserting that "JLS can be a villain although in general he is viewed as a sage if not a saint." Boring and Gregg, of course, did not like each other.[59]

Although love, jealousy, and anger pervaded the daily lives of Yenching's people, emotions generated from the fear and uncertainty of life in an occupied area overshadowed personal intrigues. To the question, "do they really arrest people?" Boring replied, "of course they do, they have arrested several of our students, and it is a miracle that they have so far taken no faculty." They tortured one of the boys that they arrested "until he promised to spy on his fellow students when he returned." Because he reported this incident to Stuart, special precautions were adopted for him. The Japanese, however, "have not followed up their advantage in this case," although other formerly well-to-do Chinese were tortured and endured hardship.[60]

To amuse themselves, faculty members took "wonderful hikes, and formed various clubs including the 'Shop Club.'" One of the Club's more unique features, Boring explained, was that no one need apologize for going to sleep. Since the faculty was composed of specialists, no one need be ashamed if he or she was bored by a specialized presentation. Nobody fell asleep, she reported proudly, when

> I reported on the Hybrid Frogs which one of my students has been raising, and discussed their relation to mules. Unfortunately it takes frogs three years to mature, so we shall have to wait two more years to know whether they are fertile or sterile. And probably we shall not be able to keep them alive that long.[61]

With dramatic readings, movies (she saw "One Hundred Men and a Girl, the one with the Philadelphia Orchestra and Stokowski"), hiking, shopping, and meetings, they managed to be entertained most of the time. "Life is full of contrasts," she wrote. "We on this campus are lucky."[62] Since a summer vacation away seemed impossible, Boring remained at Yenching, "working on Frogs in the morning and sleeping in the afternoons."[63]

Yenching's students were trapped in an untenable situation during 1938, 1939 and 1940. Like Stuart, they shuttled back and forth from the occupied North to the unoccupied South. They had to weigh the advantages of remaining in the North and having their patriotism questioned against moving to "Free China" in the South and having their future careers jeopardized. Those who felt their patriotic duty required them to return to the unoccupied South found unorganized educational institutions, inadequate equipment, and job shortages. For some, the inadequacy of facilities in the South encouraged a return to Yenching where, in exchange for excellent facilities, they endured the humiliation of living in an occupied territory. Boring observed from her vantage point as Acting Dean of Natural Sciences during the summer of 1938 that she spent much time in her office welcoming those arriving from the South and bidding farewell to those leaving—"about in even numbers."[64] By 1939, however, the balance shifted. Even though Yenching was in a potentially hazardous position and might "become more or less an oasis this winter if the balance of power in Europe should shift in some way as to aid and abet our neighbors," many students decided that they "would rather be on this oasis."[65]

A large number of students decided that they could best contribute to China's future by obtaining a superior education at Yenching. The enrollment increased to a record number in the fall of 1939. Although the average number of freshmen had remained constant at about 800 for several years, in 1938, the freshman class swelled to 950. "Unfortunately," Boring quipped, this large class "was so good that we could not flunk many." Therefore, in 1939 Yenching was confronted with a record sophomore class, "which is harder to handle as it involves more advanced classes, and is especially difficult for our science laboratories"[66]

At Yenching, hoses for air, gas, water, and oxygen allowed students access to the necessary utilities for experiments. Large storage bins and tanks were supplied for preserved animals. Well-kept microscopes were available. Boring demanded that her students behave meticulously in the laboratory. They wore lab coats and each person was in charge of keeping his or her equipment and supplies scrupulously clean, neat, and in working order. Although "Miss Boring was very fussy about this matter," they later appreciated this training which gave them "good working habits and background."[67]

The operation of the College of Natural Science mirrored the situation in the university as a whole. The university's effective operation was related to the attitude of the constituency in the United States which, in turn, was affected by the policies of the United States government in

China. Boring and her Yenching colleagues watched the Japanese engulf more and more territory and felt that the United States foreign policy must change. However, the U.S. government hesitated to commit itself to Chiang Kai Shek, or to one of the other contenders in the internecine strife.

For years, the Japanese had watched squabbling contenders destroy each other and had observed the West's timidity. In response, Japan developed its so-called "Continental Policy," a thinly disguised program of imperialistic conquest and economic exploitation, rationalized as "a sacred mission to free the peoples of Eastern Asia from bondage to their own oppressive rulers and from western encroachments." As the Japanese swept across an area to "liberate" it, they slaughtered civilians, raped women, looted, and burned. The Japanese had learned the economic value of opium from nineteenth-century Europeans who had hastened to profit from the trade by assuring the addiction of large segments of the population. Learning the lesson well, they enforced the planting of the poppy and insisted on the open sale of opium and its derivatives.[68] The anti-Japanese sentiment of the populace was so universal that both western and Chinese observers agreed "that any other fate would be better for China than Japanese military domination."[69]

In 1940 the instability of the potential leaders of an anti-Japanese front in China continued to make the United States government hesitant to throw its support behind any one faction. Bickering puppets, disorganized Soviet-influenced Communists, and opportunistic followers of Chiang Kai Shek seemed wavering allies at best. Still, both Stuart and Boring believed that the United States, in attempting to maintain a middle-of-the-road approach, was making a grave error, primarily because U.S. policy makers did not recognize "the essential difference between the various puppet leaders and General Chiang Kai Shek."[70] In addition, Hitler's aggressions were multiplying in Europe, and most policy makers considered him the most imminent threat to the United States' interests.

By January 1941, Boring's former disgust with American foreign policy toward China was replaced with a new respect.

> We are getting to be proud of America too. That victory for Roosevelt gave us real heart. All you Wilkie ites [sic] just forget your personal disappointment and rejoice with us to whom foreign policy and experience in foreign affairs means a future or no future, and at least a chance for future peaceful relations, even though war may have to come first.[71]

Even with a stronger foreign policy, day-to-day living at Yenching became increasingly perilous. Faculty and staff members who remained recognized the potential danger. As a precaution, during 1940 University authorities divided the community into three priority groups for evacuation: groups A, B, and C. Group C comprised women with children, the aged, and those who were decrepit in any way. Group B contained all other women "(an insult to our sex!) and ordinary men." Group A contained "those few men of great wisdom necessary to hold the property and lay the plans for the interim until the rest of us could come back."[72]

Boring expected that women and men who have similar responsibilities should share in both the inherent privileges and the hazards. When she as a woman was excluded from group "A" she resented the implication that her services were not sufficiently valuable to the university to merit her inclusion. Other Yenching woman faculty members shared these views. Group B, she explained, "has done some loud protesting, the women probably feeling a little hurt that no one of us was put in A." Stuart found the single women teachers a formidable force with which to reckon. Boring wrote that he had been heard to say that "I suppose those single women will do as they please! so he has learned one important lesson."[73]

III

Increased pressure from the Japanese did not tempt Boring to leave Yenching. China, she reflected, "is home." Since "our Chinese colleagues and friends can not get out of any trouble that develops, ... we would feel a bit mean to save our heads if they can not." She also found it difficult to "believe that disaster is really coming," knowing that "all U.S. officials always have magnified danger...." In spite of the dire prophecies by governmental officials, she was gratified that the United States allowed them to make their own decision about leaving and had not attempted to force them out.

> It is wonderful to belong to a country where the Consul can only advise, not order, so that a person can still feel free to use his own intelligence in making decisions. Internement [sic] would be no joke, but neither would tearing up roots and trying to find something to do in a place which is already full of the 'unemployed.'[74]

Boring wanted to assure her own participation in Yenching's future. Convinced that after the war the University would have a role in the reconstruction of China, she wanted to be a part of the process. Optimistically she reported that "we are even pricing building materials so as to have some on hand as soon as we see that it is safe to expand a bit here and there."[75]

Boring found that the "occupation" had a generally salutary effect on morale, although "there are a few long-faced pessimists on the campus who think the idea is crazy, but we have lived in a crazy world so long now that most of us are no end cheered by the thought."[76]

The discussions about A group, B group, and C group priorities did not concern Grace Boynton, for she left Yenching on July 3, 1940, for leave in the United States. The night before her departure, she "had dinner and the evening with Alice and Leighton in the Prince's Garden… the house where Alice and I spent four years as house-mates." Even though the evening was beautiful and they were served on "Alice's terrace by the lake," Boynton recalled her past unpleasant memories of the place.

Boynton found Stuart's behavior paradoxical. Although he demanded an adoring audience, he hated "to be regarded as a spell binder."[77] After Stuart left, Boring and Boynton discussed their different interpretations of the evening. Boring praised Stuart for his openness and honesty and tried to convince Boynton that he was incapable of diplomacy, which Boynton found nonsensical. She snorted, "the whole purpose of the evening was diplomacy!"[78] Boring, "who is herself, God knows, quite innocent of subtlety," had no answer when Boynton asked "if Leighton is, as you say, incapable of diplomacy, then who is capable?"[79]

After she left Beijing, Boynton became a conduit for information from Yenching to the Edwin Boring family. She was able to provide Garry with information about Alice and Yenching, for when she returned to the United States she "spent the night with the Borings in Cambridge…." During their discussion of China, they considered the rumor that non-combatant Americans would be withdrawn. Both Garry and Grace agreed that the "non-combatant" designation would not apply to Alice. "Alice, I reckon as a combatant," Garry volunteered.[80]

While Boynton and Garry were in the United States speculating about events in China, Alice followed her usual routine as much as possible. In the midst of uncertainty, the time-consuming task of grading examinations, determining grades, and administering a biology department remained. "I flunked only four out of 59 freshmen, and no upper classmen," she reported.

> We are so crowded for space in our laboratories that I have just spent a whole day trying to make schedules for Premedical, Home Economics, Physical Education, and Biology sophomores fit together so that I can admit exactly 60 students to my Vertebrate Anatomy class in the second semester, in two sections of exactly 30 each, and still allow each to get the proper courses in Chemistry and Physics and other departments which each is required to take.[81]

The result, she explained, is "like a bad jigsaw puzzle." Since she had precisely sixty sets of instruments and sixty and only sixty dogfish for dissection, class size could not exceed that number.[82]

During the school terms, required school activities absorbed most of Boring's time, and she had little time for her own research. Consequently, she looked forward to the winter vacation, "to have a chance to work with my Frogs uninterruptedly without classes and conferences to cut up the time."[83]

Boring was happy to be in the midst of the problems at Yenching and not in the United States pondering them from afar with Boynton. Away from China and the difficulties described by Boring, Boynton longed to return. Since in April 1941, a return to Yenching was unlikely, Boynton explored alternatives such as teaching at Nanjing University which "certainly [could] use me." The general situation almost kept Boynton at home, for the American Board of Missions "was about to take action providing that no women missionaries should be returned to the North China Field." The Mission Board made an exception for Boynton, belying her perception that Stuart did not want her to return.[84] However, deteriorating conditions in northern China kept the State Department from allowing her to return to Yenching, but she was permitted to return to Free China.[85]

The American missionaries continued to trust in the Chiangs even when they received reports of "Mme. Chiang's 'gambling' on the Chungking Black Market with funds for her orphanages." To counter the report, "she had to invite three Americans...to go over her books and certify how much money she had and what she did with it." Not at all horrified by the possibility, Boynton explained that "her 'gambling' was just the effort of a practical philanthropist to get more cash for her children...she was not cashing in for herself."[86]

Tensions were building in Yenching. Although food was expensive, Boring reported that it was available. Her dietary staples became "corn muffins and whole wheat bread from local grains grown and ground in the neighborhood," and proved "less expensive and more nutritious than American white flour...." Milk from Yenching's dairy and cheese from a nearby Trappist monastery provided their dairy products. Meat, however, was a luxury—"any good meat costs at least $1.50 a pound; ham is $2.80; so I am teaching my cook to make various entrees, including Philadelphia scrapple."[87]

Expecting internment "in some horrible place" Alice requested warm clothing from Lydia.[88] Concerned that her current wardrobe would not survive a long internment, she also asked Boynton to bring "dresses and pen and Christmas tree lights for me."[89]

In spite of the deteriorating world situation, Boring insisted that the summer of 1941 had been a good one.

> How could we [have a good summer] in face of what is happening in the world? Surely, we did it just because of that. Anything in the world may happen to us this winter, so we must be physically fit.[90]

In a memorandum to the Yenching Board of Trustees, September 25, 1941, Boring summarized the events in Eastern Asia as they affected the university. Although the new semester began with a total of 1,158 students, "which is more than we had set as our maximum," there was uncertainty about the opening of the university. "After the American freezing orders," university officials expected Japan to take retaliatory actions against the United States. Consequently, "all through August . . . I stayed close to the campus and watched for signs of measures aimed against Yenching as such." The uncertainty "was like living again through the suspense of August 1937 immediately after the outbreak of hostilities when we were facing a terrifying unknown." This new unknown prompted school officials to be prepared "to announce the indefinite postponement of opening the session, for we should have been impotent against Japanese violence." In spite of the inconvenience, Boring was convinced that the American action was proper, "regardless of any temporary disruption of university work or even the destruction of our property." Now "our chief anxiety . . . is coal of which we have on hand not more than enough for the next two months. It has become a literal fear of freezing."[91]

Boring described to the Board of Trustees her personal feelings that material discomfort was overcome by a spiritual vitality.

> . . . I remember vividly the relief with which it became clear to me that since Yenching was not only an educational institution but had its own distinctive moral and spiritual mission all that mattered was the witness to this in meeting whatever might happen. In other words, we might conceivably achieve more for the nation and for our religious purpose if as individuals or in our corporate existence we suffered the consequences of standing for our principles rather than by ensuring our material welfare.[92]

This underlying strength allowed for the effective functioning of the university. "The Japanese have discovered that threats of violence would not frighten us into complying with their demands."[93]

Boring reported that Japanese methods involved cultural penetration.

Although they have unquestionably marked us as an institution to be taken over by their agencies and thus utilized for their imperialistic aims, . . . that very fact has led them to wait until they are strong enough to eject the foreigners who would be their chief hindrance. They still do not want to provoke unfavorable publicity in the United States for which they have a wholesome fear.[94]

Therefore, we have been allowed to continue unmolested but with no illusions as to what our fate would be when present restraints were sufficiently removed. The body might remain unharmed but the soul of Yenching would become extinct.[95]

Although life at Yenching during this time was inconvenient, it was not intolerable. When Boring claimed that getting her hair shampooed and set was one of the worst problems that confronted her, it became clear that her major concern was not looting, starvation, and killing, but annoying disruptions of routine. Because of irregularly running busses, they were unable to get to Beijing at will, yet faculty, staff members, and students amused themselves on campus by a myriad of activities, including parties and plays.

Friday night we had a thoroughly recreative evening provided by the faculty dramatic club, which reads and half acts plays. They produced Gogol's *The Inspector General*. We rocked with laughter. And I had a dinner party before the theater, and invited in four couples from among my Chinese neighbors. . . . I served an entree instead of a roast, since meat is so expensive now. The menu was fruit cocktail (persimmons, pears, grapes, redfruit), chicken and mushroom pattes [sic], potato balls, creamed carrots, string beans, corn muffins, egg and tomatoe [sic] salad with sesame crackers; Peking Dust pudding (candied redfruit with grated chestnuts and whipped cream); coffee. Such a meal costs about $1.50 a head at present.[96]

Food, entertainment, and new items improved the quality of life at Yenching. Boring described her pleasure at the arrival of new things.

I feel as though I had Christmas already, since my nice family sent me things by Yenching people returning from furlough. I have a lovely new fountain pen, which does not leak! I have been using a leaky one for two years, and had got discouraged about buying one out here. And I have new summer dresses from Boston. They are exactly what I wanted and needed, plain ones for every day wear for class. I had just worn out two which have been my mainstays for several years. I showed them off to Friday Lunch, and was the envy of all. I had a funny time about the dresses because the Chinese girl who had been doing Physical Education at Wellesley and to whom Lucy gave them to bring to me, got them mixed with things which she was bringing for some one else at Yenching. So she invited us both to dinner to see if we could identify our dresses. Fortunately one was labelled for Cookie, and she expected only one, so I claimed the other four, and they look like Lucy's choice for me! two shirtmakers and two seersuckers. I have [been] longing for seersucker dresses—they are so practical and so cool. And then not least by any means Lydia sent me by Stephen Tsai last summer three suits of soft woolies, and this cold snap has no terrors for me now.[97]

In spite of the "entirely materialistic" tone of her letter, Boring reassured her family that "our chief occupation is still teaching youth how to think clearly, and preventing them from trying to pass their courses by memorizing."

By November 1941, the future appeared perilous. Although mail was still getting through, rumours indicated that such was not long to be the case, so Boring wished her family an early "Happy Christmas, in case no more letters should reach you!"[98]

Notes

1. Former student, Frederick Kao, considered this transference to have been her major strength, enabling her "to devote her life to educating many instead of loving only a few." Frederick F. Kao, "Remembering Miss Alice M. Boring," An essay, printed on 3 February 1989.
2. Wu Jie Ping to Marilyn Bailey Ogilvie, Interview, 13 July 1988.
3. Tang explained that the student was the answer with the difference between "A and D." Instead he explained the difference between "C and D." When Boring looked at the paper she said, "this is a good student. If he hadn't misunderstood the question he would have gotten the right answer." Tang Ji Xue to Ogilvie, Interview, PUMC, 18 July 1988. Yang Wang also came under the category of a "favorite." He found Boring's reputation as a strict taskmaster justified, but also recalled that she was "unusually warm" toward him, surprising some of his fellow students "who were rather awed by her stern facade." Yang Wang to Choquette, 1 December 1988.
4. Write concise and succinct answers!
5. Laurence T. Wu to Choquette, 2 January 1989.
6. Jin Yin Chang to Ogilvie, Interview, PUMC, 18 July 1988.
7. Boring, Premedical records of students, 1 July 1935. Contributed by Lin Chang San.
8. Zhou Hua Kang to Ogilvie, Interview, PUMC, 18 July 1988.
9. Fan Qi to Ogilvie, Interview PUMC, 18 July 1988.
10. Sun You Yun and Jiang Lijin to Ogilvie, Interview 13 July 1988.
11. Nai-hsuan Chang Shen to Choquette, 15 October 1988.
12. Gee to Lauder W. Jones, 25 November 1931, "Statement of Work of College of Science, Yenching University," Rockefeller Archive Center, RG1, Series 601, Box 41, Folder 336.

13. Wang Xiu Ying to Ogilvie, Interview, Beijing University, 13 July 1988.

14. Wang Xiu Ying to Ogilvie, Interview, PUMC, 18 July 1988.

15. Lin Chang Shan to Ogilvie, Interview, 13 July 1988.

16. Ibid.

17. Liu Ming to Ogilvie. Interview, Xi'An, 28 July 1988.

18. Boring displayed the superior student drawings. Zhou Hua Kang to Ogilvie, Interview, PUMC, 18 July 1988; Feng Chuan Yi to Ogilvie, Interview, PUMC, 18 July 1988.

19. Frederick F. Kao, "Remembering Miss Alice M. Boring," An essay, printed on 3 February 1989, p. 5.

20. Tang Xi Xue to Ogilvie, Interview, PUMC, 18 July 1988.

21. Fan mused that she still remembered the pattern of the dress. "It was thick and woolen and knitted and she turned it inside out to make a new dress." Fan Qi to Ogilvie. Interview, PUMC, 18 July 1988.

22. Chien Liu to Choquette, 14 September 1988.

23. Nai Hsuan Chang Shen to Choquette, 15 October 1988. "Dr. Boring, if my recollection is correct, was a strict marker of grades. She used to tell us that only God could get a perfect score. Students should be satisfied with only good grades."

24. Kao, "Remembering Miss Alice Boring," p. 5.

25. Jin Yin Chang to Ogilvie, Interview, PUMC, 18 July 1988.

26. Dorothy Wei King to Choquette, 3 December 1988.

27. These receptions occurred at the beginning of the school year and during the holidays. Chien Liu to Choquette, 14 September 1988.

28. Feng Chuan Yi to Ogilvie, Interview, PUMC, 18 July 1988.

29. Fan Qi to Ogilvie, Interview, PUMC, 18 July 1988.

30. Tang Xi Xue to Ogilvie. Interview, PUMC, 18 July 1988.

31. Kao, "Remembering Miss Alice M. Boring,"

32. From the school year 1925–26 to 1928–29, the number of biology majors had increased from seven to seventeen and the number of students from sixty-seven to 227. Report of the Registrar, July 1928–July 1931. During the fall semester, 1931, Boring taught general biology (86 students, 4 credit hours), animal histology (4 students, 4 credit hours), journal club (11 students, 1 credit hour), advanced vertebrate zoology (4 students, 4 credit hours), and thesis supervision (2 credit hours). During the spring semester, 1932, she taught general biology, comparative vertebrate anatomy (4 hours), journal club, advanced vertebrate zoology, and thesis supervision. Gee to Jones, 25 November 1931. Boring found that the greatest number of students came from Guangzhou in south China, rather than from Beijing as she had supposed. W.S. Carter to Gee, 16 Dec. 1930, Rockefeller Archive Center, RG 1, Series 601, Box 41, Folder 335.

33. E.G. Boring to A.M. Boring, 26 May 1936, Pusey Archive Collection, Harvard University, Boring Family Correspondence.

34. See Bibliography, 1940, Pope and Boring.

35. J. Leighton Stuart to Board of Trustees, Easter Day, 1936, Yale University Archives, Stuart Papers, RG 11, Folder 5521.
36. Alice M. Boring to People at Home, "Cut off from Yenching," 1 October 1937, Special Collection Archives, Yale Divinity School.
37. Ibid.
38. Ibid.
39. Ibid.
40. J. Leighton Stuart to Bettis A. Garside, 17 December 1937, Yale University Archives, Stuart Papers, RG11, Folder 5530.
41. Ibid.
42. Ibid.
43. Ibid.
44. After Boring's retirement, Boynton had a key to her apartment.
45. Ruth Hung Beasley to Marilyn Bailey Ogilvie, 18 Feb. 1988.
46. Boring, "Letters from an Alumna. An Academic Year in Occupied Territory," *Bryn Mawr Alumnae Bulletin,* 13 July 1938, Special Collection Archives, Yale Divinity School.
47. Frederick F. Kao, "Miss Alice M. Boring Ph.D. Professor of Biology and Head of the Department of Special Biology, Yenching University, Peking, China," 3 February 1989.
48. Boring to "Folks," 11 April 1938.
49. Ibid.
50. Ibid.
51. Boring, "Letters from an Alumna. An Academic Year in Occupied Territory," 13 July 1938, Special Collection Archives, Yale Divinity School.
52. Alice M. Boring to Friends, 26 March 1939, Special Collection Archives, Yale Divinity School.
53. Ibid.
54. Boynton noted that both Stuart and Boring had been under a great strain—"Alice registered the excitement she always shows under tension." Grace M. Boynton, "Red Leather Notebook," 1939, p. 163. Archives, Schlesinger Library, Radcliffe College, Cambridge, MA.
55. Ibid., 5 May 1939.
56. Ibid.
57. Ibid., 1939, pp. 245–46.
58. Ibid.
59. Ibid.
60. Boring to Friends, 26 March 1939, Special Collection Archives, Yale Divinity School.
61. Boring to Mrs. T.D. (Eva) MacMillan, 14 May 1939, Special Collection Archives, Yale Divinity School.
62. Ibid.
63. Boring to MacMillan, 18 June 1939, Special Collection Archives, Yale Divinity School. "Personally I have had a fine summer," in spite of inclement

weather—continuous rain or a saturated atmosphere around Beijing and drought elsewhere,—and discouraging world events. Puzzled by the "insane" international situation, she asked, "does any nation know what it wants? And are there any ideals left in the world, or any sense of humor?" Perhaps, she suggested, the hope of the world lay in the Chinese, because, unlike everybody else, they "still have both ideals and humor." Boring to Friends, 27 Aug. 1939, Special Collection Archives, Yale Divinity School.

64. Alice M. Boring to Friends, 13 July 1938, Special Collection Archives, Yale Divinity School.
65. Boring to Friends, 27 August 1939, Special Collection Archives, Yale Divinity School.
66. Ibid.
67. Ruth Hung Beasley to Marilyn Bailey Ogilvie, 18 Feb. 1988.
68. J. Leighton Stuart, "Memorandum on the Japanese Invasion of China from the Standpoint of American Concern," 4 Feb. 1940, Yale University Archives, Stuart Papers, RG 11, Folder 5541.
69. Ibid.
70. Stuart, "Memorandum on the Japanese Invasion of China."
71. Boring to Friends, 20 Jan. 1941, "New Years Greetings," Special Collection Archives, Yale Divinity School.
72. Ibid.
73. Ibid.
74. Ibid.
75. Ibid.
76. Ibid.
77. Ibid.
78. Grace M. Boynton, "Red Leather Notebook," 8 Nov. 1940, pp. 59–60, Archives, Schlesinger Library, Radcliffe College, Cambridge, MA. Boynton wrote in 1956 that

Leighton was in confidential relations with the American Embassy, the Japanese Military, the Chiang Kai Shek Government, and the guerrilla Reds who were in close touch with Michael Lindsay. Private messengers from all these factions were constantly arriving on campus and constantly asking for Leighton's advice and good offices. I was given to understand, that all four knew JLS was connected with all of the others . . . and yet they entrusted him with most delicate and dangerous information. They all asked for his advice (he did not say they all took it!) But as I have never in what little history I have studied encountered a figure who was trusted by four rival political powers . . . two of which were actually at war . . . this account of what Leighton was doing in politics was simply astounding. As for his own motives they were to serve the Chinese people, and secondarily to preserve Yenching. The Japanese had tried to frighten him and there had been a period when he had been tried out with every brutal threat they could make. When they found he didn't scare, they changed their tactics and began to ask him to carry messages to the Generalissimo. He was their only avenue to the ear of Chiang who refused to have anything to do with other approaches but would listen to Leighton. Leighton had brought back defiance from Chiang and had truthfully delivered it to the Japanese military. Somehow they admired his nerve and I gathered they were anxious to be on good terms with this American who steadfastly opposed them. But how Leighton got away with covering Michael Lindsay's teaching the guerillas how to dynamite Japanese troop trains, I do not know!

79. Ibid., pp. 60–61.
80. Ibid., 1940, p. 85.
81. Boring to Friends, 20 January 1941, "New Years Greetings," Special Collection Archives, Yale Divinity School.
82. Ibid.
83. Ibid.
84. Boynton was forced to give him the benefit of the doubt for she received a letter "from Mr. Evans in New York," that changed her "conviction when I left the campus [Yenching] that the president [Stuart] didn't want me to return." Evans reported that "JLS cabled him to approach the State Department to let me proceed to Yenching;" the Trustees took action approving her return. "Red Leather Notebook," 25 Jan. 1941, p. 19.
85. Ibid.
86. Ibid.
87. Boring to Friends, 20 Jan. 1941, "New Years Greetings."
88. A.M. Boring to Lydia T. Boring, 27 July 1941. Special Collection Archives, Yale Divinity School.
89. Before she realized that Boynton would not be returning. A.M. Boring to Family, 29 Aug. 1941, Special Collection Archives, Yale Divinity School.
90. Ibid.
91. A.M. Boring to Board of Trustees, 25 Sept. 1941, Special Collection Archives, Yale Divinity School.
92. Ibid.
93. Ibid.
94. Ibid.
95. Ibid.
96. A.M. Boring to Family, 2 Nov. 1941, Special Collection Archives, Yale Divinity School.
97. Ibid.
98. Ibid.

Chapter 6
Pearl Harbor and Internment

Boring continued to publish and work on new research amid the uncertainty, hardship, and unrest in the pre-Pearl Harbor years at Yenching. From a vast quantity of accumulated data, she and Clifford H. Pope planned a monumental collaboration on Chinese amphibians corresponding to Pope's *Reptiles of China*. Boring's contribution to Pope's reptile book had been small, but her research was to constitute the major portion of the proposed amphibian work.[1] Intervening world events dictated that a major monograph on the amphibians could not be published. Potential supporters were unwilling to pour money and supplies into collecting expeditions in a turbulent China, and publishers were less than enthusiastic about sinking large sums of money into a book on Chinese amphibia during these troubled times. Boring agreed that they should publish the results of their research in an abbreviated form in the *Peking Natural History Society Bulletin*. The resulting résumé of the species of frogs and salamanders of China based on their "study of the literature and of specimens preserved in certain museums of Europe, America, and China," proved a valuable addition to the taxonomic literature. The work was arranged hierarchically by taxa and included characteristics, distribution accounts, and keys for each group.[2]

Although amphibian taxonomy continued to dominate her research in the pre-Pearl Harbor years, Boring collaborated in a behavioral, anatomical and histological study of the Chinese toad and the pond frog; an anatomical study of the hammerhead shark; and a histological study of Bidder's organ in Chinese toads.

Boring's earlier work on the histology of the reproductive system prepared her to correlate behavior with histology and anatomy. Working with her student Ting Han Po, Boring studied the sexual rhythm of the toad, *Bufo bufo*, and the frog, *Rana nigromaculata*, compared the two, and investigated the relationship between testicular constituents and periods of sexual activity.[3]

Another non-taxonomic paper of the pre-Pearl Harbor period involved a description of the structures of the head of a hammerhead shark. Taking advantage of an available opportunity, Boring obtained the specimen from a Beijing fish market and, with student Cheng Tsai Ting, studied its anatomy. "Several specimens of this curious elasmobranch" opportunely had appeared in the market during the year, so Boring and Cheng "undertook to find out in what features its internal structures are modified to match this peculiarly extended head."[4]

Collaborating again with Ting, Boring studied the enigmatic "Bidder's Organ," an "ovary-like structure situated at the anterior end of each gonad in the toad." This organ, variously interpreted as important in the formation of testicular tissue, a rudimentary ovary, and a "rudimentary hybrid gland containing both ova and spermatozoa" had long puzzled biologists. Boring revised previous interpretations of this organ's function, incorporating her experience in embryology and histology.[5]

Boring published both individually and collaborated with others on additional taxonomic papers. These papers included a study of geographic variation, a list of specimens in the Fan Memorial Institute, and behavioral notes.[6]

During her internment, Boring continued to work on a bibliography of Chinese amphibians, both living and fossil forms. The work, written under the most difficult of circumstances, was not published until after the war (1945). Boring continued her research up until Pearl Harbor.

Ruth Beasley recalled a student perspective on those days.

> When I was attending Yenching as a student, Peiping had already fallen to the Japanese, and Japanese Imperial Army soldiers were everywhere. Every gathering of students or even faculty were [sic] personally monitored by a Japanese soldier or trusted Korean guard. The only gatherings not attended by a guard were those group activities which had to do with religious classes and Chinese literature classes.[7]

Beasley noted that science classes were especially suspect and "it bothered Miss Boring a good bit to have a Japanese soldier attending her classes, even though he sat in the back of the classroom." Since the science courses were conducted in English

> we did try a few tricks to find out if the guard knew what was going on, and we found to our delight that most of the men could not understand any English

nor any of the subject being taught, and we were able to be more relaxed in discussions.[8]

However the guard became suspicious and "reported to the Commandant that he thought we were plotting against the Japanese Conquerors and requested that an English speaking guard be posted there." The Japanese were not far wrong with their distrust, for "the Chemistry class was planning to build a bomb!" The intruder's presence put a great strain on Boring for she

> felt that she could not teach effectively under such pressure, and was very emphatic that we learn as much as we can while we had the chance. She did not think the Japanese would allow the college to be opened for much longer unless it was completely under their power and direction.[9]

She was right, as it turned out. The Japanese attack on Pearl Harbor, December 7, 1941, brought an abrupt end to the uneasy truce between the Japanese government and Yenching University. To Boring's family in Massachusetts, New York, and North Carolina, Pearl Harbor initiated a time of hovering around the radio, pouring over newspaper reports, conferring with government and mission officials, and meeting the mailman in hopes of discovering information about Alice's fate.

Boring recognized that the chances of her letters reaching their destination in the United States were minuscule, but still made the attempt. On January 12, 1942, more than a month "since the 'accident' [Pearl Harbor] as our Chinese friends call it," Boring wrote to her family that "no one has ventured to write to America, simply because we cannot figure any route by which letters can go." Since "there is no regulation against writing, . . . several of us this week-end are sending letters off into the blue, on the bare chance that they may sometime in the dim future reach you."[10] Although the letters written immediately after Pearl Harbor eventually reached their destination, the worried family had to rely on indirect sources for their information about Alice before her detailed commentaries arrived.[11]

Grace Boynton in the unoccupied South supplied some information, mostly rumors, about the Americans in the North. Although the reports indicated that all Yenching people were safe, they did not contain explicit information about Alice.[12] The suspense over Alice's fate lasted slightly over a month. On February 7, 1942, Edwin Boring received a telegram from Boynton, informing him that "Alice well."[13]

Before he heard from Alice herself, Garry worried about her "enforced inactivity." An inactive Alice seemed a fearful prospect, and coupled with the fact that she was "denied the counsel of Dr. Stuart," he was concerned about her well being.[14] His anxieties were partially relieved when the family received a form letter from Alice via the International Red Cross on May 28, 1942, indicating that she was active, comfortable, healthy, and living with a Yenching foreign faculty group. Food, money, conveniences, servants, books, and recreation were adequate. "Enjoy long hikes. Can visit Peking. Studying Amphibia. Thanks for Cable."[15]

When Boring's accounts eventually arrived in the United States, she supplied the details.

> When I was on my way to my office at 8:30 A.M. on Dec. 8, some one ran by me calling out that war had been declared, but I did not believe it—one more rumor—and was calmly teaching my freshmen at 9:40 when some one opened the door and announced that the campus was taken over by the Japanese military and students and faculty were to assemble in different places and await orders. Two weeks ago when I was allowed to get my books and papers out of my office I noticed that my outline was still on the blackboard of the lecture room![16]

In another letter she added that on Dec. 9 the university was closed, the students left the campus and the British and American faculty were moved to the South Compound where most foreign faculty members already were living.[17]

Boring and her colleagues were as insulated from the outside world as was the outside world from them. Fragments, rumors, and speculations were the source of information on global events for the Yenching detainees. Although the Yenching community did not realize it, immediately after Pearl Harbor, Chiang Kai Shek had proposed an alliance of Britain and the Commonwealth, the United States, the Soviet Union, the Netherlands, and China to protect the Pacific area from Japanese incursions. Unconvinced that events in China were central to the general war effort, Britain and the United States still declined full-scale involvement. After the failure of his proposed anti-Japanese alliance, Chiang looked to his own future. Fully expecting the eventual defeat of Japan, he concentrated on the group that he expected to be the greatest challenge to his future, the Chinese Communists.

General Joseph Stilwell, who eventually became Chief of Staff to Chiang Kai Shek and Commander of all U.S. forces in the China-Burma-India theater, harshly criticized the Chinese command for this attitude. Stilwell's demands for reform and his strong suggestions that Nationalists and Communists should unite against the Japanese met with strong resistance from Chiang. Stilwell's effectiveness in his effort to address the corruption in Chiang's ranks was hampered by the activities of his fellow

American, Chiang admirer Claire Lee Chennault. Charismatic Chennault's assertion that he could win the war for China by pitting the Chinese air force against the Japanese convinced President Franklin Delano Roosevelt to give him the opportunity to test his theories. As Chief of Staff of the Chinese Air Force, Chennault's tactics failed dismally, for the Japanese pilots outmaneuvered the American and Chinese pilots. Although Stilwell was recalled before Chennault, his position was later vindicated. In 1943, Chiang's excessive demands on the United States caused Secretary of the Treasury Henry Morgenthau to describe the Chinese as "a bunch of crooks."[18] The increasing disillusionment with Chiang resulted in the United States' conclusion that Japan must be defeated without a major campaign on the Chinese mainland.

Chiang's lack of total commitment to the Japanese war may have contributed to Japan's lackadaisical approach to her prisoners at Yenching, enabling Boring and her colleagues to exist very nicely. Boring explained that her new lodgings were quite adequate. She found her friends among the Chinese families already living in the compound, including "both Freddie and the Hungs, my best friends." Describing her new abode as satisfactory, she wrote that "House 53 is a very comfortable foreign house, three floors high. This is the first time that I have lived in a foreign house in China, and during the first few days I was out of breath and lame in the legs all the time from going up and down stairs."[19]

The six-bedroom house had a large living room and a dining room. Her house mates were "three single women, Miss Hancock (Mathematics), Miss Kramer (Home Economics) and myself." The three women shared the house with "two young American men teachers"; however, they ate "with a young crowd in another house." Strained relations sometimes occurred, for "it is not an easy task for three middle-aged single women of decided character, all of whom have been used to having their own homes and servants and managing them in their own way, to make a home together."[20]

During this stage "we have been treated very liberally." Although not allowed to enter the buildings, they had the freedom of the campus. All of the buildings except the Administration Building were sealed, but faculty members were allowed to enter their offices once in order to get books and materials for study. Faculty members had been paid their December salaries and understood that money for an additional month's salary was available. By pooling their money and food and by living economically, they had enough for several months. "A Swiss (neutral) office" was set up in Beijing "to attend to the needs of Britons and Americans, and we trust that this will arrange for further money for us in the future."[21]

Thirty foreigners inside the compound participated in this communal life; they were joined for part of their activities by twenty others who lived outside the compound. "We are all allowed to roam around within a radius of 6 kilometers, which allows for a good hike for exercise." Gradually, most of the detainees were given gate passes. Although they needed a different kind of pass in order to go into Beijing, "these can be had for any good reason."[22] Boring reported that she was to have "the thrill of going to Peking tomorrow for the first time." President Stuart's separation from the group saddened Boring. "I should love to see Leighton, but fear that this will not be possible, since he is a bit more restricted than we are, but very comfortable in a PUMC residence with several PUMC administrators."[23] Leighton Stuart's predicament concerned many people, but Boring and Boynton were among those most interested. On Easter Sunday, 1942, Boynton received a message that "JLS is locked up somewhere in Peking."[24] Boring had more detailed news and reported that JLS was "detained" with four others in a Chinese house with a "guard" of several soldiers "so that no one can enter or leave." Boring and others inside the compound were allowed to leave letters, and parcels "such as flowers, fruit and books" at the gate. The parcels were received promptly, "the letters eventually, sometimes taking ten days for the censor."[25] Boynton's information indicated that Stuart had been allowed to visit the Yenching campus with a Japanese escort to pick up some clothes.

Stuart's ability to make friends and to gain support from his "enemies" initially worked during his captivity. Boring was aware that "the young officer who was in charge of Leighton was caught in Stuart's spell and allowed the passage of short communications."[26] By sending letters to Stuart, Boring felt she was making his imprisonment more bearable, for she knew that he craved news of the outside world. After the friendly officer's superior suspected Stuart was receiving lax treatment, he cut off contacts with Boring and other internees.[27]

During April of 1942, the plans to develop Yenching in Free China developed. Stuart served as the model for the president of Yenching-in-exile, Y.P. Mei. Mei had learned his lessons from Stuart well. He "made an excellent impression; his personal charm and sense of humor captivated everyone."[28]

Yenching-in-exile provided Boynton with the opportunity to be a member of the "inner circle." After years of disappointment when "I have always longed to be at the heart of University affairs" and envious because "Alice has had so active a role," Boynton was finally "allowed a seat at Yenching's council tables." After years of assuming that her lack of acceptance by Stuart and Boring must have been "due to some grave lack in me of which I have been unconscious," she was now appreciated.[29]

Boring's information about the alternative Yenching as well as everything else was fragmentary. Freed from the day to day obligations of teaching and participating in University affairs, she had more time for study and research.

> We spend our mornings studying: I am writing a review of Pope's Reptiles for a paper published by the French Jesuit Fathers in Peking, and after that, I am working to get my Amphibian Bibliography in shape for those same Jesuits to publish.[30]

These jobs, she explained, would keep her busy for some months. Household tasks, meetings to "decide how little we can eat and still get all the calories and vitamins we need," hikes, singing, and reading for recreation occupied the remainder of the time. One household, she explained "has set up a Barber Shop and Beauty Parlor. I was given a marvelous shampoo, wave, facial massage, and etc. there this afternoon. Everybody says that I look ten years younger!"[31]

Although Boring and her colleagues constantly feared being removed from the Yenching property, "the blow did not fall until July 16 when we were told we must be out soon." Plans to move slowly were thwarted when "on Sunday, July 19, after a beautiful farewell church service, we were suddenly ordered to be all packed in the next two days and then wait for further orders." However, the situation was not as bad as it might have been for "fortunately we knew where we were going—into the beautiful Chinese houses left vacant by the American diplomats when they were repatriated."[32]

The Yenching faculty and staff lived rather luxuriously in their new quarters, Boring wrote.

> I never should have thought that I could be glad to leave the Yenching campus, but life had become a bit hectic and a bit uncertain—there was often trouble about being allowed through the campus gate and for two weeks we could get no busses to go to Peking—part of the campus is already occupied by soldiers, and the rest is to be used for a research institute in September—perhaps it is easier not to be there to watch all this change.[33]

Although repatriation was possible, Boring noted that the first American repatriation boat was filled with diplomats but very few civilians. Even if the opportunity to be repatriated surfaced, she preferred to stay, although those in authority "seem to think that it is better for most of us to go home and get refreshed and ready to return when we are needed again." Repatriation would be bittersweet without Stuart, and "I hate to come home if JLS is still here, since I have been able to do a lot for him with letters and various things to vary the monotony." She acknowledged, though, that her wish to stay might be ignored, for "the Japanese seem desirous to get rid of all of us...."[34] "Enjoy freedom of city," she wrote. "Amphibian bibliography progressing."[35]

With uninterrupted blocks of work time, this bibliography was growing rapidly. In her first letter of the New Year, to Boynton, Boring reported on the status of her manuscript.

> My paper on the Bibliography of Chinese Amphibia is already in press and I have has [sic] fifteen papers of galley proof, thanks to my friends the Jesuits. I am busy making maps for this paper. The maps can be made in Peking, while the printing is done in Shanghai. Of course we always used to print papers in Peking, but the Jesuits are fussy and consider that paper and type are better in Shanghai![36]

During the internment, visitors came at will. "Young and old they come, students and faculty, so the old bonds are cemented even tighter. I nearly embrace every old student whom I see! and pump him hard for news of others."[37]

Boring celebrated her sixtieth birthday while interned, asserting that "sixty does not feel any older than fifty did." After describing her birthday parties and gifts, she sent Grace Boynton and her brother a poem composed for the occasion.[38]

"We are not suffering" Boring assured her friends. Although for the time being, items such as soap and paper remained available, she speculated that "some day there is going to be a famine in both of those articles, unless we get repatriated soon."[39]

In addition to returning home, the possibility of concentration was a favorite topic of conversation among those interned. Boring reported that although "some people are betting 50 to 50 on repatriation against concentration," she considered repatriation more likely. Recognizing that anything could happen, she reported that "my partly packed trunks are still sitting on the porch outside of my room waiting for the next sudden announcement." This announcement did not come immediately. The trunks originally "were fully packed" and "ready to go on Sept. 1," but "I have had to unpack winter clothes to wear." Carefully, she made a list "of things to be stored in the Embassy, trunks for the hold, trunks for the baggage room and bags for the stateroom." This effort probably was futile, she declared, for "we hear that those on the British repatriation ship never got any of their baggage except what they took with them on the train...."[40]

After dipping into her packed trunks all winter to extract needed warm clothing and packed treasures, Boring ceased to be concerned about keeping everything intact for an impending trip home or for concentration camp. Relying on her instincts, she concluded that the Yenching group would be immune from concentration and would be repatriated. The half of the group that had predicted concentration rather than repatriation unfortunately prevailed. The actual proclamation to Boring and her group on Friday, March 12, 1943, stated that they would be taken by train to a "Civilian Assembly Center" near Weihsien, a city in Shandong Province. The announcement was not a complete shock, for other Yenching teachers had previously received the message.[41] Langdon Gilkey and five other bachelor teachers from Yenching had been notified in February that they would be interned at the camp. Although both Boring and Gilkey had ample time to prepare for the future, neither knew exactly what to prepare for.

Gilkey's group received a letter describing a future where "every comfort of Western culture will be yours."[42] They were allowed to send ahead "a bed or cot and one trunk apiece," whereas Boring's luggage allowance, shipped on March 18, was more liberal. She and her housemates could each send a "crate of bed and bedding and two steamer trunks." In both cases the allowances seemed reasonable for the distant future. The prospects for the immediate future were more disconcerting, for prisoners were allowed to take with them only what they could carry.[43]

Because the Yenching teachers were allowed sufficient time to consider the kinds of items they might want in an internment camp, several possibilities beyond the practical necessities occurred to each person. Since scholar Gilkey pictured endless monotony, he "rounded up copies of Aristotle, Spinoza, and Kant" to fill his days. Others accepted the promise of paradise indicated in the letter from the Japanese government and brought such nonessentials as golf clubs. Although those practical persons who suggested bringing blankets, towels, basic camping and household equipment, and medicine proved wise, others who insisted on bringing books and musical equipment helped keep morale from plummeting.[44]

Before they actually left the Beijing area, Boring's group under the Vice-Consul of Tsing Tao, "not under the military," organized itself into special interest societies, each bringing the appropriate equipment for its concerns. They formed an athletic group, a music group, and a gardening group.[45] Members of the music group collected "victrolas," records, musical instruments, and "lots of choral music...." As Gilkey and his associates had anticipated, music later became an essential way to while away long evenings.[46] Boring repacked her trunks and awaited the actual move.

On March 25, a polyglot collection of Americans assembled in the former United States Embassy compound to await relocation. Boring recognized many of the people. She clustered with the Yenching faculty members, including graduate students, young instructors, and older professors like herself. Reconnoitering, she also recognized doctors from the Peking Union Medical College, businessmen, and missionary families. The missionary families, in particular, exhibited wide age ranges. Six-month-old infants wailing in their mothers' arms, bewildered eighty-five-year-old men and women, and people of all ages, sizes, and shapes in between anxiously anticipated their futures.[47] Boring reported that "everyone is taking the situation in good spirit, and feeling that at last we shall be taking a share in the fortunes of war, as so far we have suffered nothing...."[48] The Yenching constituency had never encountered some of the approximately four hundred people assembled. A "wan, paper-thin ghost of a man, with dirty, torn clothes, scraggly beard and sea-green complexion," a "captive of a dope addiction," contrasted vividly with a cluster of wealthy older widows resplendent in furs and hats who gathered near the steps of the Embassy. Roman Catholic priests, monks, and nuns captured in Siberia gathered close to the former residence of the American Ambassador to complete the variety of civilians awaiting concentration.[49]

As the people stood, sat, or lay around waiting for orders, Boring, although slightly apprehensive, exhibited her propensity to thrive on change. She found it "interesting to see how a whole community can face a crisis like this." As she talked with people and collected their views, she concluded

> that we are determined not to be downed, and most of us are looking forward to it with real anticipation for an entirely new kind of experience in community living. There are a few pessimists who are moping, and of course we know that life will not be easy, but this will give us a concrete project to work on instead of drifting as we have been doing for some months.[50]

Although the Japanese had stated clearly that each person could bring to concentration only what he or she could carry, the collected group could not believe that their captors really meant what they said. Everything seemed necessary! Surrounded by a miscellany of "bags, duffles, coats, potties, and camp chairs,..." the crowd was horrified when a Japanese officer barked orders over the megaphone that each person must carry his or her belongings the mile to the railroad station." The procession from the Embassy to the railroad station, punctuated by "dragging and resting, of dragging some more and resting again," was viewed by the not-always-sympathetic Chinese. Even though the Japanese were supposedly the enemy, the Chinese recalled with bitterness the humiliation that they had suffered for years from the westerners. Therefore, many found it satisfying to witness the spectacle of westerners looking ridiculous, dragging their possessions through the street.[51]

After an hour, the weary marchers arrived at the railroad station only to be told that they must remain on the platform and have no contact with the Chinese until the train arrived. Since they had planned to buy food and drinks from the Chinese, this news was most unwelcome. They were dependent for food and water on what they carried with them. Eventually, the train arrived and they were herded aboard.

Infected by uncertainty, packed into the straight wooden seats characteristic of third-class Chinese rail transport, Boring speculated with her fellow passengers about the future. After spending a cold, dirty, hungry, thirsty, and sleepless night, the passengers pulled into the Weihsien City station. Although Boring would not have admitted it, she had become very accustomed to being waited on by the Chinese. Thus, when their captors announced that Chinese would not be allowed within the camp, she, as well as her companions, felt some dismay. They would be responsible for providing their own heat, food, clean clothes and water—a prospect that was somewhat disconcerting since the facilities were bound to be primitive. They were jammed on army trucks that bounced the three miles to the compound and were greeted by dirty, curious Europeans who had preceded them to the camp.

Their new home, a dank, grey compound which previously had housed a well-equipped American Presbyterian mission station, was a shambles, dismembered by many garrisons of Japanese and Chinese soldiers. The stench from the already overflowing toilets assaulted the new arrivals' sensibilities. The precious running water that was available in the camps dribbled out of the faucets, making it difficult to wash the trip grime from their hands and faces. After the long train ride without food, a forty-minute queue for dinner greeted Boring. Though the soup was thin and tasteless, the bread was filling, and both were welcome after the long ride without food.[52] The first nights were especially miserable. Since the cots, bedding, and warm clothing had not yet arrived, they slept fully clothed on the straw mats provided by their captors and shivered through the March rains.

Boring's faith in the ability of the group to form a community was justified. Many skills were available among the almost two thousand people who finally were gathered at the compound. The dreaded public health crisis did not develop, as the few doctors and nurses conscientiously organized the hospital and ordered and distributed the medicine. There were volunteers among the Catholic priests, monks, and nuns and a few of the Protestant missionaries to undertake the odorous task of cleaning up the latrines. Donning borrowed boots, with their faces swathed in cloths, they scooped and mopped until the task was completed.

Unfortunately, time blunted the cooperative spirit. As supplies became more scarce, overcrowding more severe, and chances for relief more remote, squabbling, stealing, and bullying increased. However, during the time Boring remained at the camp the worst abuses had not begun to occur.

Single women like Boring were housed dormitory style in the class-rooms and offices of the school buildings. As determined as she was to make the best of the experience of cooperative living, still it was very difficult for a sixty-year-old woman to be thrust into a large room with strangers. Privacy was non-existent and extreme tact had to be exercised in resolving disputes.

In spite of the conflicts and the heterogeneity of the group, Boring adjusted as well as possible. Her family at home relied on second-hand reports for news. Boynton wrote Edwin Boring that her chief worry was "the general food shortage in North China...."[53] Food rations were decreased drastically, and, although they were adequate to prevent starvation, everyone was always hungry. Boynton's hope that "our people may be repatriated from Weihsien" was soon realized in Alice's case.[54] After she was in the camp for six months, news came to her family in the form of a report of repatriation. On July 22, 1943, Aline Walsh of the Red Cross, relayed information to Edwin Boring concerning "continued rumors about the ship which may bring home interned civilians in the Pacific area...." She stressed that "thus far they are only rumors...." She did not want to raise hopes because "the ship has been loaded three times and ready to sail, but each time plans fell through because of lack of Japanese cooperation and the ship had to be unloaded." Once more, "a cargo is again being put on and we have hope."[55]

On August 24, 1943, a State Department list of the Yenching staff definitely scheduled for repatriation on the neutral Swedish liner, the M.S. Gripsholm, appeared, including "Boring, Miss Alice M."[56] The exchange of American and Japanese nationals was set for October 15, 1943, at Mormugao, in Portuguese India. The actual exchange occurred in Goa on October 19. On October 22, Boynton reported that she had received a letter from Charles Corbett listing Alice Boring and Margaret

Speer as among those to be repatriated but including "neither Leighton nor Lucius."[57] Those to be repatriated were on the ship Teia Maru where the conditions were "crowded and dirty" and with "insufficient food." Drinking water was available only twice a day. They "stopped at Hongkong, the Philipines [sic], Saigon, Singapore, and finally tied up at a pier in Goa, to wait for their white ship of deliverance." The Gripsholm arrived, was tied end to end with the Teia Maru, and the exchange made. The repatriates were given a joyous welcome aboard the Gripsholm. The people, however, "were warned against putting too much into famished stomachs at first." Boring reported that "she felt full for the first time in two years!" She felt unable to celebrate her own good fortune, however, because Stuart had been left behind. She explained that "Washington and Tokio [sic] arranged Leighton's repatriation," but "the Peking military prevented it, and he is in despair. He thinks his government has forgotten him."[58]

In a letter written while on the Gripsholm, Alice explained that "we have been marvelously well." In spite of what people assume, "we shall not look like physical wrecks when you see us in New York, even if our clothes may be rather dilapidated." Even this shabbiness might not occur, she speculated, for "the Red Cross has given us some things and there is a dress shop on board."[59]

Boring's prediction of a prosperous returning group was supported by a newspaper article describing the return.

> Sun-tanned, healthy and ecstatically happy, but exceedingly reticent about many of their experiences, more than 1,000 of the 1,440 passengers—1,222 Americans and 217 Canadians—aboard the diplomatic exchange liner Gripsholm debarked yesterday after the 18,353-ton Swedish ship docked at Pier F, Jersey City.[60]

Stuart's position during the final days of the war was related to the policies of the Chiang faction. Even if the Japanese had been willing to exchange Stuart, Communist Chinese groups feared his influence in peace negotiations because of his "connections with Chiang Kai-shek." The actual conditions of his imprisonment were tolerable. Boynton reported that his "Japanese-guard-interpreter has come to admire him and treats him well. He reads Leighton's autobiography and wants a copy [of his book] for himself."[61] During part of his long, shared (with Acting Director Dr. Henry Houghton and others from PUMC) captivity, Stuart was well treated, but at other times conditions were unacceptable. The first month after their arrest, they were housed in the American Embassy guard barracks with eleven other Americans and six to eight Britishers. It was during this early part of the captivity that Boring and others were able to smuggle letters and other articles to the prisoners. The Americans in the group were then moved to Tientsin and, after a short time, to the Ying compound. While they were at the compound, occasional visitors were allowed, including birthday party guests for Dr. Houghton. However, as the war progressed, Stuart and the three principal executives of PUMC (as well as Dr. Snapper's wife) were moved to the small, dank, dark back quarters of an insurance company, with unsatisfactory bathing facilities. The food was insufficient and its quality poor. Although PUMC was not looted and other American employees were allowed to move freely in Beijing, the three PUMC administrators and Stuart were singled out as examples. To the Japanese, the PUMC powers represented American cultural imperialism and Stuart, who had acted as an intermediary between the Japanese and Chinese, was a traitor.[62] Although many attempts at prisoner exchange had been made, Stuart's outspoken support for Chiang thwarted all attempts.

By this time, though, even their former supporters had begun to question the Chiangs' position. Boynton gossiped about them, noting "that it is now common knowledge that the Generalissimo and his wife are not living together, and that he has re-established relations with a former wife." Stuart's pragmatic attitude toward the Chiangs represented a change from his original "notion of the Chiangs as outstanding Christians." Boynton realized that it was Stuart's policy "to push the popular estimate of the Chiangs regardless of what he must have known of qualifying aspects." Boynton was sad when she realized "that as the world wags, the cynical view of both the Chiangs and of JLS had much justification."[63]

No matter how skeptical U.S. government officials were about Chiang, they were obliged to support him during the months after Pearl Harbor. For its part, Japan could no longer continue its former *laissez-faire* attitude in dealing with Yenching officials and teachers. The result of this change in stance on both sides was concentration for Boring and imprisonment for Stuart. Although Boring's time of hardship was limited, her optimism never wavered. Food deprivation, filth, and cold never seemed to daunt her. Her letters were invariably optimistic. It was almost as if she saw her internment as another adventure. Her only real regret was her concern over Stuart.

Notes

1. Pope noted Boring's contributions to his book in the acknowledgments. Clifford H. Pope, *The Reptiles of China Turtles, Crocodilians, Snakes, Liz-*

ards. In *Natural History of Central Asia*, Vol. 10, Central Asiatic Expeditions, Roy Chapman Andrews, Leader (New York: The American Museum of Natural History, 1935), vi.

2. Pope and Alice M. Boring, "A Survey of Chinese Amphibia," *Peking Natural History Society Bulletin*, 15 (Sept. 1940), 13. Boring's contribution to the collaboration included the study of the specimens and field notes of C.C. Liu "around Peking, Moukden, in Shangtung and now in Szechwan and Sikang;" those of T.K. Chang in Kiangsu, Anhwei, Chekiang, Kiangsi and Kwangsi; "by Herklots on Hongkong; by Pere Licent in Manchuria, Chahar, Suiyuan, Ningsia, Kansu, Shensi, Shansi, Hopeh and Shangtung; by the Fam Memorial staff in Kwangsi, Kweichow, Yunnan and Szechwan; and by various students at several places in Shansi, Shantung, Kiangsu, Hupeh and Kwangtung." Pope's own field studies in Kwangtung, Fukien, Hunan, Anhwei, Shantung, Hopeh, Suiyuan and Shansi plus his examination of Chinese specimens in European and American museums constituted his contributions. Pope's trip to Europe was financed by the expedition funds of Director of the American Museum of Natural History, Roy Chapman Andrews. Accounts of the expeditions may be found in *Asia* magazine.

3. Han Po Ting and Boring, "The Seasonal Cycle in the Reproductive Organs of the Chinese Toads *Bufo bufo* and the Pond Frog *Rana Nigromaculata*," *Peking Natural History Bulletin* 14 (Part 1, 1939–1940), pp. 49–80.

4. Tsai Tung Chen and Boring, "The Anatomy of the Hammerhead Shark, *Sphyrna Zygena*," *Peking Natural History Bulletin* 14 (Part 2, 1939–1940), pp. 99–102.

5. Han Po Ting and Boring, "A Study of Bidder's Organ in Chinese Toads," *Peking Natural History Bulletin* 13 (Part 3, 1938–39), pp. 147–60.

6. Boring, "Studies in Variation among Chinese Amphibia. II. Variation in Five Wide-Ranging Common Salientia," *Peking Natural History Bulletin* 13 (Part 2, 1938–1939), pp. 89–110; T.L. Tchang and Boring, "List of Amphibians in the Fan Memorial Institute," *Peking Natural History Bulletin* 14 (Part 4, 1939–1940), pp. 285–90; Tso Kan Chang and Boring, "Notes on Kwangsi Amphibia," *Peking Natural History Bulletin* 14 (Part 1, 1939–1940), pp. 43–47.

7. Ruth Hung Beasley to Marilyn Bailey Ogilvie, 18 February 1988.

8. Ibid.

9. Ibid.

10. Alice M. Boring to Family, 12 January 1941, Special Collection Archives, Yale Divinity School.

11. The letter of 12 January 1942 reached her family on 11 February 1943.

12. Grace M. Boynton to Edwin G. Boring and Lucy Boring, 16 January 1942, Special Collection Archives, Yale Divinity School.

13. Boynton to E.G. Boring, telegram 7 Feb. 1942, Special Collection Archives, Yale Divinity School.

14. E.G. Boring to Boynton, 26 March 1942, Pusey Archive Collection, Harvard University, Boring Family Correspondence.
15. A.M. Boring to Family, Red Cross Cable, 28 May 1942, Special Collection Archives, Yale Divinity School.
16. A.M. Boring to Family, 4 Aug. 1942, Special Collection Archives, Yale Divinity School.
17. A.M. Boring to Family, 12 Jan. 1942.
18. Jonathan Spence, *To Change China: Western Advisers in China 1620–1960* (Harmondsworth, Middlesex, England: Penguin, 1969), p. 238.
19. A.M. Boring to Family, 12 Jan. 1942.
20. Ibid.
21. Ibid.
22. Ibid.
23. Ibid.
24. Boynton, "Red Leather Notebook," 1942, p. 38, Radcliffe.
24. A.M. Boring to Family, 4 Aug. 1942.
26. Boynton, "Red Leather Notebook," 1942, p. 38.
27. Ibid. Boynton reported on Boring's actions.
28. Ibid., pp. 45–46.
29. Ibid., p. 47.
30. A.M. Boring to Family, 12 Jan. 1942.
31. Ibid.
32. A.M. Boring to Family, 4 Aug. 1942.
33. Ibid.
34. Ibid.
35. A.M. Boring to Family, International Red Cross Message, 3 Nov. 1942, Special Collection Archives, Yale Divinity School.
36. A.M. Boring to Boynton, 1 Jan. 1943, Special Collection Archives, Yale Divinity School.
37. Ibid.
38. A.M. Boring to Boynton and E.G. Boring, 28 Feb. 1943, Special Collection Archives, Yale Divinity School.

In San Kuan Miao there lives a dame
Who's full of vim and vigor
Alice Boring is her name,
Trim and upright is her figger.

She used to live in solitude
In a lotus-land-ish garden,
(Jane Newell called it jungle

A slip we'll never pardon.)

But she has had to leave her lake
Once the home of royalty,

And move to a mere legation
Now a slum for the refugee
No more is she a tenant

Of a royal Manchu Prince;
Her neighbors now are poor while
Their manners make you wince

There are dogs upon her doorstep,
There is revelry by night,
And the Stanley baby's didies

Will soon blot the sun from sight
How does she take this downfall?
Does she whimper, fret, or snort?

She acts as if she really likes it,
Like a real and royal SPORT!

> She's trim and she's nifty
> This lady of sixty
> She's no more than forty today;

And when she is eighty,
She'll be more like sixty,
And so it will go on for aye!

39. Ibid.
40. A.M. Boring to Boynton and E.G. Boring, 28 Feb. 1943.
41. Grace M. Boynton to Edwin G. Boring, 14 May 1943, Special Collection Archives, Yale Divinity School.
42. Langdon Gilkey, *Shantung Compound: The Story of Men and Women under Pressure* (New York: Harper & Row, 1966), p. 1.
43. Ibid.
44. Gilkey, *Shantung Compound*, p. 2.
45. Boynton to E.G. Boring, 14 May 1943.
46. Ibid.
47. Gilkey, *Shantung Compound*, p. 2.
48. Boynton to E.G. Boring, 14 May 1943.
49. Gilkey, *Shantung Compound*, p. 3. In his account, Gilkey describes many people, experiences, and reactions.
50. Boynton to E.G. Boring, 14 May 1943.
51. Gilkey, *Shantung Compound*, p. 4.
52. Ibid., pp. 10–11.
53. Boynton to E.G. Boring, 14 May 1943.
54. Ibid.
55. Aline B. Walsh, American Red Cross, to Boring, 22 July 1943, Pusey Archive Collection, Harvard University, Boring Family Correspondence.

56. List of those to be repatriated and returning on the M.S. Gripsholm, 24 Aug. 1943. Dwight W. Edwards, *Yenching University* (New York: United Board for Christian Higher Education in Asia, 1959), p. 451.

57. Boynton, "Red Leather Notebook," 1943, p. 68, Archives, Schlesinger Library, Radcliffe College, Cambridge, MA.

58. Ibid., p. 73; For further information see *Prisoner of War Bulletin*, 1 Oct. 1943, American Red Cross National Headquarters, Washington, D.C., 20006.

59. Alice M. Boring to Charles H. Corbett, 9 Nov. 1943, Special Collection Archives, Yale Divinity School.

60. *New York Times*, 1, 3, 5 Dec. 1943. See also *Prisoners of War Bulletin*, 1 Oct. 1943, American Red Cross National Headquarters, Washington, D.C. 20006; The Red Cross Courier, 23 Oct. 1943; 23 Nov. 1943; 23 Dec. 1943.

61. Boynton, "Red Leather Notebook," 1944, p. 50.

62. "Notes on Report Brought by Mr. McConaughy of American Embassy Staff in Peking Concerning PUMC and Conditions in Peking," 27 Aug. 1942, Rockefeller Archive Center, CMB, Inc., Box 72, Folder 509.

63. Boynton, "Red Leather Notebook," 1944, p. 51.

Chapter 7
The Return

The United States to which Boring returned seemed more foreign than the China she had left. Some of the strangeness was pleasant. It was a great relief to have enough food to eat and clothes to wear and to be able to indulge in an occasional extravagance such as a visit to the beauty parlor. At Yenching, she had cherished these periodic visits. At Weihsien, she had been lucky to have enough water available to splash over her head and enough soap purchased with U.S. "comfort money" to scrub away the dirt and dust of the compound. With coal at a premium, wet hair in the cold Chinese winter was so unpleasant that Alice and the other internees washed their hair only when absolutely necessary. Ready access to a beauty parlor and a warm, well-heated house were appreciated luxuries.

Other aspects of "home" were less attractive. Initially, friends and relatives were eager to learn of her experiences. But they wanted to be told once and then move on to subjects closer to home—the education of their children, the sales at the local grocery store, and bridge-table gossip. To Alice, their concerns seemed petty and inconsequential. To them, her conversation was strange and irrelevant. In many ways it was easier for Alice to endure the hardships of internment than it was to fit into a complacent America. She soon gravitated toward those Americans who had shared some of her experiences in China and avoided those people who had not.

Garry recognized that homecoming would present problems to his sister. He pondered whether

America's prosperity, selfishness and relative remoteness from the War and suffering is depressing thee. I should think it might.... Idealism is the capacity to substitute symbols for reality and act on them, and most people do not have a great deal of it. It has been the last step in evolution and has not got very far yet."[1]

When she first returned home, Alice moved to Lydia's home in Upstate New York. While living with Lydia, she explored teaching possibilities. Garry suggested a medical school, one of a few places still having large numbers of men students (whom Alice preferred) during wartime.[2]

Garry's advice to Alice came through letters, for she did not visit him and his family until Christmas. At this time, he suggested, she could explore job opportunities in the Cambridge area. This visit would be Garry's first chance "to get all the inside information about what has been happening to thee."[3]

Although Garry looked forward to the Christmas visit, he did not know what to expect of Alice, for "the difficult situation in which the Japs had landed" her might have profoundly affected her personality. He was relieved to be greeted by "thy old self," full of the usual "enthusiasm and verve...." In spite of finding Alice well, he recognized her difficulty in reintegrating into American society. Sympathizing with her inability to find compatible friends, he hoped a suitable job would resolve the situation. The job opportunity came more quickly than either of them expected. Alice's Christmas visit to Cambridge ended abruptly when a job appeared unexpectedly at Columbia University's College of Physicians and Surgeons.

Even though the shortened visit seemed "a little sad" to Garry, for "we had planned to see more of thee and to have thee see other people around here who wanted to see thee," he recognized Alice's good fortune in obtaining the job. The position as instructor in histology with a research assistantship in the College of Physicians and Surgeons was precisely the kind of position that he had envisioned for his sister.[4] The job, however, seemed more ideal to Garry than to Alice. To her, it reinforced the wisdom of her decision to observe amphibians in their natural habitat and to record information about museum specimens rather than peer through microscopes all day. After only two months in her new post, she recognized her own restlessness and predicted that she would "go crazy" if she had to "sit still and look through a microscope all the time."[5]

Since the job at Columbia was temporary, she looked for a replacement position. When offered "a routine Histology research job for $4000.00 at U. of Rochester," she turned it down, confessing guiltily that she would hate a pure research job because it was not active enough and would not allow her the personal contacts that she found so important. Going to work at Yenching had, for the most part, been a pleasure; at Columbia it was drudgery. At Rochester, it would have been intolerable. When a more congenial opportunity did not appear, "after all my bold declarations against getting tied down to a research job," she asked Dr. Aura Severinghaus to try to extend her appointment at Columbia for another year. The thought of leaving New York, where she had contact with people from China and could easily visit her family and old friends, was unappealing.[6] Meanwhile, in New York, she watched Chinese politics and the American China policy carefully, hoping to return at the first opportunity.

Some of the actions of Chiang Kai Shek's Nationalist government became increasingly suspect. With an eye to the inevitable power struggle after the war, some of Chiang's more outspoken ministers reinterpreted Sun Yat Sen's Three Principles, nationalism, democracy, and livelihood, into suppression, autocracy, and favoritism. When Chen Li Fu, China's Minister of Education, decreed that bureaus would be established in foreign countries to "guide and control thought and conduct" of Chinese students studying abroad, the British and American Nationals were predictably indignant. The regulations were broadened to include professors and instructors working abroad, further incensing the British and Americans.[7]

Harvard philosopher, Ralph Barton Perry, leader of Harvard's American Defense Faculty Group, alarmed by the similarity between the new rules and the Japanese system of thought control, asked the State Department to investigate. Harvard students and faculty members joined in the protest, reassuring the Chinese students in the United States that this country recognized the injustice. Edwin Boring was one of the sponsors of the American Defense Harvard Protest group, and Alice wrote him that she "glowed with pride to think that thee was one of the original sponsors of that group."[8] Alice found from her conversations with the New York Chinese that they were troubled by the Minister of Education's pronouncements, and were gratified by the Harvard protests.[9] The extent of the reaction in this country surprised the Nationalist government. Backpedalling furiously, Guomintang spokesman P.H. Chang claimed the controversy was a misunderstanding, based on a poor translation.[10]

The problem went much deeper than a poor translation, claimed Sun Yat Sen's son, Dr. Sun Fo. Sun Fo accused the Guomintang of dictatorial methods, suppressing elections, and misusing his father's ideas. If such tactics were not abandoned, Sun warned, the United States and Britain would cease to support the Nationalist government and, instead, support their rivals, the Communists.[11]

Boring blamed the errant ministers, rather than Chiang. She claimed that the very fact that Sun Fo could make a speech critical of the government, supported her interpretation. Two extremely conservative brothers, Chen Li Fu and Chen Kuo Fu, Ministers of Education and War respectively, were largely responsible for turning Chinese youth against the

Nationalist government and toward the Communists. Although she exculpated Chiang, she admitted that he could not control these two men, but deferred to their wishes in order to avoid an upset in the middle of the war. Recalling Stuart's support of Chiang, she found it inconceivable that anyone could think that Chiang himself was undemocratic; "what China is fighting for is real freedom."[12] However, she admitted that the storm produced by the Harvard protest encouraged Chen Li Fu to claim that he had not meant "thought control."

Boring downplayed the opinions of those who were convinced that corruption and graft swallowed the good in the Chiang government. Such views served no positive purpose and led to misunderstanding. She cringed when she thought of "hothead" anti-Chiang Agnes Smedley indoctrinating the uninformed at the Columbia Women's Faculty Club with "anti-Chiang propaganda." Unfortunately, because of her class and research schedule, Boring was unable to attend the luncheon and speech. "I was sorry," she wrote Garry, "as we China-hands were afraid she would give a one-sided picture so vividly that many would swallow it whole."[13] In her general support of Chiang and the Nationalists, Boring admitted that "there is graft and there is strict censorship and very little democracy as yet."[14]

Fretting about conditions in China, teaching classes, and working on assigned research did not take up all of Boring's time. She also considered items of long neglected personal and family business, such as revising her will and visiting friends and family in different cities.[15]

Even though she loved her family, had learned to tolerate her job, and enjoyed American conveniences, hardly a day passed during which Boring did not think about returning to China. The obvious place to go was Yenching in exile at Chengtu. After vacillating back and forth between deciding to go and deciding to stay, she made plans to go to Chengtu. She collected information on the proper clothes to bring, passed the necessary medical examination, and was to the point of packing when she was "held up by the passport section of the Department of State because she was a woman."[16] However, women nurses were flying back and forth daily. Flying over the hump in old C-47s was a dangerous undertaking for anybody. It involved bouncing all over the sky, being air sick, sitting on a bucket at 25–30,000 feet, and breathing oxygen. At any rate, Boring's application was denied. She was very disappointed, because she had begun to think that returning to China, even if it were to Free China in the South rather than to Yenching, would be a reality. It proved fortunate that Dr. Severinghaus was able to get her appointment at Columbia extended.

Boring's appointment at the College of Physicians and Surgeons ended in June, 1945, and she took another temporary position, this time as Visiting Professor in Zoology at Mt. Holyoke College. Joining an all-female staff in the zoology department of three professors, one associate professor, one assistant professor, and three instructors, Boring taught invertebrate zoology and parasitology, a course which she had not taught at Yenching.[17] Although she was pleased to be able to look away from her microscope, the students at Mt. Holyoke seemed frivolous after those at Yenching.

While at Mount Holyoke, Boring maintained membership in numerous scientific societies, including the American Association for the Advancement of Science, the American Society of Zoologists, the American Society of Naturalists, the Society of Ichthyologists and Herpetologists, and the Peking Natural History Society.[18] Knowing that the position was temporary, she became involved with the college only superficially, teaching her classes, but not developing a commitment to the institution. The Japanese war was over and negotiations were occurring that would allow her return to Yenching.

The success of the Occupation would determine the time and conditions of Boring's return. Garry wrote Alice that in his opinion the Japanese occupation was going well, and, even though he disliked "MacArthur's egoism as a leader in a democratic army, especially as compared with Eisenhower and Marshall,... as a tough overlord for an emperor I am getting really to like him." Jokingly, he suggested that the latest contribution "to the peace effort from 21 Bowdoin is the suggestion that Leighton be made Emperor of Japan. He seems to have all the necessary attributes, so why not?" Garry, however, was more sympathetic to the occupation policy than were some other members of the family. Lydia and "Aunt Mollie," feared that the United States was "being too kind to Hirohito.[19]

By November 1945, the civil war in China became more serious, and Garry was concerned about the effect of this renewed tension on Alice's return. Some of the former teachers, including Grace Boynton, had become increasingly disillusioned with the Chiangs, and even seemed to hope "the Communists would get hold of Peking and keep Chiang out." However, Garry questioned whether the State Department might refuse to allow Americans "into a region where they might need to be protected."[20] During Leighton Stuart's visit to New York in December 1945, it became clear that westerners were returning to China, and that he wanted Alice to be among them.[21]

During what proved to be Alice's last Christmas in the United States before returning to China, she and Lydia went to visit Garry and his family in Cambridge. After the holidays, she spent all of her free time preparing to return to Yenching. She first attacked medical and financial concerns. By acquiring a special "belt" she hoped to minimize the back problems that had long annoyed her. Finally, she completed the new will and had it witnessed. By June 2, 1946, she still did not have her passport or passage, "but the office advises to pack and be ready to be alerted at any time." Confident that the details would be worked out, she wrote Garry that her trunks were in her room, and she planned to "begin tomorrow to fit spices and stockings and casseroles together!"[22]

Her optimism justified, about one year after V-J Day Boring arrived at a war-torn Yenching to begin the fall semester of 1946. Even though she was intellectually prepared for the alterations in Yenching's appearance, the reality was painful. The formerly tidy landscape was unkempt, the fine porcelain and carved redwood furniture from the Chinese faculty houses had been sold to buy food, and even the white bathtubs had been replaced by wooden "Tokyo style" tubs. The impact of inflation, the scarcity of coal, and temporary living quarters contributed to the bleakness of the homecoming. Although she hoped eventually to return to her old home in the Prince's Garden, the interim living arrangement with six single American women was not entirely satisfactory.[23]

Although Grace Boynton also returned to Yenching, she did not arrive until after Boring was settled. Knowing that Boring had preceded her and that they would be living together again, Boynton apprehensively recalled their former experience as housemates. The first words Boynton heard after landing, "Alice is here," were not altogether welcome. The old anxieties welled up again, the weather was "iron cold," and the dark hills appeared forbidding—hardly a propitious beginning for Boynton. She and the other returnees were piled into trucks and hustled to the campus. Once they arrived, the world appeared brighter. Boynton was ushered into a warm living room "furnished with Alice's things" and met "familiar people doing familiar things such as correcting English Entrance Examinations." Even the old conflict with Alice was muted. Alice seemed glad for Grace's companionship. Boynton vowed to make a conscious effort not to be a "nuisance," recognizing that the severe winter, fuel shortages, and high prices would result in uncomfortably low temperatures and other conditions that might try tempers.[24]

By the time Boynton arrived, Boring had already taken inventory of supplies and equipment available to teach biology. Microscopes, of course, were essential, and all of Yenching's were missing. Although they had ordered new ones from the United States, their arrival was delayed. "Nothing has arrived from America," she complained to Mary Ferguson of the Rockefeller Foundation. Even the microscopes that Spencer Lens promised would leave the United States in June (1946) had not been shipped by October. In the interim, they borrowed microscopes from PUMC which were not very satisfactory, because "the Japs were hard on them;...they are minus some of the lenses and not all parfocal...." Nevertheless, Boring hastened to add, "we do not look a gift horse in the mouth and are most grateful for the use of them."[25]

Much of Yenching's equipment had been rescued by a Japanese biologist who understood its value. After V-J Day, a surprising amount of glassware, demonstration specimens, and microscope slides were returned. This equipment made it possible for Boring to "give decent courses in Embryology and Histology and Comparative Anatomy," a possibility that she had not dreamed of when she left the United States.[26]

Although Boring found it difficult to maintain the characteristic optimism of her pre-war experience in China, she recognized that Yenching had made "a marvelous comeback." On the one hand, she proclaimed that post-war teaching was "practically up to pre-war standards," while on the other, she admitted that it was difficult to maintain standards in the face of lowered English competency and make-shift equipment.[27]

Through heroic efforts, Boring and the other teachers could minimize the consequences of inferior equipment and poor student preparation. They had, however, little control over the powerful political presences pawing over converts and territory. The festering conflict between the Communists and Nationalists infiltrated Yenching as well as other Chinese institutions. A willingness to compromise eluded both parties. The idealism of the Communists that originally had appealed to many Chinese faculty members became tainted by their pursuit of power, disillusioning many of their former supporters. The graft-ridden Guomintang was incapable of inspiring nationalism in those who genuinely sought a unified China. Whereas Boring admitted the failings of the Guomintang regime, in 1947, she favored it over the Communist alternative, claiming that there was "not so much gestapo business as is generally supposed in America"[28]

As Boring pondered the alternatives, she concluded that an apolitical stance was her most productive path. Apparently others agreed, for Boring reported that on the Yenching campus, "we go ahead with our work as though no civil war were going on almost at our very gates." In spite of the uncertainty, "the morale here is wonderful." Even though "expenses are high and salaries are low, ... " the faculty "all feel that on this campus there is a freedom, and a friendliness, and a fairness to all that makes them rather stay here than go where they might receive more salary."[29]

Nevertheless, it was clear to all involved that some kind of a political solution must be reached. General Wedemeyer recognized that a stable China was possible only if Chiang Kai Shek negotiated an acceptable accommodation with the Communists. In agreement with Wedemeyer's assessment, President Truman sent General George Marshall to China to attempt to hammer out such an accord. In spite of massive infusions of money into the country from the United States, inflation spiralled, peasants became increasingly discontented, and the Nationalist army became bloated and complacent. Marshall and his delegation were unable to convince Chiang that a military solution to the problem was unfeasible.

Taken altogether, the problems of post-war China seemed insurmountable. However, administration officials in Washington, D.C., had a proposal that they hoped would help. On July 9, 1946, Dean Acheson sent a memorandum to President Truman recommending the nomination of J. Leighton Stuart as Ambassador to China.[30] Acheson stressed Stuart's favorable reputation in Chinese education, religious, and governmental circles. He hoped Stuart could convince Chiang to see reason, since "he has enjoyed close relations over a period of years with Generalissimo and Madame Chiang Kai-shek and other high Chinese Governmental leaders."

Optimistic and exhilarated over the opportunity to change the course of events in his new position, Stuart saw himself as an impartial mediator between the Communists and the Nationalists. Others, however, saw him as biased toward Chiang Kai Shek.[31]

In the early heady days of his ambassadorship, Stuart often returned to the Yenching campus, where William Adolph had replaced him as Chancellor. Adolph, who lacked Stuart's charisma and made drastic personnel cuts, was not immediately popular.[32] Stuart reported on one of these visits that he enjoyed being ambassador and regaled his flattered after-dinner audience of Boring and Boynton with his interpretation of the Nationalist-Communist conflict. He predicted the emergence of a new era of warlords if the Guomintang collapsed. However, he was convinced that the Communists knew they did "not have the personnel to run all of China," so only wanted a coalition government. Their terms would include retaining control over their own areas and sharing power in other places, but they would not want to accept responsibility for the entire country.[33]

As it became evident that Chiang had no intentions of allowing the Communists to "become a constitutional party with complete freedom for the spread of their political ideology" (as Stuart had previously claimed) and that the Communists did not plan to be satisfied with a coalition government, Stuart became increasingly disillusioned. As Washington considered Stuart's ineffectiveness, officials became less supportive and rumors were generated about Stuart leaving the ambassadorship.[34]

By 1947, Stuart's dispatches reflected pessimism for China's political future. Negotiations between the Communists and Nationalists had broken down and, although reorganization of the Chinese government was taking place, it was without Communist participation. Even Stuart's faith in Chiang began to waver; the powerful political cliques were still formidable and showed no sign of melding into Chiang's government.[35] Confiding in Boring and Boynton, he admitted that if Chiang did not change, revolt would result.[36]

When Stuart first accepted the Ambassador's job, he was enthusiastic, optimistic, and confident. The ambassadorship proved to be "one crushing humiliation." Toward the end of his tenure both his enthusiasm and his confidence waned.[37]

In spite of the political realities, the personal crises, and educational struggles, Boring remained optimistic about the conditions at Yenching. She wrote a letter for the *Bryn Mawr Alumnae Bulletin* during the Christmas season of 1947, explaining that in spite of her apprehensions, "the first year was a wonderful one," and the second "bids fair to be even better." The streamlining that Yenching had undergone for efficiency after Adolph became president resulted in the faculty doing "less research and better teaching. . . ." Some of the old institutions were revived including the Peking Branch of the American Association of University Women and the Peking Natural History Society.[38]

By December 19, 1948, events made optimism for the future difficult, even for Boring. She watched as columns of Nationalist troops retreated in an orderly fashion, sequestering the houses of Yenching faculty members' servants for their quarters.

> Fearing trouble, the employees or their families who lived outside the campus came onto our campus carrying all sorts of bundles of beding [sic] and stores of food. Our cook's wife and five small children slept in his one room, and some of the ammah's family slept with her on the ironing table in the laundry—she usually does not stay here over night. Our lab buildings and classrooms were fully [sic] of families at night.[39]

The Red soldiers followed "close on the heels of the retreating troops. . . ." Boring observed that the young Communist soldiers were not the ogres that they were supposed to be, but orderly professionals who soon made friends with the local police. Protected by both the local police and the occupying Red army, she felt very safe.[40] Admittedly, she heard distant firing near Beijing. It, however, was sporadic and "classes began again on Friday after only three days suspension." Her faith in the good sense of the Chinese on both sides was undiminished. She could not believe that either the Communist or Nationalist armies would "allow beautiful historic Peking to be shelled and spoiled; that sort of thing is not done in China!"[41] The good conduct of the Red soldiers so impressed Yenching's students and faculty that many "have been hobnobbing with the Red soldiers."[42]

The Communists remained pleasant to those at Yenching and classes continued as usual. Recognizing that education was vital if Communism was to succeed, the new government had some definite ideas about the curriculum. However, instead of pushing ahead blindly, they sought the advice of Boring and other Yenching faculty members. Boring was relieved to find that they wanted pure subjects taught as well as applied ones. It might be, she speculated, that the faculty would be in a position to try educational experiments.[43]

Although during the early part of 1949 Beijing was still not in Communist hands, change was expected momentarily. There were several false alarms about an impending invasion. Many of the Yenching students and faculty members were anxious for the transition to occur. Predictably, the students were excited by the "revolution." Supporters of the Communists grew in numbers until "a very large group of Chinese faculty and several foreigners believe sincerely that a Red future is the best future for China." Boring wrote that she was "surprised to find that in spite of my opposition in the past, I now am full of hope!"[44]

By January 23, Chiang Kai Shek had resigned and Fu Tso Yi had surrendered to the Communists. "This week will be historic," prophesied Boring. Much anti-imperialist literature was circulated, "even cartoons of Leighton." In spite of all the propaganda, there was no unpleasantness against individual Americans. The fate of U.S. officials was uncertain. "Will Leighton be kept as Ambassador?" Another unknown was the attitude of the United States toward the new government. "Will she recognize the new government?"[45]

The Nationalist troops were still in Beijing on January 30, and their presence thwarted the triumphant entry of the Communists that the students awaited. Although Chinese were allowed to freely enter and leave Beijing, foreigners were restricted.[46] On February 6, the "triumphal entry of the Communists into Beijing" finally occurred. "The recalcitrant Nationalist general submitted and the city has been turned over to the new government." Yenching students, Boring reported, went to the city to join the huge parade. "The big shots have not yet arrived, such as Mao Tse Tung, Chow En Lai and Chu Teh, but are coming soon." Perhaps, she speculated, there will be peace talks. In spite of all the excitement of the external situation, she expressed hope that the spring semester would start soon.[47]

Such a hope was ill founded, for the students celebrated so continuously that the beginning of spring semester was postponed until March 2. Even after cancelling spring vacation and postponing commencement, the semester would be a week short, Boring lamented.

The isolation from the outside world that Boring felt now that "Peking city has been liberated," became uncomfortable. The "Bamboo Curtain in between us and the outside world" became less penetrable. The last regularly scheduled plane left Beijing on January 29, 1949. Others were more fearful than Boring, who commented hopefully that the curtain was not yet made of iron.[48] If Boring considered the past disruptions in China—warlord incursions, student riots, and the Japanese invasion—the current Communist takeover seemed mild indeed. Of course, there was always the uncertainty, but she had lived with the unknown for many years. "We have been at work again for two and half [sic] weeks, and all goes well." Life for foreigners "has been looking up." Foreign faculty members finally got passes to Beijing, and "I dashed right in the next day, which happened to be my freest day, and got a shampoo and a wave, had lunch with Freddie Li, my best Chinese friend, and visited all my cronies at the P.U.M.C."[49]

The "New Democracy as it is called," was tolerable, since Boring and the other foreigners now had the freedom to go and come as they pleased. They were allowed to communicate with the West and were no longer concerned about having sufficient money for a livelihood.

> Both Chinese faculty and students have taken a new lease on life and feel truly optimistic. I am so glad that I have been here to share this experience. I am sorry for all those who left before the turnover, but nobody expected things to be so simple and peaceful. And now of course we are all watching every development and thinking hopefully of the future.[50]

Boring did not consider that this future might not include westerners. The fate of the West in China became more clear, as on April 25, the Communists broke into Ambassador Stuart's bedroom in Nanjing. He had chosen to remain, approved by the State Department, after the Nationalist government left. Other western diplomats followed Stuart's example. On April 25, the Communists stationed guards around the Embassy compounds. Just as in Beijing, although they were subjected to annoying restrictions, no one was harmed. Although Stuart wanted to meet with the Communists, hoping to influence their policies, the State

Department refused to give him permission. Stuart, accredited to the Nationalist government, could not remain indefinitely. Since he could not meet with Mao, Communist officials obstructed his departure until August 2, when he left, never to return to China.[51]

Stuart's inability to meet with Mao indicated a hardening of the divisions between China and the United States. Mao's philosophical pronouncement of June 30, 1949, "On the People's Democratic Dictatorship," hinted at the subsequent fate of westerners in China. After he described the untold hardships suffered by the Chinese in their quest for truth from the West, he indicated the necessity for a new approach. The Chinese had been deceived when they were told that modernization after the pattern of western capitalist countries could save China. Western "bourgeoisie [sic] civilization, bourgeois democracy and the plan for a bourgeois republic have all gone bankrupt in the eyes of the Chinese people." In his moderate views of 1949, he declared that the Communist policy was to "regulate capitalism, not to destroy it." However, their new teacher was to be the Communist Party of the Soviet Union, not the West.[52] From Mao's manifesto, it is apparent why the expatriate community swung from optimism to despair at the prospects for the future. Boring remained confident that the Communist regime would be acceptable, for she did not remain in China long enough to be affected by this new development.

Notes

1. E.G. Boring to A.M. Boring, 11 Dec. 1943, Pusey Archive Collection, Harvard University, Boring Family Correspondence.
2. Ibid.
3. E.G. Boring to A.M. Boring, 5 Jan. 1944, Pusey Archive Collection, Harvard University, Boring Family Correspondence.
4. A.M. Boring to E.G. Boring, 2 March 1944, Pusey Archive Collection, Harvard University, Boring Family Correspondence.
5. Ibid.
6. A.M. Boring to E.G. Boring, 6 April 1944, Pusey Archive Collection, Harvard University, Boring Family Correspondence.
7. *Time*, 24 April 1944, pp. 34–36.
8. A.M. Boring to E.G. Boring, 16 April 1944, Pusey Archive Colleciton, Harvard University, Boring Family Correspondence.
9. Ibid.
10. *Time*, 24 April 1944, p. 36.
11. *New York Times*, 18 April 1944, p. 4.

12. A.M. Boring to E.G. Boring, 16 April 1944, Pusey Archive Collection, Harvard University, Boring Family Correspondence.
13. Ibid.
14. Ibid.
15. A.M. Boring to E.G. Boring 6 April 1944, Pusey Archive Collection, Harvard University, Boring Family Correspondence.
16. Dwight W. Edwards, *Yenching University* (New York: United Board for Christian Higher Education in Asia, 1959), p. 388.
17. Mount Holyoke College, Catalogue, 1945–1946, pp. 115–118.
18. Boring, Mount Holyoke College, "Biographical Data for the College Press Bureau," September 1945.
19. E.G. Boring to A.M. Boring, 5 September 1945, Pusey Archive Collection, Harvard University, Boring Family Correspondence.
20. Ibid.
21. Ibid.
22. A.M. Boring to E.G. Boring, 2 June 1946, Pusey Archive Collection, Harvard University, Boring Family Correspondence.
23. A.M. Boring to "All," 15 Nov. 1946, Bryn Mawr College Bulletin, April 1947.
24. Boynton, "Red Leather Notebook," 1947, p. 12, Radcliffe.
25. Boring to Mary Ferguson, 5 Oct. 1946, Rockefeller Archive Center.
26. Ibid.
27. Ibid.
28. Boring to "All," 15 Nov. 1946. Boring felt that there was hope in General Chen Cheng who replaced General Ho Ying Chin, "the grafter." Chen belonged to "a fine group of elder statesmen called the Political Science Group." Another individual whom she trusted was Sun Fo, the son of Sun Yat Sen and "by far the most liberal of the Kuomintang."
29. Ibid.
30. "Memorandum for the President," Acting Secretary, Dean Acheson to President Harry Truman Subject: Nomination of J. Leighton Stuart as Ambassador to China, July 9, 1946, Dept. of State, Washington, 1957.
31. *The Forgotten Ambassador: The Reports of John Leighton Stuart, 1946–1948*, eds. Kenneth W. Rea and John C. Brewer (Boulder, Colorado: Westview Press, n.d.), p. 1.
32. Boynton, "Red Leather Notebook," p. 22.
33. Ibid., p. 39.
34. Ibid., p. 45.
35. *The Forgotten Ambassador*, pp. 57–58.
36. Boynton, "Red Leather Notebook," 1947, pp. 44–46.
37. Ibid., p. 55.
38. Boring to Bryn Mawr College Alumnae Bulletin (April 1948).
39. Boring to Family, 19 Dec. 1948 (Composite of several dates), Special Collection Archives, Yale Divinity School.

40. Ibid.
41. Ibid.
42. Ibid.
43. Boring to Family, 2 Jan. 1949, Special Collection Archives, Yale Divinity School.
44. Boring to Family, 9 Jan. 1949, Special Collection Archives, Yale Divinity School.
45. Boring to Family, 23 Jan. 1949, Special Collection Archives, Yale Divinity School.
46. Boring to Family, 30 Jan. 1949, Special Collection Archives, Yale Divinity School.
47. Boring to Family, 6 Feb. 1949, Special Collection Archives, Yale Divinity School.
48. Boring to Family, 20 Feb. 1949, Special Collection Archives, Yale Divinity School.
49. Boring to Family, 12 March 1949, Special Collection Archives, Yale Divinity School.
50. Ibid.
51. *The Forgotten Ambassador*, p. 319.
52. J. Mason Gentzler, *Changing China: Readings in the History of China from the Opium War to the Present* (New York: Praeger, 1977), pp. 242–46.

Chapter 8
The Finale

Boring's confidence in China's Communist future was strengthened when she found that many former Yenching students had become high officials in the new government. Since two hundred Yenching students had worked in the Communist underground movement, the University was favored by Communist leaders who consulted Yenching officials on educational policies. "None of the dire results expected by cautious people like myself, have as yet happened." She hoped that the Chinese "with their gift of reasonableness and practicality" would manage a synthesis of ideologies.[1] Boring, however, did not remain at Yenching long enough to observe the failure of her dream.

Neither age nor politics but an accident suffered by her sister, Lydia, caused Alice to consider leaving China. In December 1948, Lydia fell at the Bankers Trust Company and was taken, unconscious, to the Roosevelt hospital. The accident and astronomical care expenses had a huge impact on the entire family. Although it was doubtful whether Lydia could ever live outside a hospital or nursing home, if she improved enough to come home the family agreed that the two sisters should live together. Perhaps Alice was more willing to consider returning to the United States at this time than previously, for, in spite of her brave words, she had begun to feel her usefulness at Yenching had diminished.[2]

Lydia's accident also involved the question of liability and the nature of the responsibility of Lydia's long-time friend and companion, Helen Fogg, toward her care.[3] As family burdens escalated, Garry increasingly resented Alice's distance from the problem. Although previously he had boasted about her accomplishments, his pride became subsumed to a conviction that her continued presence in China was a means of escaping responsibility. As he pondered the advisability of pressuring Alice to return, he commented that "it would be a new thought to her that she might have family responsibility."[4]

Although Lydia improved toward the end of January, she remained incontinent, tended "to be a little querulous," and alternated between rationality and confusion. The family settled Lydia in a nursing center in Waltham. At this point, Edwin and Katharine no longer saw the necessity or desirability of Alice's immediate return. Garry telegraphed Kat on February 2, 1949, stating that he felt "strongly that Alice should plan to stay in Peiping." He felt confident that Lydia would recover eventually and return to live with Helen; if Alice were to be on the scene matters would be greatly complicated.[5] Kat supported Garry and promised to write Alice and "reinforce what we have agreed to say."[6]

When Helen refused to go along with their plan, Garry and Katharine recognized that they would need Alice after all.[7] Katharine wrote Garry that "what Alice will do or what she can do is anybody's bet. But I think that thee and I can decide things from now on."[8] Garry welcomed the arrangement and wrote to Kat that "Thee and I are in control, and I welcome the partnership."[9]

Although the uncertainty of Lydia's physical condition made it impossible to make any firm plans, if she recovered sufficiently, Garry and Lucy agreed to provide the apartment next door to them as a home for Lydia and Alice. In spite of Kat's concern about the effect on Garry of having his sisters so close, he assured her that he was comfortable with the arrangement.[10]

Alice was not in a hurry to leave China and did not plan to return until August 1950. The family, well aware of Alice's attachment to Leighton Stuart, wondered if hearing of the stroke Stuart had suffered "would have anything to do with hurrying Alice up!"[11]

Garry reported that the family was apprehensive about Alice's impending return. "Everybody is scared of Alice, Helen, Ly and me." Since Lydia's condition deteriorated rather than improved, it became evident that she would not be able to live in the apartment with Alice after all. When Alice asked him when she should return, Garry told her "to aim at the middle of August."[12]

In the meantime, a family tragedy far larger than Lydia's accident was developing. Edwin and Lucy Boring's youngest daughter, Barbara (Bobs), seemed unable to cope with the demands of living in the Boring household. Although she rebelled against her family she nevertheless developed many of her strong-willed parents' values. Obsessed with being the "best" in high school, she found that she could achieve her goal by hard work. When she left for Swarthmore College, she expected to maintain her record. Unable to match her own expectations for herself, she became depressed, seemingly incapable of managing her own life, and resentful of her parents' suggestions. She tried suicide repeatedly with gas and pills.[13]

During this time, the family was in constant turmoil. Not only were they concerned with solutions to Lydia's problems, but they trembled every morning for fear that they would find Bobs dead in her bed. In spite of all of their efforts, Barbara succeeded in suicide in late February or early March.[14]

Insulated by distance from the events at home, Alice was undergoing emotional turmoil of her own. It was clear to her that once she left China, she would never return. Her life's work would be, in essence, finished. In spite of Garry's contentions, Alice felt her family responsibilities keenly. If she was needed, she was more than willing to devote the remainder of her life to her sister. In the end, Lydia's predicament served as the catalyst that allowed her to leave China. In August 1950, she packed her accumulation of furniture and Chinese artifacts, booked passage, and left China for the last time.

When Alice arrived in Cambridge, she inspired mixed emotions in her stay-at-home family. Garry reported that it was a joy to have her back, but he also admitted that they lived "more intensely with an extra Boring around."[15] The qualities that made Alice successful in China—tenacity, certainty, and optimism—sometimes were not appreciated in her new culture. Even before she walked in the door of 21 Bowdoin Street, the family dreaded the flood of memorabilia that would accompany her. Kat wrote to Garry complaining about "Alice and her goods and chatels [sic]."[16] Katharine was dismayed because Alice talked about colors of kimonos and rugs as China was being engulfed by communism. Kat found it strange, but "Alice-like," that she did not appear to be upset by the world situation. Alice was indeed concerned about China's plight, but unlike her sister she had lived through a variety of catyclysms in that country. What was "Alice-like" was her optimism and faith that the Chinese people would develop an appropriate, successful solution for their problem.

Lydia remained in the nursing home, and Alice temporarily moved into the Edwin Boring house. Close quarters required constant restraint both on Alice's part and that of Garry and Lucy so that they refrained from irritating each other. Since both parties recognized that the arrangements were temporary, they were able to cope precariously with the situation. Garry saw no chance of Alice's being able to move out until January, and considered it possible that she might remain until April. The arrangement was difficult "for Lucia and me, and . . . for Alice." It was not impossible, however, since "both parties realize the difficulties and both are deter-mined to make the thing work. . . ."[17]

Alice's main topic of conversation was, of course, China—what it had been and her hopes for its future. Although at first Garry and Lucy were intrigued by her stories, after a while they found them repetitious and annoying. It did not occur to Alice that those who had not shared her experience might not share her continued fascination.

Apart from Alice's presence, Garry and Lucy's lives were marred by the emotional strain of Lydia's law suit with, of course, Barbara's death lurking in the shadows. Thus, it was not surprising when Alice, with her positive assertions, appeared, that more of the harmony disap-peared. Much of the conflict surfaced around petty situations—the kind of annoyances that can build up tremendous pressure and even-tually result in an explosion. Garry and Lucy had spent their lives in Cam-bridge, operating under a very conservative system of protocol. Alice, on the other hand, had spent her life in an environment where the little niceties were affectations. When a revolution was on her doorstep, protocol hardly seemed important. To Garry and Lucy, however, man-ners reflected a civilized culture. Edwin noted that "there are dozens of little ways in which our cultural patterns differ." As an example he noted that

> For thirty-five years now we have all of us refrained from eating until Lucia has got the first bite to her mouth. That takes hard work because Lucia is not too prompt and will also get bite no. 1 half up to her mouth with all of us straining to start, and then put it down because she has forgotten something or wants to make a remark in oro vacui.
>
>   The protocol behind such a delay never penetrated Alice's mind. Alice reaches for the bread, gets her piece buttered before she is served, starts eating before all others are served. All right. The People's Republic of China is for youth and against these old inefficient conservatisms that represent a false spir-itualism and are not consistent with dialectical materialism.[18]

This sort of thing, Garry complained, "can not be mentioned because it is artificial and has no real biological importance, and yet it prevents that harmonious living together that is the essence of a family life and that occurs between hosts and invited guests, because the invitation is based on preknowledge of community of custom."[19] In spite of their disagree-ments, a strong current of family loyalty undergirded differences. They might bicker among themselves but unite against outsiders. When Alice moved to her own apartment next door to Edwin's, some of the tension was eliminated.

Although she occasionally associated with her former scientific friends, China took precedence over biology. Continuing to retain her faith in the Chinese, Alice protested against the anti-Communist mania that was sweeping the United States. Even Leighton, she lamented, had forsaken the ideals that had formerly dominated his life. Although while at Yenching he had always sided with the young, he complained in a 1951 letter to Alice that the young people had been duped by Communist propaganda and failed to see the larger issues. According to Stuart, these "larger issues" involved a plot by "the two great nations of Russia and China... to enslave the world." Garry agreed with Stuart's assessment, but such ideas seemed nonsensical to Alice. She indignantly sputtered that Leighton had been "captured by the State Department in Washington." If he had only remained at Yenching, he would not have defected, for "he always sided with the young group." Garry, who equated the "young mind" with the naive mind, pronounced that "it is youth and the youthful mind that is endangering the world now." To him, Alice's "young mind" and Leighton's earlier views reflected immaturity.[20]

Although Yenching remained as one of the last remnants of western-created and supported educational institutions in China, it ceased to exist in its former state in 1952. Rather than dwell on its disappearance, Boring was encouraged, because many of her friends continued to teach in the government university into which it merged.[21] She had no patience with doom-prophesying Cassandras. Already disappointed with Stuart for selling out to the State Department, she was equally distressed by her brother's opinions. She flounced out of the room when Garry expressed his ideas of a Communist plot in an especially condescending way.[22]

Since it appeared that Alice would not have to be constantly with Lydia, she could consider part-time employment. Smith College persuaded her to commute to Northhampton two days a week, where she taught from 1951–1953, claiming that the "teaching habit" was sufficiently strong to lure her away from conversations about China and its fate. She found, however, that American students "are not much fun to teach...." Thirty years of teaching Chinese students had spoiled her, "for higher education is still a privilege to a Chinese."[23]

By November 1951, Alice was showing physical aging. Although she wanted to spend Christmas with Katharine and Howard Rondthaler in North Carolina, the Rondthalers questioned the advisability of her making the trip. Edwin assured them that she could manage, although she no longer was able to walk briskly nor to negotiate stairs regularly. He explained that "she will not want to be up and down stairs in your house all the time, ... " but there is "no reason why she should not go up and down two or three times a day. ..."[24]

Following a strong Quaker and familial tradition of writing family histories, as the family aged its members became more committed to recording its history. Garry became the official family historian, but solicited contributions from other members. After the history was completed, another tragedy struck the family. Katharine, who had been Garry's confidant and strong supporter, died.[25]

Alice gradually adjusted to the "obliteration" of the Chinese culture in which she lived happily for so many years. She became more concerned with local matters, including Cambridge politics, and as that happened she felt "less and less a responsibility for Chiang Kai Shek and Mao Tse Tung."[26] As her local interests increased, she was less inclined to commute to Smith. When the college invited her to stay for a third year she declined. Although she claimed that her decision was based on the establishment of her Social Security, her involvement in Cambridge and her lack of enthusiasm for the American student may have played important roles in her decision.[27]

The year 1953–54 was Boring's "first one of real retirement." Retirement to Alice meant having the freedom to devote all of her time to her "causes." Favored among many were "The American Friends' Service Committee's Refugee Clothing Room and the League of Women Voters." The Cambridge Civic Association, the American Civil Liberties Union, the Bryn Mawr Club of Boston, a travel club, the Boston Symphony, and the Theatre Guild also claimed time. She did not forsake international concerns and, in particular, her Chinese interests, being active in the International Institute and the Chinese Students' Centre.[28] Although she promised "to begin to discriminate a bit more and stop running around to so many places," it simply was not in her nature to slow down.

Part of her activity involved subletting a portion of her apartment. She was generous with the lessee, offering her a free telephone and other amenities. This generosity brought down Garry's wrath, for since he rented the apartment to Alice he felt she was being generous with *his* money. Edwin's proverbial "nearness" in money matters had not tempered over the years, nor had his interpretation that Alice's lack of interest in such matters was a sign of immaturity. "Thee likes to be generous," he ranted. "Thee hates quibbling over small financial details and collecting debts from people who forget to pay, and that is another form of generosity. ..." But self interest, claimed Garry, was involved in this magnanimity. By granting her tenant certain favors, she could expect in return reciprocities, like "thy dominant role in the kitchen." It was his property that was involved, chided Garry, and he would lose money by the arrangement.[29]

Alice was not able to appreciate her "retirement" for long. During the two years before her death, she suffered from what Garry called cerebral arteriosclerosis. The major symptom was sleepiness. She would ride by her car stop and end up at the end of the line or drop off to sleep at the Friends' Service Committee clothing storage room. The experience of "suspension of consciousness" came without warning. She described the situation in the Friends' workroom as being "asleep with my eyes open." The situation did not seem to bother her greatly, and she remained cheerful. Luckily, she did not drive, for if she had been able to, no one would have been able to convince her not to try.[30]

During the summer of 1954, she went to her Bryn Mawr 50th reunion and became very tired. On the way home, she visited a niece in New York, blacked out, was taken to Cambridge and put to bed. She said little about the incident, fearing checks would be put on her activities. In November 1954, when she went to Waltham to see Lydia, she went to "sleep" walking along the sidewalk, fell down, injured her head, and had to be taken to the hospital. She woke up on the operating table after the surgeon had taken 36 stitches in a gash in her forehead. Edwin and Lucy were out of town, so the people living in the apartment contacted Grace Boynton. After numerous telephone calls, Grace located her, went to the hospital to visit, and found an irate Alice who "was quite annoyed to see me!" She had "wanted to put through this little episode without observation."[31]

The prognosis, which Alice fortunately did not know, involved progressive, prolonged mental and physical deterioration. On Christmas Eve, 1954, she suffered what Garry called a cerebral thrombosis. Although she did not wake up in the morning, she kept breathing and regained consciousness toward evening in the hospital. After ten days in a Cambridge hospital, she returned to her apartment "very nervous and belligerant [sic]—evidently afraid she was going to have limitations put to her established routine." Her doctor, however, apparently understood that "she needs liberty more than life" and simply urged her to slow down.[32]

In spite of physical deterioration, Boring championed a new cause during the summer of 1954. Chinese students studying technological subjects in the United States had been refused exit visas; essentially, they were held hostages by the United States government. Twenty-six of these students signed letters, protesting the refusal by immigration authorities to provide them with exit permits allowing them to return to China or other places. Boring wrote a letter to President Dwight D. Eisenhower on behalf of these students. "America is a free country," she wrote. "What right have we to prevent persons of other nationalities from leaving this country to return to their families and their country?" Incensed that the United States would make them "prisoners," she appealed to "American" ideas of reciprocity. "We do not like it when another country keeps our citizens from returning to their home country." In pleading the case of the students she noted that she could not "imagine them doing anything against America when they return to China." She begged Eisenhower to "kindly not throw away either this letter or the one from the Chinese students, but take time to consider it carefully. There is a principle at stake— Freedom, which means so much to us as Americans."[33] Secretary of State John Foster Dulles responded more pragmatically than idealistically as he discussed the problem in a memorandum to Eisenhower. Originally, he had hoped that the detention of the Chinese students would encourage the Chinese Communists to release imprisoned Americans. When this goal was not realized, he suggested a change in policy, assuming that the "release of the students would enable the U.S. to press its case against the Chinese Communists more effectively in the United Nations and elsewhere." Subsequently, most of the students were given permission to depart.[34]

The plight of the detained Chinese students became Boring's last crusade. During the early part of September 1955, Alice had spent some time with Garry and Lucy in Maine and seemed "to have an exceptionally good time. . . ." She returned to Cambridge, but they remained in Maine. On Saturday, September 17, Alice visited Lydia in the morning, and lunched with a friend. She had a "gay time" with both of them and in the afternoon told a woman friend how happy she was in Cambridge. She went to bed that night and never woke up, apparently dying in her sleep from what was "undoubtedly a cerebral thrombosis," early Sunday morning, September 18. Her roomer, a young Chinese chemist, became alarmed when she did not appear as usual, but hesitated to open the door. When he became sufficiently alarmed, he called in others and her body was found that afternoon.[35] The sudden death was the way that active Alice would have wanted to go.

Expressions of condolence swept in from classmates, colleagues, former students, and friends from all over the world. Letters were from those who had known Alice for a long time as well as those who had only known her during the last years of her life. Lucy Burtt, her associate through so many events in China, characterized Alice's life as one of great beauty and "loving service" to her fellows.[36] Eleanor Rubsam Barstow, who as a graduate student at Radcliffe shared Alice's apartment in 1951–52, reported that she understood how much Alice meant to students who came to visit "years after she had taught them." She too concluded that Alice had lived a good and productive life.[37]

To respond to the many expressions of sympathy, Garry turned to Grace Boynton, whom he characterized as Alice's "best friend." Asked to compile a tribute, she avoided anything "emotional or too personal," knowing that Alice would object. She also knew that an "in depth" treatment would unearth their personal disputes. Eulogies require selective memories, and Grace was fastidious about her selections. She summed up the facts of Alice's life. Depending on the specific audience, she emphasized the appropriate phases.[38]

Candid Garry considered Alice's weaknesses as well as her strengths. In a letter to Boynton, he referred to enthusiastic Alice as a "menace to society." To Edwin Boring, Boynton answered, "I must deprecate the idea that Alice was ever a menace to society, although I recognize the right of a candid brother to express himself freely! She went on to note that "Alice's spontaneity was a stimulus—it made people feel waked up. In a way, it made us share her youthful quality. So there now!" Boynton chided him while recognizing his brotherly right to express himself freely.[39] Garry persisted, however, describing her love affair with China as "an adolescent and not wholly rational enthusiasm."[40] Boynton's apparently positive view of Alice's "spontaneity" to Garry was quite different from her earlier view of that same spontaneity. When writing to Mary E. Ferguson, Associate Executive Secretary of the United Board for Christian Colleges in China, shortly before Boring's death, she purported to present only the "facts" about Alice's situation. Since Ferguson was "more or less of a clearing house for Yenching news," Boynton thought that it seemed "sensible" for her to be fully informed. Only the tone of the "facts" indicated Boynton's below the surface resentment of Boring. The emphasis on her stubbornness in insisting to go on with her ordinary activities after she had her spells of "falling asleep" was reminiscent of her earlier feelings when Alice had used other people to smuggle letters out of occupied China.

Alice had named sixty-nine-year-old Edwin Boring executor of her estate.[41] Since Lydia was most in need, she was the sole beneficiary. Garry worked with Grace Boynton to decide on the disposition of Alice's papers. They deemed certain letters to have value beyond that of personal family treasures, so sent folders of general letters about Yenching's role in Chinese history to the United Missions Board to be microfilmed and made available to researchers. After microfilming, Grace Boynton would receive any of the originals that she wanted to keep.[42]

This disposition of her letters would have pleased Boring. She would have the opportunity to share her observations and experiences with many others. The wish to share, to give, and thus to make her own life worthwhile would be accomplished.

Notes

1. Alice M. Boring to Class of 1904, 17 March 1949, Bryn Mawr College Archives.
2. Grace M. Boynton, "Red Leather Notebook," 1949, p. 26, Radcliffe.
3. E.G. Boring to K. Rondthaler, 7 March 1950, Pusey Archive Collection, Harvard Univ., Rondthaler Family Correspondence, 1949–1950, Box 51, Folder 1143. E.G. Boring to E. Rondthaler, 22 July 1949, Pusey Archive Collection, Harvard University, Rondthaler Family Correspondence, 1949–1950, Box 51, Folder 1143. Family members blamed Helen for the fact that Lydia had not continued teaching long enough to be eligible for a pension. Years before, Helen had encouraged Lydia to quit her job, convincing her of future support. E.G. Boring to K. Rondthaler, 19 Jan. 1949, Pusey Archive Collection, Harvard University, Rondthaler Family Correspondence, 1949–1950, Box 51, Folder 1143.
4. E.G. Boring to K. Rondthaler, 19 Jan. 1949.
5. E.G. Boring to K. Rondthaler [telegram], 2 Feb. 1949, Pusey Archive Collection, Harvard University, Rondthaler Family Correspondence, 1949–1950, Box 51, Folder 1143.
6. They agreed that Alice should stay in Beijing, for at least one more year. "If a change of decision should be necessary later, why, the possibility of that can be considered in due course, that is to say we do not need to say that to her now." Rondthaler to E.G. Boring, 9 Feb. 1949, Pusey Archive Collection, Harvard University, Rondthaler Family Correspondence, 1949–1950, Box 51, Folder 1143.
7. Rondthaler to E.G. Boring, 9 Feb. 1949.
8. Rondthaler to E.G. Boring 17 Feb. 1949.
9. E.G. Boring to Rondthaler, 20 Oct. 1949, Pusey Archive Collection, Harvard University, Rondthaler Family Correspondence, 1949–1950, Box 51, Folder 1143.
10. Ibid.
11. Rondthaler to E.G. Boring, 12 Dec. 1949, Pusey Archive Collection, Harvard University, Rondthaler Family Correspondence, 1949–1950, Box 51, Folder 1143.
12. E.G. Boring to K. Rondthaler, 24 Jan. 1950, Pusey Archive Collection, Harvard University, Rondthaler Family Correspondence, 1949–1950, Box 51, Folder 1143.
13. E.G. Boring to Kath and Wayne, 13 Feb. 1950, Pusey Archive Collection, Harvard University, Rondthaler Family Correspondence, 1949–1950, Box 51, Folder 1143.

14. On March 22, 1950, when the remaining children got together with their parents, "the talk was all about Bobs." Even though the conversation freshened the pain, it served as a catharsis. E.G. Boring to K. Rondthaler, 22 March 1950, Pusey Archive Collection, Harvard University, Rondthaler Family Correspondence, 1949–1950, Box 51, Folder 1143.

15. Edwin G. Boring to Katharine Rondthaler, 21 Oct. 1950, Pusey Archive Collection, Harvard University, Rondthaler Family Correspondence, Box 51, Folder 1143.

16. Rondthaler to Boring, 9 March 1950, Harvard University Library, Archives.

17. Boring to Rondthaler, 28 Oct. 1950, Harvard University Library, Archives.

18. Ibid.

19. Ibid.

20. E.G. Boring to Rondthaler, 5 March 1951, Pusey Archive Collection, Harvard University, Rondthaler Family Correspondence, 1951–1952, Box 51, Folder 1144.

21. E.G. Boring to Clara Woodruff Hull, 4 Oct. 1955, Pusey Archive Collection, Harvard University, Boring Family Correspondence.

22. E.G. Boring to Rondthaler, 5 March 1951.

23. A.M. Boring to Class of 1904; E.G. Boring to Clara Woodruff Hull, 4 Oct. 1955.

24. E.G. Boring to Rondthaler, 20 Nov. 1951, Pusey Archive Collection, Harvard University, 1951–1952, Rondthaler Family Correspondence, Box 51, Folder 1144.

25. E.G. Boring to Howard Rondthaler, 10 Oct. 1952, Pusey Archive Collection, Harvard University, Rondthaler Family Correspondence, Box 51, Folder 1144.

26. E.G. Boring to H. Rondthaler, 10 Oct. 1952.

27. E.G. Boring to Hull, 4 Oct. 1955.

28. A.M. Boring to Class of 1904, 1 April 1954, Bryn Mawr College Archives.

29. E.G. Boring to A.M. Boring, 3 Jan. 1953, Pusey Archive Collection, Harvard University, Boring Family Correspondence.

30. Grace M. Boynton to Mary Ferguson, 2 March 1955, Special Collection Archives, Yale Divinity School; E.G. Boring to Hull, 4 Oct. 1955.

31. Ibid.

32. Ibid.

33. A.M. Boring to Dwight D. Eisenhower, 26 Aug. 1954. Dwight D. Eisenhower Library, Abilene, KS. The petitions were referred to the Department of Justice for attention. Reference to letter by Hwei Yuen Lo to President Eisenhower, 25 Aug. 1954. Dwight D. Eisenhower Library, Abilene, KS. On 5 August 1954, the United States Government issued a restraining order to prevent Chinese scholars with technical knowledge of special military value from leaving the country. The petitions to the President pleaded for him to revoke the order.

34. John Foster Dulles to Eisenhower, Memorandum, 1 April 1955, Dwight D. Eisenhower Library, Abilene, KS.

35. E.G. Boring to Hull, 4 Oct. 1955.

36. Lucy Burtt to E.G. Boring, 3 Nov. 1955, Pusey Archive Collection, Harvard University, Boring Family Correspondence.

37. Eleanor Rubsam Barstow to E.G. Boring, 12 March 1956, Pusey Archive Collection, Harvard University, Boring Family Correspondence.

38. Boynton to E.G. Boring, 20 Dec. 1955, Pusey Archive Collection, Harvard University, Boring Family Correspondence.

39. Ibid.

40. E.G. Boring to Hull, 4 Oct. 1955.

41. E.G. Boring to Mary Ferguson, 15 Nov. 1955; Ferguson to E.G. Boring, 28 November 1955; E.G. Boring to Ferguson, 5 Dec. 1955; Ferguson to E.G. Boring, 9 Dec. 1955.

42. Ibid.

Chapter 9
A Retrospective

Alice Boring was a part of the mainstream of American zoology. A member of a select cadre of women scientists, she was a professional in the best sense of the word. She possessed a doctorate, studied under well-known teachers, published in professional journals, participated in scientific societies, and earned her living from science. Her scientific interests, including the relationship of the chromosomes to heredity, reproductive biology, and the classifying of hitherto undescribed animals coincided with those of her colleagues. By participating in the foundation-supported expansion of American zoology beyond the North American continent, she experienced an additional career dimension.

Traditional symbols of a successful scientific career were less important to Boring than those human factors that extended into all of her scientific work. For Boring, science did not exist without people. Boring's family of brother, sisters, nieces, and nephews spilled over to include students and colleagues. Throughout much of her life, her relationship with this extended family took precedence over that with her biological family. Whether or not a student was one of her favorites or male or female, Boring professed a mission to teach each of them western science.

Many of her students attested to her attempts to positively influence their lives. Mediocre teachers soon fade from students' minds, whereas very good or very bad ones are remembered. The clear and lasting images invoked by Boring's former students, some over a period of sixty years, make it evident that they remembered her for excellence.

Although students' anecdotes indicate Alice Boring's impact on their lives, her importance can also be evaluated by considering the achievements of her professional progeny. Since the same political uncertainties that trailed Boring's career in China plagued her students, they pursued their careers in many parts of the world. In some cases, political stances and research opportunities outside of China forced the young Chinese professionals to make agonizing choices. Some decided that for the sake of family and career they would pursue their medical research and/or practice in other countries. China's loss translated into the adopted country's gain, for they used their expertise in medical research and in humanitarian pursuits. *Vitae* indicate that most of these expatriates attempted to keep contact with their families and colleagues in China. Others chose to serve by remaining in China and becoming a part of China's new medical and scientific establishment. Many of the physicians who remained aided in the new government's program of "barefoot" doctors, addressing the charges of elitism that had plagued western-trained physicians for many years. Others pursued their scientific careers quietly in the universities or in the newly created scientific institutes. Many of these people faced severe hardships during the "Cultural Revolution," yet they returned to their careers and made contributions important both to their own country and to the world.

Two attractive women who chose to remain in China, Sun You Yun, formerly of the Institute of Languages and Jiang Lijin, Professor of Chemistry and member of the chemistry division of the Academia Sinica, modified their original career plans because of the political situation. Jiang was in Boring's premedical courses and entered the PUMC medical school just when the Japanese came. Rather than finish a medical degree after the war, she went to the University of Minnesota where she completed a Ph.D. degree in chemistry in 1955. She visited Boring in Cambridge, Massachusetts, in 1955, just before Boring's death and found a somewhat "softer" person than she had been as a teacher. Sun explained that although she had started out in nursing, after the war she changed to sociology. Although she began teaching at Yenching when it changed to Beijing University, the sociology department was moved to the Institute of Foreign Languages. Rather than sociology, Sun ended up teaching mathematics.

Through letters and personal interviews, Cliff Choquette and Marilyn Ogilvie have become acquainted with many of Alice Boring's former students both in the United States and China. Eight individuals have been selected to illustrate the variety and quality of the achievements of Boring's students. Many others could just as well have been selected, and many of their recollections are included in other places in this biography. Four of those selected pursued careers outside of China, and four remained in their home country. Of the four expatriates, the work of

Katharine H.K. Hsu and Tao Jung Chin emphasized medical practice rather than research, whereas Frederick F. Kao and Liu Chien specialized in biomedical research. Of the four who remained in China, Liu Shilian pursued a career at Peking Union Medical College, Liu Chen Chao (C.C. Liu) became widely known for his expertise on Chinese amphibians, Lin Chang Shan modified his original research in entomology to human ecology, and Ding Han Bo became an expert on the amphibians and reptiles of Fujian province.

KATHARINE H.K. HSU, M.D. (1914–)

Hsu, Boring's advisee from 1931 to 1933, was awarded a post-doctoral fellowship in 1948 at the Cincinnati Children's Hospital. Rather than return to China immediately, she arranged to attend the University of Pennsylvania and learn current techniques in tuberculosis prevention and treatment. By the time she had completed this preparation, the Korean War had broken out, preventing her return.[1] Unable to use her skills in China, she transferred her talents to the United States. In 1953, she went to Houston, Texas, after an outbreak of tuberculosis threatened the health of many inhabitants. She became the first Director of Tuberculosis control in the Houston City Health Department, established a network of tuberculosis clinics, and in 1969 was promoted to Professor of Pediatrics at the Baylor College of Medicine. Alpha Omega Alpha Honorary Medical Society honored Boring's former student by selecting her to be the single faculty member elected to honorary membership in 1984.

Hsu's medical contributions involved practical ways of applying theoretical principles. She published thirty-eight papers, a book, *Tuberculosis in Children and Finding Tuberculosis through Examination of Contacts*; was co-author of *Guide for Follow-up of Tuberculosis Cases, Contacts, Suspects*; co-author of a chapter in *Treatment of Tuberculosis in Children*: *Pediatric Clinics of North America*; and author of a chapter on "Cervical Lymphadenitis Due to *Mycobacterium scrofulaceum*," in *Current Therapy in Respiratory Medicine 1984–1985*.[2]

TAO JUNG CHIN, M.D. (1915–)

Tuberculosis prevention and treatment also constituted a major part of Tao Jung Chin's life work. Like Katharine Hsu, Tao practiced medicine outside of China. Like Hsu, he used his skills to improve world health. The Korean National Tuberculosis Association recognized his achievements in 1984 by awarding him a Plaque of Appreciation, "in recognition and appreciation of outstanding service in tuberculosis treatment as well as devotion to the national tuberculosis control in Korea."[3]

Tao was a premedical student at Yenching from 1934 to 1937. During this period, he was under the supervision of Boring, who had the responsibility of "observing, scrutinizing, and guiding pre-medical students during the whole period of study."[4] While stressing the importance of Boring's recommendation for entrance to PUMC, he also noted that her relationship with students transcended the purely academic. She behaved like a mother hen to her students and they, in turn, treated her "as a motherly figure, tender, affectionate, and above all, with respect."[5] It seemed natural for Boring to be one of the wedding guests when Tao and Lo Hsiu Chen (Dorothy) were married by Dr. Leighton Stuart.

Tao's over thirteen publications stressed practical applications of medical principles. His last position (he retired in 1977) was as a regional adviser on chronic diseases, at the World Health Organization regional office. His duties included advising member governments of the WHO western Pacific region on the planning, organization, operation, and evaluation of the control services against tuberculosis, leprosy, cardiovascular disorders, cancer, and metabolic and other chronic diseases.[6]

Tao took his entrance examination for PUMC from July 6–8, 1937, and the Sino-Japanese War broke out on July 7. Because of the war, his studies at PUMC were interrupted. He elected to go to Free China to enroll in the medical school of the Western University in Chengdu, where, dissatisfied with the teaching standards, he remained only a short time. Persuaded by his army general father to return to PUMC, he completed his medical studies at that institution.

After graduating in 1943, Tao worked for the Chinese government for sixteen years in the Tuberculosis Control Service of the National Institute of Health. The well-received program emphasized the principle of early diagnosis and early treatment of pulmonary tuberculosis among apparently healthy people (especially high school and college students). Tao's interest in public health medicine continued, and he was awarded a Rockefeller Foundation Fellowship to study at Johns Hopkins School of Public Health. He returned to mainland China for a short time and was then ordered by the Ministry of Health to move to Taiwan. From 1959 until retirement in 1977, Tao practiced medicine in the Pacific Region.[7]

FREDERICK F. KAO (KAO FENGTIEN), M.D., Ph.D. (19..–)

Frederick F. Kao's scientific credentials are impressive. He came to the United States in 1948 as an invited trainee at the Wesley Memorial Hospital in Chicago, now renamed the Northwestern Memorial Hospital. Since he knew he could not return to China, he prepared to be a biomedical scientist in the United States. During the time Kao was trying to establish his credentials, Senator Joseph McCarthy was vigilantly looking for Communists among the young Chinese students. Kao was "interrogated by a tall blond young woman in Chicago" who told him that she was from the F.B.I.[8] Finding that he harbored "no taint of communism" he was allowed to remain, unlike many Chinese scholars who were deported.[9]

Kao used his medical expertise both in the United States and internationally. From 1965 through the present (1989), he has been Professor of Physiology and Biophysics at the State University of New York, Downstate Medical Center (now renamed Health Science Center at Brooklyn). His work has included visiting professorships in Taiwan, England, Germany, Hong Kong, Turkey, and Sweden. In 1973, he was head of the Delegation of the Chinese American Scholars to China, the first medical delegation to visit the mainland after the Cultural Revolution. He has recently been Professor of Physiology, Shanghai First Medical College and has conducted research at the respiration laboratory, Shanghai Medical University. Since 1977, he has been an advisor to the World Health Organization.

Kao has received numerous awards, several million dollars in grants (1988 dollar value), trained Ph.D. students and postdoctoral fellows, lectured and presented papers in many parts of the world, and is a member of many scientific and professional societies.

Kao's over 119 published scientific papers from 1951 to the present and eight edited and authored books include a variety of subjects: the regulation of respiration, physiological adjustment in muscular exercise, chemical environment of the brain, environmental stress, and respiratory pharmacology. He expanded his work to include comparative medicine and physiology between the East and West as well as the historical development of medicine in China.[10]

LIU CHIEN (CHIEN LIU), M.D.(1921–)

Pearl Harbor prevented Liu Chien's Yenching class of 1941 from entering PUMC. Liu transferred to West China Union University in Chengtu and finished his medical education at that institution in 1946.

Liu, who originally came to the United States for post-graduate training, elected to remain in this country. His successful medical career has been centered on the University of Kansas College of Health Sciences Center, where he has held a variety of positions from 1958 through the present. A classmate of Dr. Kao at Yenching, Liu's contributions include 131 research papers, dating from his experience at the Johns Hopkins School of Medicine (1949–1951) to 1988. After leaving Johns Hopkins in 1952, Liu went to the Harvard University Medical School where he was Research Associate in Bacteriology and Immunology (1952–1955), and Assistant Professor of Bacteriology and Immunology (1958). After he left Harvard for Kansas City, Kansas, in 1958, Dr. Liu was involved with Children's Mercy Hospital in Kansas City, Missouri, as well as with the University of Kansas Health Sciences Center. From 1958–1962, he was Chief of the Infectious Disease Section and during 1962–1963, Chairman of the Department of Pediatrics at Mercy Hospital.[11]

LIU SHILIAN, M.D. (1926–)

Dr. Liu, who received his B.S. degree from Yenching University in 1948, did not begin his university work until 1945, when Yenching reopened after World War II. He entered PUMC in 1948 and received an M.D. degree in 1953. Although Liu has engaged in many overseas activities, he had made his career in China, including teaching and research at PUMC. In 1983, he moved from his position as Acting Director, Institute of Basic Medical Sciences, to Dean, Capital Medical College of China (PUMC's name from 1983–1985). From 1985 to the present (1989) he has remained in the Dean's position at this institution (although the institution's name was changed back to Peking Union Medical College of China). Dr. Liu's research has centered around immunology, and he has published over forty papers since 1974.[12]

LIU CHENG CHAO (C.C. LIU), Ph.D. (1900–1976)

Liu Cheng Chao has been characterized as China's "most prominent herpetologist."[13] Boring was closely associated with Liu. Although Liu, who received B.S. and M.S. degrees from Yenching, was officially a student of Li Ju Chi (J.C. Li), he had classes from Boring, she provided him with research advice, and the two collaborated on three papers.[14] After he became prominent, Liu credited Boring with help in two of his major publications. In "Secondary Sex Characters of Chinese Frogs and Toads" (1936), Liu noted that "at Peiping, during the spring breeding season, Professor Alice M. Boring of the Biology Department of Yenching University has collected frogs and toads in the interests of my project, and I gratefully extend to her my appreciation of her long-continued help and interest."[15] In his 1950 classic publication, "Amphibians of Western China," he thanked his "former teacher at Yenching University, Dr. Alice M. Boring," and stated his "grateful remembrance for her continued encouragement and help during the war years."[16]

After Liu left Yenching University with an M.S. degree in 1929, he taught at Northeastern University in Muckden (Shenyang) (1929–1931). With Boring's help, he received aid from the Rockefeller Foundation for a project on the life histories and distribution of North China Amphibia. In a letter to N. Gist Gee she wrote, "I heartily recommend Mr. Liu as an intelligent and conscientious worker, and know that this grant will be put to good use."[17] Liu continued to receive grants throughout his career. The escalating conflict between China and Japan resulted in Liu's losing his library and collections during this time. He and Boring both knew that he needed to obtain an advanced degree. Boring wrote her friend, G.K. Noble at the American Museum of Natural History, to get advice on ways to help Liu prepare for his future. Liu had obtained a Rockefeller Foundation fellowship to work for his Ph.D. in the United States, and Boring wanted to know "where to send him to get good solid training in general Vertebrate work and give him a chance to go ahead with Amphibian problems." She inquired whether Liu might "work with you [Noble] and get a Ph.D. at Columbia?" Another alternative involved the University of Michigan. "Would Michigan be better for his Ph.D. and then could he spend a summer in New York with you to widen his horizon?"[18] After additional correspondence, they decided that Liu should attend Cornell University and study with Albert H. Wright.

Armed with his new degree, Liu returned to China, to teach at Suzhou University in Jiangsu Province. As Japan advanced, Liu moved to Chengdu in western China, to West China Union University, where he became Professor of Biology. The "forced emigration to western China in 1938," enabled Liu to engage in herpetological studies in a new region. He found West China Union University a favorable base of operations, for he could make repeated field trips into the escarpment of the Tibetan Plateau. These field studies made possible his major work on the western

Chinese amphibians.[19] After he had completed the field work, Liu visited the United States again, and finished writing the work at the Field Museum in Chicago. Liu returned to Yenching in 1950, and in 1950–1951, was head of the biology department. In 1951, he again came to Chengdu, this time as President of Sichuan Medical College. He later became an elected member of the Chinese Academy of Sciences.[20] Liu's wife, Hu Shu Qing, was also a well-known herpetologist. Hu and Liu collaborated on a book, *Chinese Tailless Amphibians* (1961).

Although the greatest number of Liu's over fifty-five papers appeared in the *Peking Natural History Society Bulletin*, he also published in a variety of journals, including *Copeia*, *The Journal of Morphology*, and publications of the Field Museum of Natural History.

LIN CHANG SHAN, Ph.D. (1913–)

Yenching students who remained in China tended to modify their research as conditions in their country dictated. Lin Chang Shan, Boring's student and laboratory assistant, did his research under entomologist Wu Cheng Fu. Lin's early publications reflected an interest in entomology. Originally absorbed by insects of economic importance, he broadened his interests to include ecological interrelationships that would affect human populations. As Lin studied population growth in different animal populations, he drew analogies to the devastating population explosion in China. Passionately convinced that China's problems stemmed from overpopulation and could only be solved by a new plan, he became involved in population modelling. Human ecology replaced insect ecology as his primary concern.

Lin, who received his B.S. degree from Yenching in 1935 and an M.S. in 1938, completed his doctorate in insect ecology at the University of Minnesota (1951). After he completed his Master's degree and before he began work on his doctorate, Lin served as Lecturer in Biology, Peking Catholic University and China University (1941–1945), and Associate Professor in Biology, Yenching University (1945–1947). From 1948 to 1951, Lin worked on his doctorate. In 1952, he obtained the position that he continued to hold in 1992, Professor of Entomology, Environmental Biology, and Ecology, Peking University.

Lin has published more than seventy papers, books, and translations and has received awards in both China and the United States. He credits Alice Boring with teaching him an approach to science that helped him throughout his career.[21]

DING HAN BO, Ph.D. (1912–)

Like his classmate Lin Chang Shan, Ding Han Bo has made a scientific career in China building on the foundation that he received from Boring and other members of the Yenching biology department. Originally a pre-medical major, Ding changed his major to biology after he contracted tuberculosis and was forced to spend a year in a sanitarium recuperating.[22] Ding received B.S. (1936) and M.S. (1939) degrees from Yenching. Boring was his advisor for his M.S. degree, and he was a laboratory assistant for her comparative vertebrate anatomy and histology courses. He credits Boring with initiating his interest in amphibians. She suggested several research problems to him, including research on the seasonal changes of the reproductive organs of amphibians found in Beijing, the Bidder's organ of Chinese toads, and hybridization experiments between different species of amphibians. According to Ding, these early research problems provided excellent training for his future studies on amphibians.[23]

In 1940, Ding returned to his native province, Fujian, where he first became a lecturer and then Associate Professor of Biology at Fukien Christian University, Fuzhou, Fujian. In 1947, he went to Ohio State University to work on his Ph.D. degree, which he received in 1949. He remained in the United States through 1950, as a Muellhaupt Postdoctoral Scholar.

Ding returned to Fuzhou, Fujian, in 1951, when he became Professor of Biology at Fujian Teachers University. In addition to this position, at various times he has been Vice President of the University, Chairman of the Biology Department, and Director of the Developmental Biology Research Laboratory.

Ding Han Bo has established himself as one of China's outstanding herpetologists. He has published over sixty-eight papers in both English and Chinese, has been associate editor for two scientific journals, Head of the Zoological Survey Division, Wuyishan Natural Reserve, an officer in several scientific societies, and a committee member of the First World Congress of Herpetology.[24] Ding considered Boring one of the pioneers in the study of the amphibian fauna of China, "especially on the variations and distribution of the amphibians of northern and eastern China."

BORING'S INFLUENCE ON STUDENTS

The accomplishments of her students indicate Boring's ultimate impact. Wu Jie Ping noted that when he entered Yenching in 1933, there were fifty-two students in the premedical program, but only seventeen of the fifty-two entered Peking Union Medical College. These students might be considered the "cream of the crop," and were the ones who fulfilled the promise of biomedical research in all parts of the world. If we consider that Boring was in China for approximately thirty years, then the number of her students making significant contributions in this field is close to 600. During the Chinese "diaspora," many of Boring's premedical students migrated to different parts of the world (many to the United States) and made outstanding contributions to the research science of their new homes. Many other students who did not meet Boring's rigid requirements for entrance to PUMC attended other less research-oriented medical schools and made contributions to health care in China.

Although the success of her premedical students by virtue of numbers overshadows her successful biology majors who were interested in taxonomic, distributional, anatomical, and descriptive projects, her students demonstrate her success in this area as well. Most of these students elected to remain in China, for many of their Boring-inspired interests involved the fauna of that country. For a list of graduates from the Yenching Biology Department, 1924–1932, see *A Brief History of the Department of Biology of Yenching University.*

In the list of graduate and senior theses produced during this period, Boring's role as teacher and adviser is clear. From 1921–1932, she supervised the following theses (the names are transliterated as they appear on the theses, the Wade-Giles spellings).

1921–1922. Chen, Tse-Ying, B.S. (Soochow 1921). "The Genetics of Two Mutations in the Fruit-Fly."

1926–1927. Yui, Hsi-Chiu, B.S. (Soochow 1922). "The Nephridial System of the Chinese Earthworm *Pheretima hupchensis Michaelson.*"

1927–1928. Liu, Ch'eng Chao. "The Changes in the Digestive System during Metamorphosis of Salientia (Amphibia)."

1929–1930. Chang, Miss Pin Hui, B.S. (Yenching 1929). "The Comparative Study of the Visceral System of the Common North China Frog and Toad: *Rana nigromaculinaa* and *Bufo bufo asiaticus.*"

1930–1931. Meng, Ting-Hsiu, B.S. (Yenching 1930). "A Comparative Study of the Muscular System of the North China Frogs and Toads."

1931–1932. Hsaio, Chi-Ti, B.S. (Shanghai 1925). "The Musculature and Skeletal Parts of the Pectoral Girdle of the North China Frogs and Toads."

1931–1932. Lu, Chin-Jen, B.S. (Soochow 1926). *"Anatomy of Bombina orientalis."*

1931–1932. Yang, Ching Tse, B.S. (Lingnan 1930). "An Analytical Study of the Stomach Contents of the Birds in Canton."

In addition to these graduate theses, during the same years Boring supervised fourteen senior theses on a variety of topics including anatomy, histology, and systematics.

The product (her successful students) is one measure of Boring's success. Another gauge is her own research. When she left the eastern United States in 1918, Boring had already produced enough publications to make her remembered in the history of science. Undoubtedly had she remained there, she would have continued to produce competent, but largely uninspired publications. China, however, offered her an opportunity to engage in creative taxonomic research—a field to which she never would have turned had she remained in the United States.

A far more nebulous framework based upon acquisition of power is interwoven with Boring's clearly successful teaching/research career in China. Within the Third World environment, she enjoyed a type of power that she would have been unlikely to attain in the United States. During the early twentieth century, when the United States presumed that its mission was to "civilize" the world according to its own pattern, western science and medicine provided the one who "civilized" with a great sense of control. Whereas within the United States power was concentrated in the hands of white males, in China accoutrements of power could be acquired by both western men and women. Part of the reason may have been that some of the men who chose to go to China were interested in the relational aspects of teaching, and saw little problem with sharing this feature as well as "control" with women. Consequently, when Boring appeared able and willing, she was given the opportunity to be a policy maker in Yenching's "inner circle," while at the same time, she (as well as some of the men teachers) became involved in the lives of their students.

Alice Boring's story, then, portrays a fine teacher, good research person, influential decision broker, and friend to students, plying her career amidst a chaotic background of civil strife and world war. Among her students and colleagues in China, she was able to ignore gender strictures that would have fettered her work had she remained in the United States, pursue science as the cure for the ills of civilization, and display unwavering faith in the integrity and good will of the Chinese people.[25]

ADDENDA

When Frederick Kao visited Alice Boring in 1955, after they had lost contact for nearly fourteen years, he found that "she had not changed a bit, in appearance or her way of speaking."

Miss Boring still had on her door the signs made in China transphonoliterating her name as Po Ai Li. The characters chosen to represent those sounds we had always translated as LOVE PRINCIPLES BROADLY. In her apartment was still the same carpet that I had trodden upon many times at her Yenching residence. It brought back many of my sweet memories of the Yenching years.

Miss Boring told me that she had sewed pieces of paper with the names of her students in her jacket before she was interned in China and again before she returned to Boston. That was the only way, she said with a laugh, to smuggle the papers out of China, adding, "I was always afraid of forgetting the names of my students." Those are the last words I remember her saying to me. Are there better words to define uncommon dedication?[26]

Notes

1. June Dove Leong, "God's Ambassador, Dr. Katharine H.K. Hsu," *U.S. Asia News*, Part 2, Nov. 18, 1988, p. 1.
2. Katharine H.K. Hsu, "Curriculum Vitae."
3. Tao Jung Chin to Choquette, 16 Dec. 1988; Tao Jung Chin, "Curriculum Vitae."
4. Ibid.
5. Ibid.
6. Ibid.
7. Ibid.
8. Frederick F. Kao, "Remembering Miss Alice M. Boring," An essay, printed on 3 Feb., 1989.
9. Ibid. The expelled Chinese included Guggenheim Professor, H.S. Tsien, the rocket scientist who built guided missiles in China after his return in 1955.
10. Ibid; Frederick F. Kao, "Curriculum Vitae."
11. Ibid.
12. Liu Shilian, "Curriculum Vitae."
13. *Contributions to the History of Herpetology*, Kraig Adler, ed. Issued to commemorate the First World Congress of Herpetology, Canterbury (n.p., Society for the Study of Amphibians and Reptiles, 1989), p. 123.
14. See bibliography.
15. Liu Cheng Chao, "Secondary Sex Characters of Chinese Frogs and Toads," *Zoological Series, Field Museum of Natural History*, 22, No. 2 (Oct. 31, 1936), Publication 368, pp. 115–156 (117).

16. Liu, *Amphibians of Western China*, Fieldiana: Zoological Memoirs, Volume 2 (Chicago, IL: Chicago Natural History Museum, June 15, 1950), p. 5.

17. N. Gist Gee to Boring, 5 May 1930, Rockefeller Archive Center.

18. Alice M. Boring to G.K. Noble, 16 February 1931, Special Collection Archives, Yale University.

19. Liu, *Amphibians of Western China*, p. 17.

20. *Contributions to the History of Herpetology*, p. 123.

21. Lin Chang Shan, "Curriculum Vitae;" Lin Chang Shan to Marilyn Bailey Ogilvie, Interview, 13 July 1988.

22. Lin Chang Shan to Marilyn Bailey Ogilvie.

23. Ding Han Bo to Marilyn Bailey Ogilvie, 20 May 1984.

24. Ding Han Bo, "Curriculum Vitae."

25. The transliteration of the names of individuals are the forms that they use today. It may well be Pinyin in one case and Wade-Giles in another. In Chinese, the family name is given first; however, some people have adopted the European style with the family name last. Many have also adopted European names. The form of the name, then, is the form in which they were introduced to us.

26. Kao, "Miss Alice M. Boring, Ph.D."

Bibliography
Alice M. Boring

Morgan, Thomas Hunt and Boring, Alice Middleton. (1903) "The Relation of the First Plane of Cleavage and the Grey Crescent to the Median Plane of the Embryo of the Frog." *Archiv für Entwickelungsmechanik der Organismen* 16, 1903: 680–90. *Bryn Mawr College Monographs.* Reprint Series, Vol. 1, No. 3, 1904.

Boring, Alice Middleton. (1904) "Closure of Longitudinally Split Tubularia Stems." *Biological Bulletin* 7, No. 3, Aug. 1904: 154–59. *Bryn Mawr College Monographs.* Reprint Series, Vol. 5, 1905.

Stevens, Nettie Maria and Boring, Alice Middleton. (1905) "Regeneration in Polychoerus caudatus." *Journal of Experimental Zoology* 2, No. 3, Aug. 1905: 335–346. *Bryn Mawr College Monographs.* Reprint Series, Vol. 6, 1906.

——. (1906) "Planaria morgani n. sp." (1906) *Proceedings of the Academy of Natural Sciences, Philadelphia.* May 1906. *Bryn Mawr College Monographs.* Reprint Series, Vol. 6, 1906.

Boring, Alice Middleton. (1907) "A Study of the Spermatogenesis of Twenty-Two Species of the Membracidae, Jassidae, Cercopidae, and Fulgoridae, with Especial Reference to the Behavior of the Odd Chromosome." *Journal of Experimental Zoology* 4, No. 4, Oct. 1907: 469–512. *Bryn Mawr College Monographs.* Reprint Series, Vol. 7, 1908.

——. (1909) "On the Effect of Different Temperatures on the Size of the Nuclei in the Embryo of Ascaris Megalocephala, with Remarks on the Size Relations of the Nuclei of univalens and bivalens." *Archiv für Entwickelungsmechanik der Organismen* 28, No. 1, Sept. 1909. *Bryn Mawr College Monographs.* Reprint Series, Vol. 9, 1910.

——. "A Small Chromosome in Ascaris megalocephala." *Archiv zur Zellforschung* 4, No. 1, 1909: 120–131.

——. (1912) "Interstitial Cells and the Supposed Internal Secretion of the Chicken Testis." *Biological Bulletin* 23, No. 3, 1912: 141–42.

Pearl, Raymond and Boring, Alice Middleton. "Fat Deposition in the Testis of the Domestic Fowl," *Science* 36 (937), 1912: 833–835.

Boring, Alice M. (1913) "The Odd Chromosome in Cerastipsocus venosus." *Biological Bulletin* 24, No. 3, 1913: 125–28.

——. (1914) "The Chromosome of the Cercopidae." *Biological Bulletin* 24, 193: 133–46.

Pearl, Raymond and Boring, Alice Middleton. (1914) "Some Physiological Observations Regarding Plumage Patterns." *Science* 39 (995), 23 Jan. 1914: 143–44.

Boring, Alice Middleton and Pearl, Raymond. "The Odd Chromosome in the Spermatogenesis of the Domestic Chicken." *Journal of Experimental Zoology* 16, No. 1, 1914: 53–71.

Boring, Alice Middleton. (1915) "Further Notes on the Chromosomes of the Cercopidae." *Biological Bulletin* 29, No. 5, 1915: 312–15. In collaboration with R. Folger.

Pearl, Raymond and Boring, Alice Middleton. (1917) "Sex Studies, Interstitial Cells in the Reproductive Organs of the Chicken." *Anatomical Record* 13, 1917: 253–68.

——. (1918) "Sex Studies, Corpus Luteum in the Ovary of the Domestic Fowl." *American Journal of Anatomy* 23 (1), 1918: 1–35.

——. Hermaphrodite Birds." *Journal of Experimental Zoology* 25 (1), 1918: 1–47.

Boring, Alice Middleton and Morgan, Thomas Hunt. (1923) "Lutear Cells and Hen-Feathering." *Journal of General Physiology* 1, 1918: 127–131.

Boring, Alice Middleton. "Notes by Stevens on Chromosomes of Domestic Chickens." *Science* 58 (1491), 1923: 73–74.

——. (1927) "Varieties of Monocephora bicincta from the Point of View of a Cytologist." *Psyche* 30 (2) 1923: 89–92.

Gee, Nathaniel Gist and Boring, Alice Middleton, with C.F. Wu. (1929) "A Chinese Earthworm." *Lingnan Agricultural Review* 4 (1): 1–12.

——. "A Checklist of Chinese Amphibia with Notes on Geographical Distribution." *Peking Natural History Bulletin* 4, Dec. 1929: 15–51.

Boring, Alice Middleton. (1932) "Distribution Problems of North China Amphibia." *Peking Natural History Bulletin* 5, Dec. 1930: 39–47.

Boring, Alice Middleton and Li, Hui Lin. "Is the Chinese Amphioxus a Separate Species?" *Peking Natural History Bulletin* 6 March 1932: 9–17.

Boring, Alice Middleton and Liu, Ch'eng Chao. "A New Species of Kaloula with a Discussion of the Genus in China." *Peking Natural History Bulletin* 6, March 1932: 19–23.

Boring, Alice Middleton. "List of Fukien Amphibia and Reptiles." *Marine Biological Association of China*. First Annual Report, 1932.

Liu, Ch'eng Chao, Chow, Shu Ch'un, and Boring, Alice Middleton. *Handbook of North China Amphibia and Reptiles*. (Herpetology of North China). Peking: Peking Natural History Society, 1932.

Boring, Alice Middleton and Chang, Tso Kan. (1933) "The Distribution of the Amphibia of Chekiang Province." *Peking Natural History Bulletin* 8 Sept. 1933: 63–74.

Boring, Alice Middleton and Liu, Ch'eng Chao. (1934) "Giant Toads in China." *Copeia* 1, 1934: 14–15.

Boring, Alice Middleton. "Amphibia of Hongkong." *Hongkong Naturalist*. Parts I and II. 5, March–June 1934: 8–22, 95–107; 7.

Chang, Tso Kan and Boring, Alice Middleton. (1935) "Studies in Variation among the Chinese Amphibia. I. Salamandridae." *Peking Natural History Society Bulletin 9*, June 1935: 327–60.

——. (1936) "A Survey of the Amphibia of Southeast China; an Analysis of the Basis of Species Distribution." *Peking Natural History Society Bulletin* 10, March 1936: 253–73.

Boring, Alice Middleton. "A Survey of the Amphibia of North China Based on the Collection by E. Licent S.J. in the Musee Hoangho-Paiho." *Peking Natural History Society Bulletin* 10, June 1936: 327–351.

Boring, Alice Middleton and Wei, Han Hsin. "The Reversal of Symmetry in Two Chinese Dogfish." *Peking Natural History Society Bulletin* 11, Sept. 1936: 17–20.

Boring, Alice Middleton and Kao, Y. "Two Hermaphrodite Goats." *Peking Natural History Society Bulletin* 11, Dec. 1936: 115–18.

Boring, Alice Middleton. "The Amphibia of Hong Kong." *Hong Kong Naturalist* 7, April 1936: 11–14.

Boring, Alice Middleton and Liu, Ch'eng Chao. (1937) "Studies of the Rainfrog, Kaloula Borealis." III. An Analysis of the Skeletal Features." *Peking Natural History Society Bulletin* 12, Sept. 1937: 43–46.

Boring, Alice Middleton. (1938) "Studies in Variation among Chinese Amphibia. II. Variation in Five Wide-Ranging Common Salientia." *Peking Natural History Society Bulletin* 13, Dec. 1938: 89–110.

Ting, Han Po and Boring, Alice Middleton. (1939) "A Study of Bidder's Organ in Chinese Toads." *Peking Natural History Society Bulletin* 13, March 1939: 147–60.

Chang, Tso Kan and Boring, Alice Middleton. "Notes on Kwangsi Amphibia." *Peking Natural History Society Bulletin* 14, Sept. 1939: 43–48.

Ting, Han Po and Boring, Alice Middleton. "The Seasonal Cycle in the Reproductive Organs of the Chinese Toad Bufo bufo and the Pond Frog Rana nigromaculata." *Peking Natural History Society Bulletin* 14, Sept. 1939: 49–89.

Cheng, Tsai Tung and Boring, Alice Middleton. "The Anatomy of the Hammerhead Shark Sphyrna zygena." *Peking Natural History Society Bulletin* 14, Dec. 1939: 99–101.

Tchang, T.L. and Boring, Alice Middleton. (1940) "List of Amphibians in the Fan Memorial Institute." *Peking Natural History Society Bulletin* 14, June 1940: 285–290.

Pope, Clifford H. and Boring, Alice M. "A Survey of Chinese Amphibia." *Peking Natural History Society Bulletin* 15, Sept. 1940: 13–86.

Boring, Alice Middleton. (1945) *Chinese Amphibians, Living and Fossil Forms; a Complete Bibliography, Analysed, Tabulated, Annotated and Indexed by Alice*

M. Boring. Edited by Pierre Leroy, S.J., Peking: Institut de geobiologie, Peking. Publication No. 13, 1945.

Boring, Alice Middleton, Chang, Lan Fen, and Chang, Wei Hsi. (1948) "Autotomy and Regeneration in the Tails of Lizards." *Peking Natural History Society Bulletin* 17, Dec. 1948: 85–107.

Boring, Alice Middleton. (1949) "In Memoriam: Bernard Emms Read (May 17, 1887–June 13, 1949)." *Peking Natural History Society Bulletin* 18, Sept. 1949: i–ii.

——. "Early Days of the Peking Natural History Society." *Peking Natural History Society Bulletin* 18, Sept. 1950.

Index

Abbreviations and shortened forms used in this index are: AMB for Alice M. Boring, EGB for Edwin G. Boring, GB for Grace Boynton, JLS for John L. Stuart, LTB for Lydia T. Boring, PUMC for Peking Union Medical College and Yenching for Yenching University. Page numbers followed by "n" refer to a note.